Thailand: Land of the Free

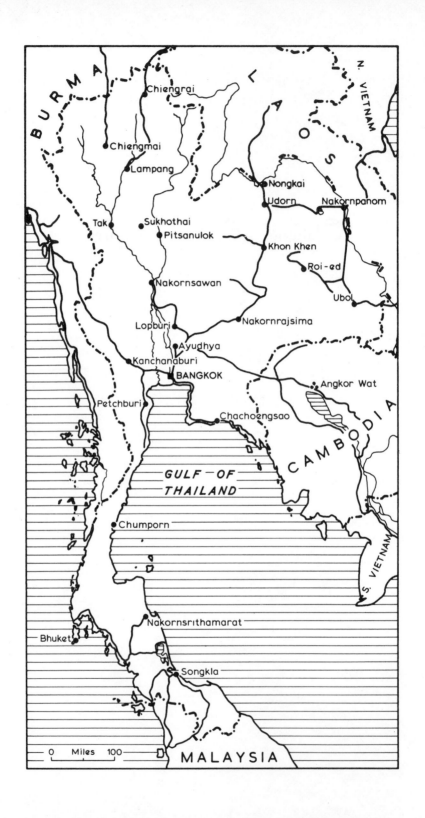

Thailand:
Land of the Free

JAMES BASCHE

Taplinger Publishing Co., Inc.
New York

First Published in the United States in 1971 by
TAPLINGER PUBLISHING CO., INC.
New York, New York
ISBN 0-8008-7607-5
Library of Congress Catalog Card Number 71-122250
Published simultaneously in the Dominion of Canada by
Burns & MacEachern Ltd., Ontario

Printed in the United States of America

This book is dedicated
to my mother and father

Contents

Preface

Every year thousands of visitors arrive in Thailand (pronounced Tie-land) from all over the world. Most of these visitors are tourists. Some are there for business or trade. A few are there to take up residence as businessmen or as representatives of their home governments or international organizations.

For the short-term visitor the Thailand he sees is often the Thailand of the guidebook—the magnificent luxury or first-class hotels which have sprung up all over Bangkok; the fine restaurants serving Thai, Chinese, and European food; a few of the more noted Buddhist temples; the floating market; a Thai boxing match; a sample of Thai dancing; and perhaps Timland, a small park not far from the Bangkok airport.

The resident foreigner, or *farang,* is more fortunate. Not only does he have the opportunity to live among a kind and warm-hearted people, but he has the time to learn about them and to explore the fascinating countryside, history, and culture of the Thai people.

For a period of time I was one of those fortunate resident farangs, as they are called by Thai and foreigner alike, who had the chance to live in this exciting country among these pleasant people.

This book is a report of what I have learned about Thailand and its people. It does not pretend to be an exhaustive, scholarly monograph on any specific topic about Thailand, but is a general introduction for the reader who has never been to Thailand, for the short-term visitor who wants to learn more about the country, and for the resident or former resident who wants to refresh his memories about his "second home."

For the reader who wants to explore more fully the politics and economics, the history and the anthropology of Thailand, there are many fine, detailed works by scholars in Thai and in all major Western languages to which he can turn.

One final comment should be made about the spelling of Thai names which have been used in this book. There are several systems for spelling Thai names in English. These spellings may vary depending on whether the writer uses the Thai or Sanskrit base of the name or whether he spells phonetically. I have followed a simple and useful (although thoroughly unscientific) method. For place names I have used the spellings found on a map which has been my constant companion since my first arrival in Thailand almost a decade ago, and I have changed those spellings only when there has been some other widely used form of the particular place name which might be more familiar to Western readers. For personal names I have used the spelling used by the individual or the spelling most commonly used by English-language publications in Bangkok. I have used the name Thailand, the name by which the country is presently known, all the way through the book despite the fact that early Thai kingdoms were often known mainly by the name of their capital city and the country was known to the West for several centuries as Siam.

Prologue

Don Muang Airport is located about twenty miles north of the old central area of Bangkok. The airport is one of the busiest in the world, serving more than a score of international airlines. For most visitors to Thailand it is the entry port to this exciting and ancient land in the center of the Southeast Asian peninsula.

A little to the west of the airport, the Chao Phya River, lord of all rivers to the Thai, flows by as its course twists and turns down from the hills of north-central Thailand to the Gulf of Thailand. On the river, boats pull strings of barges, often so low in the water they appear to be sinking, full of rice and other farm products down to Bangkok and city-made products back to the towns and villages upriver.

At regularly spaced intervals great canals, or *klongs,* stretch outward from the river as far as the eye can see. The major klongs are intersected by smaller ones which in turn are crossed by still smaller ones. Much of the Central Plain area of Thailand is divided and cross-divided by this extensive network of klongs built up over several centuries. The river and canal system provides arteries of water transportation to supplement the limited road network and distributes the water essential to the wet rice grown in the paddy fields which cover much of the Central Plain on both sides of the river. During the six months of the rainy season in central Thailand the river and klongs are filled, but during the dry season the river level drops and many of the canals are empty, their courses outlined only by the trees which grow along their banks.

Near the airport another form of agriculture can be seen. The fields consist of long, narrow ridges of earth separated by still narrower ditches for water. The ridges are raised up to permit the farmers to grow new dry crops in the area of low elevation which has traditionally been inundated to permit the growth of wet rice.

1

Around the airport other features which have become common symbols of this nation, both ancient and modern at one time, can be seen. The delicate spires of Buddhist *wats,* or temples, reach skyward in several areas outside the airport grounds. These wats are so numerous throughout the country they have become a Thai trademark. Trucks, which provide most of the freight transportation in the country, are parked in loading zones waiting to take on air cargoes for delivery to all sections of the nation. The trucks have teakwood bodies—built in Thailand—on frames and cabs that are imported. The teakwood is often polished to a very high gloss and the plain red or yellow steel cabs are usually decorated with chrome or tin figures or paintings of traditional Thai scenes from real or mythical life. And, finally, making use of all available space, a modern golf course has been built between the two long parallel runways of the airport.

Unlike the temperate zone countries of the Americas and Europe, most of Thailand, affected by monsoons, has three main seasons instead of four. A rainy season, which extends roughly from May to November, is the rice-growing season. Temperatures during this season generally range from the seventies to the nineties with little diurnal variation. At this time of the year moist winds from the Indian Ocean to the southwest and from other large bodies of water to the south blow landward bringing almost daily rainfalls, which fill up the rivers and the klongs and by September or October usually flood part of the country. When I first went to Thailand ten years ago, before the country had as many all-weather roads as it has now, the floods covered all roads and railroad lines out of Bangkok for a short period of time. For that period the capital was effectively isolated from all other parts of the country, except by air. Although steps have been taken by the Thai government to build fine, new all-weather roads in all directions from the capital, there are still many remote areas in upcountry Thailand which become isolated during parts of the rainy season.

The long rainy season is followed by a short cool season from the end of November to some time in February. During this time the winds are reversed and fresh breezes blow from the mountains of central Asia, bringing cooler temperatures to the countries of Southeast Asia. In the northern mountains of Thailand it can become so cool a fire is needed for comfort. However, this season never brings cold weather as Europeans and North Americans know it, and snow is never seen. Bangkok temperatures rarely drop below sixty degrees and that happens usually in the early morning hours during the cool season in January. Nonetheless, this season is a refreshing and delightful time of the year with rarely any rain to mar the pleasant days.

The third season is the hot, dry season extending from February until the beginning of the rains in May. In these few months temperatures are often in the high nineties during the day and may stay well up in the eighties at night. The winds still come down from the Asian land mass, but they are dry and hot. This is the summer season for Thailand. Schools close and many government officials and others who work in Bangkok take their vacations in the northern mountains or at the seashore to get away from Bangkok's heat.

When anyone steps down from an air-conditioned plane at Don Muang Airport, regardless of the season of the year, he knows he is in a tropical country. If it happens to be the hot season, he is faced with an initial blast of hot air not unlike that felt when opening the door of a furnace. But after that first gust, he can, with proper care and the right attitude, quickly adjust to the tropical climate. Millions of people do so every year.

If the visitor is fortunate enough to be met by a Thai acquaintance, he will probably be greeted by the traditional Thai form of greeting called the *wai.* The two palms are pressed together, fingers touching gently and pointed straight upward, and the hands are brought up to the chest or higher with the elbows kept close to the side of the body and not allowed to stick out awkwardly. The height to which the hands are brought is determined by the amount of respect the greeter wishes to extend to the person greeted. Roughly, the higher the hands are raised, the greater is the respect intended. If the greeter raises his hands before his face he is signifying his belief that the greeted is of equal status; if the hands go higher and the head is bowed slightly, as would be the case in greeting monks or members of royalty, for example, the greeted is of higher status; and if the hands are brought only to chest level, the greeted is of lower status than the greeter. Th wai is not only charming, but a useful determinant of one's regard by and for the persons being met. When one greets a Thai with a wai, he will almost always receive one in response except if the person greeted is a Buddhist monk. Thai social manners prohibit the return of a wai greeting by a monk.

In recent years the Western practice of handshaking has become common in Bangkok and other cities where there are many Westerners, but it is generally limited to greetings between Thai and Westerners. The greetings exchanged between Thai are still the traditional wai.

Thailand is a relatively recent name for the country of the Thai, although Thai as the name of the people who inhabit that land and some neighboring areas is very ancient. For several centuries before 1939, and again for a short period after World War II, the country was known to the international community and officially as Siam and that name is still often heard. During some of the early debates on the newly adopted Constitution of 1968, time was spent on the question of what the country's name should be. The debate was finally settled by adopting the name Thailand.

Both names, Siam and Thailand, are names by which the country is known to foreigners. To the Thai their country's name is *Prades Thai,* meaning land of the Thai. Thailand would appear, then, to be an accurate westernization of the name by which the Thai know their own country. Thai will also refer to their country often as *Muang Thai,* which is more vague in meaning, but which can be translated as the Thai nation or people.

The word Thai means free and Prades Thai, therefore, means land of the free. The Thai are justly proud of their country's name as the "land of the free," and the name may well be taken in two senses. First, it may mean the land of the free people. While both slavery and the corvée were known in Thailand up to recent times, there have always been large numbers of free and independent peasant farmers just as there are today. A second and newer meaning stems from the more recent confrontation between the nations of Southeast Asia and the major Western colonial powers. Burma, Laos, Cambodia, North and South Vietnam, Malaysia, Singapore, Indonesia, and the Philippines all were dominated for a period of their history by one or more Western imperialist nations. Only Thailand remained free of this colonial control, a fact of pride among Thai and of important, even though unmeasurable, consequences in the development of contemporary Thai relationships with other nations.

The name Siam, sometimes earlier spelled Sayam, has a somewhat obscure origin, believed to be Chinese, and is the name used in the memoirs and letters of many of the earliest Western explorers, traders, and missionaries to call at the Kingdom of Ayudhya in the sixteenth and seventeenth centuries. During the early centuries of Thai history their kings were often known by the names of the particular kingdoms which dominated the land at a specific time period, such as the king of Sukhothai or the king of Ayudhya, as much or more than they were known as the king of Siam.

A look at a map of the area of the world known as Southeast Asia will show that Thailand occupies a central position in the mainland part of that region. North and west of Thailand is Burma, to the northeast is Laos, to the southeast is Cambodia, and far down the narrow Malay Peninsula is Malaysia, bordering Thailand on the south. Thailand has about 1,200 miles of coastline along the Gulf of Thailand and about 450 miles along the west coast of the Malay Peninsula fronting on the Andaman Sea, part of the Bay of Bengal. This west coast area is generally rugged and, except for Phuket on an island off the coast and one or two other smaller towns, there are few useful ports on that coast today.

Unlike Burma and Laos, Thailand does not share any common border with Communist China. The two countries are nearest about at the point where Thailand, Laos, and Burma meet. From there Communist China is about one hundred miles or slightly less from the Thai border. With modern transportation and weapons the Chinese colossus is too close for complacency on the part of the Thai; still, the fact that it does not share a common border at any point has played a role in determining Thailand's policy on the Asian and general international scenes differing from that of some of its neighboring Southeast Asian states which face mainland China across an invisible line on a day-by-day basis.

When I was first in Thailand I made an error which was gently and humorously, but firmly, corrected. I had read many times, even in books written by Thai, reference to Thailand as a "small" country in Southeast Asia, and I had absorbed that idea and automatically referred to the country as a small one. It was pointed out to me that Thailand was a small country only if one related it to such giants as the Soviet Union, Canada, the United States, India, and China.

Southeast Asia is usually considered to comprise ten countries. The ten I will consider in this book are Burma, Cambodia, Indonesia, Laos, Malaysia, the Philippines, Singapore, Thailand, North Vietnam, and South Vietnam. The total land area of these ten nations is almost 1,750,000 square miles, of which Thailand has 198,455 square miles and ranks third in size behind Indonesia and Burma. The total population of Southeast Asia is approximately 250 million. With an estimated population of 33 or 34 million Thailand again ranks third behind Indonesia and the Philippines this time, although Thailand is close to the latter in population and may in time overtake it.

It should be noted that Thailand is larger than Spain (about 195,000 square miles), the country to which it is closest in size, and almost as large as France (about 212,000 square miles). France's population, however, is about 50 percent greater than that of Thailand, while Spain's population is about the same as Thailand's. Still, with an area slightly smaller than that of Thailand and a population about the same size, Spain is not often referred to in ordinary conversation as a small country.

Within Asia Japan looms large as a major power. Its economic growth in the last hundred years, and especially since the end of World War II, has been phenomenal. With a population around 100 million it is one of the most heavily populated nations in Asia. But in land area Japan is substantially smaller than Thailand; Japan has approximately 143,000 square miles of territory.

Thailand extends more than one thousand miles from the border with Malaysia in the south to that with Burma and Laos in the north, a distance almost equal to that from New York to Miami. From Laos in the east to Burma in the west Thailand is more than five hundred miles wide.

The term small when applied to nations is sometimes meant to refer to more than the physical size of a country. The word encompasses a complex configuration of meanings referring to power, history, past extent of domination of other lands, and many others. Even with this broadened definition of small, one should hesitate before using it without qulification as a label for Thailand. There were periods during the last few hundred years when Thailand controlled or was suzerain over large sections of Burma, Laos, Cambodia, and Malaysia, and dominated all of the Southeast Asian peninsula. Japan, China, India, and Persia all sought trade with the Thai kingdoms, and European nations tried to arrange agreements, even alliances, with the kings of Siam. In some historical periods Thailand might more properly have been considered one of the major powers of Asia.

Yet today, Thailand is often visualized as a small, rather quaint, rather picturesque country in Asia. This partly erroneous image of Thailand can only be understood as the result of years of Western accumulation of misinformation and myths about the land and life of the people of Thailand. Recent years have seen scholars unwrapping the layers of myth around Thailand and revealing more accurate knowledge about this important country.

Visitors to any country bring more than their luggage with them, for they bring unseen, but often significant, prejudgments, preconceptions, prejudices which in many cases may determine what they see in the country and what they learn about it. For a visitor to Thailand these preconceptions are often misconceptions formed from some scattered facts about Siamese cats or Siamese twins or shaped by the distortions in the various book, play, and widely shown motion-picture versions of *Anna and the King of Siam* or its musical partner, *The King and I.* Mrs. Anna Leonowens, on whose memoirs of her experiences as a teacher in King Mongkut's court in the 1860's these popular books and dramatic presentations have been based, often distorted her facts by her creative imagination. Each writer who has worked on the later dramatized versions has applied his own imagination to twist the tales still further from the truth in order to make a fascinating story, but one that is irrelevant to Thailand today or even to Thailand as it was in the 1860's.

In the recent musical version of Mrs. Leonowens' memoirs, for example, she is shown at King Mongkut's deathbed promising to help his son. In reality the English woman left Thailand for her own country a year before the king died and could not have been present at such a scene. While liberties with facts are permitted in a novel or play, it is unfortunate that many Westerners have gleaned what little information they have about Thailand from such a source without understanding it as the fiction that it is. Many years after Mrs. Leonowens' departure from Thailand her son, who had been with her in Thailand, returned to Bangkok to start a company in teakwood lumbering. The company is still active in several business fields in Bangkok.

Aside from the limitations to the visitor's knowledge of Thailand, he may have accepted, sometimes without realizing it, certain generalized errors which contribute to the misunderstanding of Thailand and its people. One of these pervasive errors is to think of all nations in a geographical region as similar solely because they are contiguous. Americans in the United States have been doing this for decades about the countries of South America with unfortunate results. The failure to see the cultural, historical, economic, political, and social differences—as well as similarities—among the countries of a particular geographical region can often lead to misunderstandings and to mistaken decisions.

The failure to differentiate among countries of Southeast Asia has appeared in some recent writings about Thailand. Some writers have turned to Thailand and, viewing it in the light of the Vietnam war, have asked if Thailand is another potential Vietnam. Whether the answer is yes or no, the implication in such a question is that Thailand *can* be another Vietnam and that the only real difference in the situation in the two countries is a factor of timing. Unless one recognizes the differences between these countries and among all countries in Southeast Asia (for example, differences in the historical relationship to China, differences in relationships to Western nations in the colonial period, differences in landholding patterns, differences in religions, and so on), it is too easy to suggest solutions to problems which appear the same, but which may have different causes in each country. Thailand may at some future time have political upheavals, but to assume that these will be caused by factors identical to those creating upheavals in Vietnam, Malaysia, Indonesia, or the Philippines and to react accordingly is to take much too simplistic a view. Each country in Southeast Asia has its own past, its own present, and its own future, and despite similarities—sometimes more apparent than real— each must be understood separately and independently.

One myth about Thailand which I have heard often repeated by American and European friends is the belief that the country is one great flat rice paddy. If one sees only Bangkok and Thonburi, the city across the Chao Phya River from Bangkok, and perhaps the old capital of Ayudhya about forty miles farther up the river, the places usually visited by tourists, it is easy to understand how the idea of Thailand as a flat country has been widely believed. This part of Thailand is flat and very close to sea level. Bangkok, approximately twenty miles from the coast, is only about six feet above sea level and Ayudhya, sixty miles from the coast, is only about thirteen feet higher than sea level. This low level and very gradual increase in the elevation in the Central Plain of Thailand seen by most writers and tourists account for the foreigners' belief that all Thailand is flat.

Thailand, however, is far from being a flat country. Indeed, it is far from being uniform in any of its geographical features. These variations can be seen easily if one is able to travel for a time throughout the country.

Usually Thailand is divided into four main regions—the Central Plain, the North, the Northeast, and the South or peninsular area. Sometimes a fifth region is added when the southeast provinces of Cholburi, Rayong, Chantaburi, and Trad are considered separately from the huge Northeast area with which they are usually associated.

The Central Plain region, drained by the Chao Phya River, is the heartland of Thailand. The area extends northward from the Gulf of Thailand about three hundred miles, rising gradually to the foothills and mountains surrounding it on all sides except the south. The width of the plain varies from one hundred to one hundred and fifty miles, and in this great valley is centered one of the richest rice-growing areas in the world. The plains and the rivers that flow through them are Thailand's most valuable geographical assets.

Unlike the Salween River, which forms a short part of the Thai-Burmese border, and the Mekong River, which forms a much longer part of the Thai-Laos border, the Chao Phya does not rise in the Himalayan mountain highlands of Asia. Lying entirely within the borders of Thailand, the Chao Phya is a much shorter river than those that make up part of the country's boundaries with its neighbors. The Chao Phya is formed by the joining of the Ping River, the Yom River, and the Nan River near Nakorn Sawan. The Ping has a major tributary, the Wang River, which joins it farther to the north. All four rivers flow southward from the northern mountains to the Central Plain. The Chao Phya itself, from the point of junction of the Ping with the Nan and Yom, flows about 225 miles to the sea. The total drainage area of the river and its tributaries, which includes the area of the rich Central Plain, is more than sixty thousand square miles in which are located the main rice-farming districts for the country.

The principal rivers making up this system originate in northern mountain ranges which run generally in north-south directions throughout northern Thailand, down the western side of the country bordering Burma, and continuing right on down the peninsular area into Malaysia. These mountain areas are sparsely inhabited for the most part and are heavily covered with forest growth. Thailand's northern forests are especially well known for their valuable teakwood. The highest mountain peak in Thailand is found in a northern range between the Ping River and one of its smaller tributaries. The mountain is Doi Inthanon and is 8,452 feet high.

The third major region is the northeast Khorat Plateau. As you drive along one of Thailand's new highways heading northeast from Saraburi toward Nakornrajsima (Khorat), you soon enter the foothills which rise from the Central Plain to a plateau height which averages three to five hundred feet higher than the plain. Once on the plateau you are in a great concave, saucer-like geographical region covering almost sixty thousand square miles and extending all the way in the north and east to the Mekong River with Laos on the other side. This huge region with its sandy soils and its relatively low rainfall is the poorest section of the entire country. In recent years, for economic, political, and security reasons, the central government of Thailand has been giving increasing attention to the needs of this territory, which faces the troubled areas of former French Indo-China across the boundary.

The area southeast of Bangkok, bordering on Cambodia, is a partly mountainous, partly coastal plain area which is often lumped together with the northeast region in general discussions.

The fourth major region of Thailand is the long narrow peninsular area extending down the Malay Peninsula to the border between Thailand and Malaysia. In the northern part of this region Thailand shares the peninsula with Burma, and at its narrowest point the Thai portion is less than twenty miles wide. Farther south Thailand covers the whole width of the peninsula with coasts along the Gulf of Thailand on the east and the Andaman Sea on the west, giving Thailand access to both the China Sea and the Bay of Bengal. The region of the south is largely mountainous, with the Tenassarim Range and several smaller ranges covered with dense forests running through the entire area.

Far from being a flat country most of Thailand is hilly and mountainous and only the Central Plain area in the immediate environs of Bangkok and Ayudhya is out of sight of hills and mountains. Some of the hilly areas with their immense trees, thick undergrowth, and rocky streams are among the most beautiful parts of the country.

If one is lucky, one will see some of the animals for which the mountains of the country are famous. I was riding a train once heading south from Chiengmai, the main city of the northern region of Thailand. As the train struggled through the valley of the Yom River, climbing so slowly at times it was difficult to tell we were moving at all in the dimness of the late afternoon, I looked across the clear rocky stream at a few fishermen at work. Then, out of the forest about a half mile distant, moving slowly, heavily, two huge elephants with their masters riding on top shuffled into sight. They could hardly be seen, for the sun striking them turned their gray skins to a light faded brown which blended with the dry brush behind them. The children in the railway car became excited, chattering and pointing, and the adults smiled happily as we all watched those massive beasts of the forest tread along a distant riverside path on their way home after a day's work.

Myths about Thailand have not been limited to misconceptions about its size and physical characteristics. They have also grown up about its people. In the case of Thailand's people, of which there are about 34 million today, the generalizations have often been extreme and sometimes contradictory. In the late 1860's, Mrs. Anna Leonowens made the sweeping statement in her memoirs that the Thai "in common with most of the Asiatic races" were apt to be "indolent, improvident, greedy, intemperate, servile, cruel, vain, inquisitive, superstitious, and cowardly." A hundred years later, with what we have learned about all Asians in that century, we can justifiably wonder if she was talking about the same people we know as Thai. Even with what we have learned about Thailand (and much of our studying about Asia until very recently, except for a few students and scholars, has been confined to Japan, China, and India), we still find the Thai described in stereotypes which often are as unreal as those of Mrs. Leonowens.

Before going to Thailand the first time I had heard and read that the Thai people were mild-mannered, without tendencies toward anger or aggression. They were, I was told, carefree, often lazy, uncomplicated, and simple people, easily pleased and ready to smile. I was soon sharply awakened to the false-ness of much of what I had been told. A few days after I arrived I was riding on Rama IV Road in Bangkok along the edge of Lumpini Park, the city's largest. Traffic was fairly heavy and while seemingly reckless, it was not mov-ing too fast. In the distance in the lane of traffic coming toward us I saw a bicycle suddenly turn out from the side of the road into a center lane. It was hit by a taxi. Fortunately the cyclist was not hurt—at least not in the accident. But in the seconds it took for my car to pass the site of the collision the rider and the taxi driver had come to blows. They were rolling on the side of the road, pummeling each other vigorously and almost falling into the klong. (In those days no one bothered to call the police when there was an accident. Instead, a more direct settlement was sought while avoiding the risk of having to pay a bribe to a policeman so that the other fellow would be blamed for the accident.) As we drove past the fighters I wondered what had happened to the mild-mannered, slow-to-anger, nonaggressive Thai about whom I had heard so much.

Much later I discussed this incident and other similar ones with a well-educated and knowledgeable Thai friend, who was by coincidence a descend-ant of King Mongkut, Rama IV, after whom the road on which I had seen the accident was named. My friend pointed out to me his belief that the Thai are reluctant to use force, as I had been told, but they will not hesitate to do so if they feel it is necessary. Usually their reluctance to do anything to em-barrass another person will be a restraint on their anger. He said a Thai will accept a scolding provided it is not done in front of other persons so that he loses face. He also said, however, that no one should ever use physical force against a Thai because the latter will often respond with a quick temper and may react with his own physical force. If his strength is not great enough to respond with his own body, "He may get a gun and shoot you." To emphasize his point he lifted the tail of his sport shirt to show the pistol he had pushed in the waistband of his trousers and told me he kept a second pistol in his car. As he spoke, I remembered a small hotel at which I had stayed in Sakolna-korn, a town in the Northeast. As in many small upcountry hotels the wide halls near the stairs on the upper floors were used as lounges. Walking through the lounge on my floor I noticed that I was the only one of eight or nine men in the hall not carrying a pistol stuck into his waistband.

One alleged Thai trait troubled me when I heard about it; that was the description of the Thai by several Westerners over the last century as lazy. Once I had questioned the trait of eternal pacificism in the Thai, I began to question other descriptive characteristics I had heard. I feel their alleged laziness is one of the easiest myths to dispel once one has come to learn a little about these people.

The idea of Thai laziness seems to stem from several sources. One is that many Thai farmers apparently work only a few hours a day. I believe this fact, when true, can be explained by reasons other than laziness. Working a few hours a day may, in a hot tropical climate, be a sign more of wisdom than of laziness. Furthermore, in Thailand many farmers suffer from liver flukes and other debilitating parasites and diseases which tend to reduce the energy and the time which can be spent in strenuous work. We must remember that illness is not laziness. Only when these illnesses are eliminated—and steps are being taken to that end—will the Thai have more energy for his daily work. Another reason for feeling that laziness is a Thai trait is that much of modern business and industrial development in cities and towns is in foreign hands or controlled by Thai of Chinese descent. These people are living in the same climate and yet appear to be more lively and industrious than the Thai. The conclusion is reached that the Thai must be too lazy to join vigorously in these newer economic activities. The real reason may well be, instead, a difference in values. A Thai cultural value that places rice farming higher than business and manufacturing is wrongly seen as laziness. The critic has failed to give due weight to the Thai value system. Certainly anyone who has seen (or tried) the backbreaking work of rice transplanting would not call the Thai farmer lazy. And yet these myths persist.

Another incident soon after my first visit to Thailand dispelled for me the pleasant image of the "eternally happy, smiling Thai" without the usual problems of mankind, with plenty to eat, and with nothing to worry about. I was walking one sunny Saturday morning near my home and saw two boys with bamboo poles fishing in a klong. One of the boys was about seven years old and the other about eleven. At first they did not see me, but when they did, they walked over with their hands extended. These were the first Thai I had encountered begging for money and I was surprised. I shook my head and kept on my way.

The older boy sent the younger one back to fish and then followed me. When he caught up to me I heard him asking for *"roi baht"* (100 baht, or $5). I shook my head again, but he persisted. He began to rub his stomach to show that he was hungry. I continued walking and shaking my head. He continued to follow just a step behind and to the side of me making his hunger signs and repeating his request. As I continued to walk away the boy slowed down and I heard his request go to 50 baht, then 20, 10, and finally 5 as he stopped somewhere behind me. Farther on down the lane I turned to look back. Apparently I was already forgotten. The older boy had returned to the side of the younger one and they were again fishing in the klong. I realize this was not a shattering experience and may not even have been typical, but it affected me. I felt saddened as I saw this myth—that of the carefree Thai—dissolve before me. Life in Thailand, as elsewhere, was not as simple as the legends had it.

These two experiences, disillusioning as they were, were an important part of my real education about the country. They made me take a new, revised look at the people and the land of Thailand, and what I had read and heard about them. I began to learn again. Everything I had previously read or heard was questioned in the light of what I experienced and of everything new I was to read and hear.

Fortunately for me, that learning process continued. Some of the views I had before going to Thailand were confirmed and others were discarded after what I saw and learned in the country. I do not believe I will ever fully understand the Thai people—or even one Thai person. Perhaps it is not possible for a foreigner ever to understand fully the people of another nation. It has been pointed out often that it is difficult for a *farang* to understand the Thai fully, and the experiences of farangs who have lived in Thailand much longer than I seem to bear this out. Still, it is possible to go beyond the rather romantic picture of silk-clad, long-fingernailed beauties with pointed crowns on their heads, dressed in a kind of funny pantaloon, smiling broadly for the camera in full Technicolor. In its place one can discover a Thai people with lives and problems and solutions similar to those of people in many other lands, but unique, too, because of the dramatic history, the rich culture, the particular geography that have shaped the Thai people and the Thai nation. I learned that replacing the myth by sounder facts and information made the Thai land and people more fascinating and more exciting to know.

When I first stepped onto Thai soil and met my first Thai I found one of the traits I had heard about often was accurate, and on this one item at least my opinion has never changed. Thailand has been called the land of smiles and its people are said to be always ready with a smile. More than any other people I have seen in my homeland or in other countries I have visited, the Thai are a smiling people.

The foreign visitor to Asia finds himself the center of stares. At first this may be disconcerting, but in time the visitor accepts the stares and learns to ignore them or to react in some innocuous, but hopefully pleasant way. My reaction in these countries is to smile at whomever I catch staring at me.

Sometimes he is the one disconcerted or embarrassed and looks away. At other times he may be suspicious or resentful or filled with hate, or he may scowl or just stare back with no expression. But not so with a Thai. When a Thai has stared at me and I have smiled at him, I have invariably received a smile back and often a grin of genuine joy that the stranger has noticed him. If the Thai happens to be a girl, the smile will often turn into inexplicable giggles, and if a boy or young man, he will often glance around to collect companions to join in the pleasure of grinning at the funny foreigner. This smile, this grin, is probably the most delightful and charming characteristic of a people with many fine traits, and it can be useful, too, as an introduction, as a pacifier, as an agent to smooth the pathways between individuals and peoples of vastly different backgrounds.

The visitor's first encounter with Thai officialdom, English-speaking Thai, and the Thai language itself usually comes on entering the immigration and customs area at Don Muang. The Thai officials are no more and no less annoying than similar officials in most countries, but the Thai bureaucrat may lessen the visitor's frustration with a smile. Most of the officials the visitor or the resident meets will speak at least a few words of English. For some years now in Thailand English has been taught as a second language from the lower grades on up to the university level so that most educated persons in Thailand have some knowledge of English. Within the last decade the large numbers of native English speakers, especially American soldiers and Peace Corps volunteers and British Voluntary Service personnel, who have been stationed all around the country, have taught an increasing number of Thai a little English.

The number of English-speaking Westerners, on the other hand, who know Thai is very small. Many foreign residents may learn a kind of "market Thai" or enough to enable them to ask directions, to make purchases in the markets, and to converse with servants, with the help of sign language.

The Thai language is tonal, monosyllabic, and uninflected. In theory, at least, Thai has five tones—lower, middle, higher, rising, and falling. Each of the lower, middle, and higher can be sharp and short or long and drawn out. In practice there may be more tones because there are some differences in pronunciation among the Thai of Bangkok and the Central Plain and that version spoken in the North, in the Northeast, and in the South. Because Thai is monosyllabic it is necessary to combine several one-syllable words to get a more complex one. For example, the word for match would combine wood, strike, and fire. There are some polysyllabic words in Thai, but these have usually been incorporated from other languages such as Pali, Sanskrit, or Khmer, or more recently from some Western languages. Since Thai is uninflected, verb conjugations are not necessary. One says, in effect, "I go home today, I go home yesterday, I go home tomorrow." This spoken language may seem simple and its grammar may well be, but the complications of a tonal vocabulary make the spoken language difficult for most Westerners and often lead to merry situations.

The written Thai language is traditionally dated back to A.D. 1283 when one of Thailand's greatest kings, King Ramkamheng, adapted and modified the Khmer alphabet to suit the Thai language. The language has forty-four consonants and thirty-two vowel signs which may be written above, below, before, or after the consonants on a line. These signs indicate the meaning by specifying the tones for the vowels in the words. To a Westerner, printed Thai looks strange because it does not use punctuation or spaces between words except to indicate the end of main phrases, sentences, and paragraphs. Thus, the words in one sentence are strung together, looking like one long word. Picture the preceding sentence as "Thusthewordsinonesentenceare-strungtogetherlookinglikeonelongword" followed by a space and then the next sentence. This can only be an approximation because, of course, the Thai sentence would not have the complications of polysyllabic words and inflections or the phrasing pattern of the English sentence. Fortunately for America and Europe more schools and colleges are beginning to teach written and spoken Thai, which should help Westerners to learn more about Thailand, its history, and its important cultural developments.

Part One

Bangkok

1

The Phra Mane Ground

Spreading out from its original site in a great bend of the Chao Phya River, Bangkok sprawls over a large area on the east, or left, bank about twenty miles up the river from its mouth. Directly across the river from Bangkok is the adjoining city of Thonburi, linked with the capital city by several bridges spanning the wide river. Together these two cities and their suburban towns comprise the only large metropolitan area in the country. As in many other nations where such a situation exists it has led at times to the statement that Thailand is really two countries. On the one hand, urban, Western, modern, hectic Bangkok and Thonburi, and on the other, the rest of the country, rural, traditional, and slower-paced. While there may be some truth in this statement, it is too simple and broad-sweeping to be entirely accurate, for the metropolitan area with all its physical, sometimes glaring, sometimes glittering, differences is truly a part and a product of the nation, its history, and its culture as a whole.

In the most recent national census in 1960 Bangkok had a population of more than one and a half million and Thonburi of more than half a million. In the last decade the two cities have grown much faster than ever before and faster than the country as a whole. Some recent estimates have placed the present metropolitan population at somewhere around three and a half to four million. In other words, about 10 percent of the total population of Thailand lives in this major metropolitan complex. Some idea of the great difference in size between this area and the other cities of Thailand can be realized from the fact that the next largest cities, Chiengmai in the North and Khorat in the Northeast, for example, are less than one-twentieth the size of Bangkok-Thonburi.

Bangkok has been the capital of Thailand since 1782, and for the fifteen years before Thonburi was the capital. Long before it became Thailand's

17

capital, however, a village and at times a fort were located at the present site of Bangkok.

The exact origin of the name Bangkok seems obscure, and, like the name of the country itself, Bangkok is the name by which the city is known internationally, while the Thai have a different name for their capital. They call it *Krung Theb*, a shortened version of a much longer name which is probably best translated to mean the Divine City. Theb is a Thai translation of the Hindu *Deva*, which is a word used for certain celestial beings in Brahmanical cosmology. These celestial beings are sometimes referred to loosely in English as angels, although they differ from angels in the Christian sense. Because of this meaning of Theb, Krung Theb is sometimes translated in English as "city of angels." I believe that the Christian connotations of the word angels are out of place in a Buddhist country and, therefore, prefer the more general term of Divine City. Traveling in distant upcountry areas of Thailand I have found persons who did not know where I came from when I used the name Bangkok, but who immediately recognized their capital and the city of my residence when I said Krung Theb.

Bangkok and Thonburi are located in separate provinces. Thonburi's province is also called Thonburi. The province in which Bangkok is located is named Phra Nakorn.

Unlike many cities in America and other lands of the Occidental world Bangkok has no one section that can be called the center of the city, no one spot where the visitor finds the business, financial, entertainment, government, and hotel sections of the city situated together. Instead, these activities are found all over the city and with the continual growth of the city they are spreading more and more widely throughout the area. There are, however, a few districts in which certain activities are concentrated. For example, in the area of the Grand Palace and the old city and along the nearby broad, handsome Rajadamnoen Road are found many government offices. Along Yawarat Road and Charoen Krung Road (New Road) are found hundreds of small retail shops whose proprietors are mainly Chinese, and crowded around the shops are the residences of Bangkok's large Chinese population. Out in Bangkapi, an eastern district of Bangkok, on many lanes extending north and south from wide Sukhumvidh Road are the large, new, modern homes often surrounded with broad, well-tended lawns and gardens, of resident foreigners and well-to-do Thai and Chinese.

In my early days in Thailand my favorite district name, although it covered a very poor district at the time, was the Din Daeng Dump. There, in an area of what had once been rice fields, the city had a huge mountain of garbage and refuse and around its edges were wooden houses, little more than shacks, built on stilts above the wet, soggy, often flooded ground beneath them, in which lived some of Bangkok's poorest residents. Today, with the spread of

the city into that outlying area and the construction of the new airport highway which traverses the Din Daeng district, the area has been considerably
upgraded.

The many districts of the sprawling capital city are an open invitation to
exploration and in the act of exploring to learn not only about the city, but
about the country as a whole and its people. Like most other cities the best
way to explore Bangkok is by walking. While that means of getting around
may seem foolish in a city with temperatures often in the nineties, still it can
be more comfortable than sweating out some of the worst traffic jams in Asia
in a taxi or private car.

One of the best places to begin any exploration of Bangkok is the Phra
Mane Ground, a large, oval-shaped open field in front of the Grand Palace.
The Phra Mane Ground is like a large racetrack in shape with a wide sidewalk around its periphery where the running track might ordinarily be, and
is a great open area except for trees which border the sidewalk at its edge.
The field, which is the site for the elaborate royal cremations, is now also
used for many other ceremonies and for a weekend market. It is also a
park and a playground and children and young people can be seen frequently
flying kites or playing English soccer-style football. American-style football
seems almost unknown.

The Phra Mane Ground is located near, but not on, the bank of the Chao
Phya River. It is far from being the geographical center of modern Bangkok,
although if Bangkok and Thonburi were considered as one large city, the
Phra Mane Ground would be much closer to the center.

In another sense, however, the Phra Mane Ground is the center of Bangkok. At its south end lies the Grand Palace. From the park can be seen the
palace's towers and spires soaring above its gleaming white crenelated walls.
Within those walls stands, too, the Wat Phra Keo, or Temple of the Emerald
Buddha, the king's temple and probably the most revered temple in the country for most Thai people. Until recently, the Grand Palace, with its many
buildings actually a city within the city, was the residence of the king and as
such, under the absolute monarchy that existed until 1932, was the governing
center of the country.

At the northwest corner of the Phra Mane Ground stands the former palace
of the deputy king, or second king, as he was often referred to in Western
writings of the past. His palace is now the home of the National Museum,
with its rich collections on Thai history. Next to it is the new National Theater and along the western or river side of the Phra Mane Ground are other
cultural institutions such as the National Library, Thammasat University,
and Silpakorn University (the University of Fine Arts). Along the east side
of the Phra Mane Ground and the Grand Palace are the Ministries of Justice,

Foreign Affairs, and Defense, as well as other government offices. In a very real sense then, the Phra Mane Ground may be considered the center of Bangkok.

Every Saturday and Sunday, with a few possible special exceptions, throughout the year the Phra Mane Ground becomes the most fascinating and exciting place in Bangkok. The great open area is used on those two days for Bangkok's weekend market, the largest market to be found in the metropolitan area and, therefore, in the country. Few foreigners visit the market and by not doing so they miss the opportunity to mingle in pleasant surroundings with a wide cross section of Bangkok's populace.

On Friday evenings after dark I sometimes walked around the Phra Mane Ground. It was always quiet, almost still, except for a few street noises. The imposing government buildings were dark except for the few lights of night workers and guards. The edge of the Ground was lighted with soft circles from the street lights spaced along the sidewalk. Few people were about. On the east side of the Ground, along Rajadamnoen Nai Road, several persons stood silently in shadowy lines as buses roared up to the loading areas and after swallowing the waiting lines of people leaped away to other parts of the city. The buses and a few cars on the same street were the only noises to disturb the quiet of the park.

Across the street along the base of the wall surrounding the Ministry of Justice there were a few bright lantern lights scattered many yards apart. Beside each one sat a man or a woman, usually elderly, on a mat or a blanket which also held the lantern and some drawings. At a few of the mats one or two other Thai squatted on their heels listening intently to the elder speaking to them in low tones. When I approached closer without disturbing the speakers or listeners I could see that the drawings were diagrams of hands and heads with various segments carefully marked off. At other mats the drawings were circles representing the universe with the signs of the zodiac drawn upon them. For these were astrologers, palmists, and other fortunetellers helping their clients to select auspicious times for special events or to choose winning numbers in the national lottery, or to prepare in other ways for the days ahead.

Back on the park side of the street a few cars were pulled up beside the curb. Their drivers, usually with one or two helpers, were busily unloading poles and boards, boxes and canvas or other cloth, and stacking all these supplies at designated spots on the inside of the sidewalk around the great oval park. A few were beginning to put up poles to erect the skeletons of the first booths for the market which opened early the following morning. There was no hurry about the work. There was plenty of time to set up the crude stalls before the market began. The men worked quietly adding little noise to the peaceful park in the heart of Bangkok.

Early the next morning I would return to the Phra Mane Ground. A miracle had occurred while I had slept. The quiet, peaceful park of the night before had become a noisy, busy, bustling, crowded, colorful market place where almost anything could be bought. The sidewalk surrounding the Ground was completely lined on both sides with hundreds of flimsy stalls made of cloth and wood. Canvas and cotton sunshades were extended over the sidewalk from both sides, held in place with ropes and strings which crisscrossed and hung down in all directions. The makeshift awnings provided shade for the thousands of milling customers strolling along in search of weekend bargains. In some parts of the oval a second row of stalls was erected behind the first, and all the crosswalks of the Phra Mane Ground were similarly lined with stalls on both sides.

One could buy fruits and fish and meat and vegetables of all kinds—fresh, dried, salted, pulverized. If the customer wanted to eat while shopping, there were restaurants at several spots around the oval where he could quench his thirst by stopping for a refreshing cold drink and a rest for a few minutes. Men's shirts, boys' short pants, girls' blouses and skirts, women's sarongs, shoes for all, undershirts and undershorts for men and boys, Chinese pants worn wrapped and tied around the waist, *pakomas* (the unique short man's sarong that has many uses), shoelaces, combs, fingernail clippers, dishes, pots, pans, knives, can openers, jewelry, nielloware, lacquerware, bronzeware, teakwood carvings, laundry detergents, soap, cosmetics, and caged birds to be freed to gain merit, all were available for purchase at numerous stalls. Almost every conceivable item could be bought with the exception of large hard goods such as heavy furniture, refrigerators, and automobiles. I would not be surprised if even these were available, if one knew the right merchants.

Huge crowds strolled around the oval in both directions. Some of the men were in the uniform of the Thai army, navy, air force, police, or civilian government services. But most were neatly dressed in white shirts with open collars and in long dark trousers. No self-respecting Thai man would wear short pants when he was not working no matter how high the temperature. Only foreigners who know no better wear shorts other than for work. The women at the market wear colorful long saronglike skirts and white blouses or Western skirts and blouses. A few can be seen in slacks, and occasionally an older woman with close-cropped hair, lips and mouth stained a deep red from years of chewing betel, will walk by wearing a traditional *phanung*, a wide skirt which is caught up between the legs and fastened at the waist in back to form a kind of pantaloon.

Merchants standing or sitting in their stalls among their wares call out their prices and their special bargains. Itinerant vendors of smaller items such as combs, soap, and nail files plant themselves in the middle of the sidewalk hawking their merchandise and adding to the general din.

On Saturday nights the scene changes again. The crowds of shoppers are gone. Many of the cloth awnings have been lowered or taken down to cover the merchandise, which is tied down under the cloths for protection against weather or thieves. Most merchants have gone home although some stay to protect their stalls. Others leave sons or daughters to watch through the night. Frequently mosquito nets are set up right on the stall in the middle of the covered merchandise and, walking past them, one can hear the murmur of quiet voices and sometimes the squealing of youngsters still playing under their nets when they should be asleep. Lighted by lanterns, a few of the restaurants remain open as coffee shops where the merchants can drink coffee or Mekong whisky and talk quietly with their friends. Except for the shadowy stalls that surround the Phra Mane Ground the area is almost as quiet as the night before. Across the street the fortunetellers are stationed along the wall, and at the bus stops a few persons are again lined up waiting for the trembling monsters to take them home.

On Sunday the market is again awake and colorful and noisy throughout the day. But when night comes the awnings are taken down, the platforms are dismantled, the poles are pulled from the ground, and all the paraphernalia, along with the unsold merchandise, is packed into cars or trucks or taxis or vehicles of one kind or another and hauled away to the merchant's usual store or his home until the next weekend. By Monday morning the Phra Mane Ground is once more a quiet park with the white walls of the Grand Palace shining in the distance.

The Grand Palace was built by the early kings of the Chakri dynasty of which the present sovereign, King Bhumibol Adulyadej, is the ninth ruler and carries the title of Rama IX. The Chakri dynasty was established in 1782 when Rama I succeeded King Taksin, who had earlier established his capital in Thonburi across the river. When Rama I became king he moved the capital to the east bank of the Chao Phya and built a new palace and city in a great bend of the river to the west. By linking the northern and southern ends of the river's bend with several klongs, in effect he created man-made islands for his palace and his capital city. The canals and river provided not only avenues for water transportation, but also effective defense barriers. The wide river epecially could be useful as a barrier against the Burmese in the west who had invaded the Thai kingdom several times and in 1767 had captured and completely sacked the city of Ayudhya, which had been the Thai capital for more than four centuries.

The history of Thailand can be divided into several major periods. In the centuries before the Thai people, moving southward from Yunnan in what is now southern China, established their first major kingdom in 1238 in the area that is modern Thailand, the territory was governed by many kingdoms. Some were small city-kingdoms while others were large empires which ruled major portions of the entire Southeast Asian peninsula.

One of the earliest-known large empires was that of the Mons, who moved eastward into central Thailand from their main area in southern Burma in the period from the sixth to the eleventh centuries. From the eighth century onward the Mons were in contact in the east with the Khmers, the ancestors of present-day Cambodians, as the Khmers extended their control westward into Thailand from the valley of the Mekong River. The Khmers had built an important empire, with their capital at Angkor Thom, best known in the present century for the awe-inspiring ruins of the temple of Angkor Wat outside the walls of the ruined city.

During the same centuries that the Mons were meeting the Khmers in central Thailand, the Srivijayan empire, which is believed to have had its main centers on the island of Sumatra, pushed northward on the Malay Peninsula until it controlled all of present-day Malaya and much of southern Thailand.

Sukhothai in Northern Thailand was a Khmer city when it was seized by Thai chieftains in 1238 and became the first Thai kingdom to begin expansion on a large scale into the area of what is now Thailand. Although Sukhothai lasted about one and a half centuries, its strength as the leading Thai kingdom in this area had disappeared by the middle of the fourteenth century when a new Thai kingdom centered at Ayudhya rose in power. The king of Ayudhya soon became the king of all the Thai territory in the center of Southeast Asia.

It was early in the sixteenth century that the Thai of Ayudhya first received traders and emissaries from Western European nations. The number of Westerners grew until, after a Thai revolution of 1688 in which Westerners were involved, the Thai rulers for the next century and a half limited Western contacts and relationships with their country.

Shortly before the Burmese captured Ayudhya in 1767 a Thai general in his early thirties fled the capital with a few hundred followers. This young general was a half-Chinese citizen of Ayudhya born with the name of Sin, who, later when he served as governor of Tak, added that prefix to his name and became Taksin. General Taksin fled to the southeastern part of Thailand around Rayong, where he reorganized his forces and added new followers to his ranks. With his new strength he turned back against the Burmese who, once they had captured and destroyed Ayudhya, had marched back to Burma with thousands of prisoners, leaving only a small force behind. General Taksin within a few months accomplished the remarkable military feats of rallying the Thai people, driving the Burmese out of the country, and re-establishing the Thai kingdom almost to the size it had been before the Burmese conquest. He proclaimed himself king to replace the king who had disappeared with the fall of Ayudhya.

When he surveyed the total destruction of Ayudhya King Taksin decided to move his capital farther down the Chao Phya River and built his new capital at what is now Thonburi. During the fifteen years of his reign King Taksin engaged in several military ventures against the Burmese, the Cambodians, and several of the Lao kingdoms north of Thailand. In almost all of these ventures he emerged victorious.

Among the followers of King Taksin who fled with him from Ayudhya was a man three years younger than the general. This man, named Thong Duang, was the son of an official in the government of Ayudhya. During Taksin's campaigns this young follower distinguished himself as a military leader, and in 1772 King Taksin named Thong Duang, Chao Phya Chakri, commander in chief of Taksin's armies.

It should be noted that the name Chakri by which the present dynasty is known is a title rather than a family or personal name. The title of Chao Phya Chakri is found at various times in Thai history and is usually given to the commander in chief or ranking military officer. Usually when a military man received that title he was known henceforth by that title rather than by the name he was given as a child. Persons known by this title in Thai history are usually not related by blood, although they may be.

This system of using titles instead of names is a common practice in Thailand, one that has been followed right down until modern times. As individuals were promoted in service to the king they were given appropriate titles and were then called by their titles instead of their names. Even foreigners employed in the service of the Thai king have received such titles at times and may be called in Thai history by their titles rather than by their real names. This practice is still true also within the permanent Buddhist hierarchy. As a monk is promoted to a higher grade he receives a new title and is known by that title rather than by any earlier name or title. A monk may have several names, therefore, during his lifetime. Thus, the chief monk in the country is known as the Somdech Phra Sangharaj (with many more titles added) which indicates that he is the Supreme Patriarch of the *Sangha,* or body or community of monks. He is not called by a personal name or any earlier title.

General Chao Phya Chakri continued to be King Taksin's most outstanding military leader and in time subdued the Lao kingdoms of Wieng Chan (Vientiane), Luang Prabang, and Chiengmai. In Vientiane General Chakri found the Emerald Buddha, a small green Buddha with a legendary past which was first known in Chiengrai, a far northern city, early in the fifteenth century, but which is probably much older. The Emerald Buddha had gone from one Lao capital to another and was in Vientiane when General Chakri took that city in 1778. He removed the Emerald Buddha from Vientiane to Thonburi and later, after becoming king, General Chakri moved the famous statue to his new palace in Bangkok, where it now rests in its own temple, the Wat Phra Keo, within the walls of the Grand Palace.

Toward the end of his short reign, a militarily successful reign, King Taksin was reported to have developed a form of megalomania. It was rumored that he had begun to think he was the Buddha and made extraordinary demands upon his noble followers and also upon the Buddhist hierarchy for obeisance and complete servitude as if he were the Buddha. A revolt broke out in Thonburi and the nobles seized the king. At that time General Chakri was leading an army in the east against the Cambodians. He hurried back to Thonburi as soon as he heard the news of the revolt, and on his arrival this popular general was declared king with the support of the army and the nobility. At first he held Taksin a prisoner, but in order to prevent any opposition forces from rallying around the deposed king, General Chakri, now King Rama I, had ex-King Taksin executed in the usual manner for royalty: the king was tied in a velvet bag and beaten to death with sandalwood clubs. In that way no royal blood was spilled.

King Rama I moved his capital across the river to the village of Bangkok and in doing so put the Chao Phya River between it and any possible resurgent invaders from Burma. He named the capital Krung Theb Ratanakosin (now usually shortened still further to Krung Theb) and supervised the construction of the new city with his Grand Palace at the center.

During his long reign from 1782 to 1809, Rama I continued to protect the country from new invasions by the Burmese and from revolts among some of the tributary states on the borders. In addition, he made some major reforms within Thai society. A new law code was prepared with old laws revised and some new laws drafted. An attempt was made to save what could be saved from the lore and learning of the destroyed capital of Ayudhya. The Buddhist hierarchy had suffered and become demoralized to some extent in the wars with the Burmese and under the strange injunctions and regulations of the deranged King Taksin toward the end of his life. Rama I tried to bring new order and discipline to a reorganized Buddhist leadership. He also began the task of rediscovering and rewriting the Buddhist scripture and canons, much of which had been lost with the destruction of Ayudhya. To do this he sent for text copies from old temples in Nakornsrithammarat and other areas under his jurisdiction. On quite a different level, the king had constructed from giant teakwood trees the first of the imposing, colorful royal barges which are still used for the annual *kathin* ceremonies by water at which the king presents new robes to monks in the royal temples.

It should be noted that Rama I, like most Thai kings and other royal leaders in Thai history, had many different names and titles. Indeed, the title

Rama I was not given to him until many years after he died. But to avoid confusion I am using only one name for each king and that is the name by which he is best known in the West.

In 1809 Rama I died and was succeeded by his son, Prince Isarasuntorn, who is now generally known as Rama II. He ruled until 1824. Rama II was a great artist in several fields and is especially remembered as a poet. He was also much interested in Thai classical ballet and did much to preserve and enrich that art form. He was also responsible for the conception and design of the magnificent Wat Arun (Temple of the Dawn) built on the Thonburi bank of the Chao Phya across the river from the Grand Palace, although the temple was not completed until the reign of his successor.

Rama II also made some changes in the laws and administration of the kingdom. For one thing, he enacted laws against the use of opium, although opium has continued in use down to the present time. During much of the century and a half since Rama II, this has been legally permitted, contrary to the kings' wishes at times. Under the present government it is illegal. Rama II began another major political practice. He started the custom of appointing senior princes of the kingdom to supervise different departments of the government. These departments were headed by noblemen ministers who under this new system became permanent under-secretaries with the actual responsibility for running the departments, but who had to report to a senior prince. This system of using senior princes in supervisory capacities lasted until the revolution of 1932 and contributed to the dissatisfaction of some of the senior civil servants who supported the revolution.

During Rama II's reign he appointed one of his brothers as *uparaja,* a position which has usually been known in the West as second king, or vice-king, or deputy king. This royal position, second only to that of the first, or major, king himself, was known in other Southeast Asian kingdoms, but unknown in Europe. It has sometimes been suggested that the uparaja was comparable to a European crown prince, but this is not really accurate. The crown prince is usually the successor to the throne and frequently the son of the king. The uparaja, on the other hand, might be a successor, but not necessarily so. He was frequently a brother or other relative of the king and not necessarily a son. Because he was often about the same age as the king, it was not unusual for the uparaja to predecease the king. The deputy king shared many of the king's duties and responsibilities at the king's request and usually was a leader of the king's military forces. Sometimes the uparaja also maintained his own military forces independent of the king's. The deputy king had many of the royal prerogatives and received much the same obedience and honor due the major king himself.

The institution of the uparaja, or deputy king, had existed for centuries and

Rama II, in appointing his brother to that position, was following long-established custom. The uparaja Rama II appointed, however, died in 1817. The king was inconsolable over the loss of his brother and during the seven remaining years in his reign never appointed another uparaja. Thus when Rama II died in 1824, there was no uparaja to succeed to the throne even if that had been the general rule.

In Thailand, however, succession to the throne was not guaranteed to the uparaja and also not to the crown prince or any particular prince. When a king died his successor was chosen by an Accession Council consisting of senior princes of the kingdom and senior officials. The previous ruler often suggested before he died whom he would like to have succeed him and the council often followed his suggestion, but it was not bound to do so. Usually the council would choose a king from among the princes of highest rank, that is, the princes who were sons of kings by the wives who had been elevated to the rank of queens.

Thai kings traditionally had numerous wives. Many of these women had become wives for political or similar reasons. To cement an alliance or to guarantee the loyalty of a vassal state, the king of Thailand would marry a daughter of that prince. Many high-ranking nobles and officials of the kingdom offered daughters to the king, thus hoping to achieve future gains by mixing their blood with the royal family. Many of these wives were wives in name only. The king usually had children by a relatively small number of his total harem. Only a very small number of the king's wives were named queens, never more than four as far as is known. The remainder of the wives were consorts. Only the small number of children who were born of the king and a queen were princes and princesses of the highest rank.

With a large number of wives and an even larger number of royal children it would appear, if one visualized the future, that Thailand might in time be overrun with royal nobility. But in one of many farsighted acts the Thai had foreseen this possibility and established a system whereby royal descendants declined in rank with each generation until the fifth generation, when the royal descendants became commoners again. The later generations were all called plain *Nai* (mister). The children of a king and queen had the title of *Chao Fa* (roughly equivalent in English to Royal Highness). The children of a king and a consort who was not a queen had the title of *Pra Ong Chao* (Highness). The grandchildren of kings were *Mom Chao* (Serene Highness); great-grandchildren were *Mom Rajawongse* (no equivalent); great-great-grandchildren were *Mom Luang* (no equivalent); and their children were commoners. The king could and sometimes did alter these ranks by decree and raised a prince in rank from the one into which he had been born.

The institution of multiple wives for Thai kings died out in the twentieth century with the death of King Chulalongkorn. Recent kings have limited their wives to one.

It was from the group of princes designated Chao Fa that the Accession Council usually chose the successor king, but the council was not bound even to a rule of that kind, and in choosing a successor to Rama II it did not choose a son of the king by a queen. The eldest son of Rama II by a queen was Prince Mongkut who, a few days before Rama II became ill and died, entered a monastery to serve the usual short period as a monk, which was an obligation for most Thai men. The eldest son of Rama II was Prince Chesda who was a child of the king by a consort *not* a queen, and who had been active in government affairs for many years. The Accession Council chose Prince Chesda as king and he became Rama III. Prince Mongkut then decided to stay in the Sangha (the monastic order or community of monks) and remained a monk for twenty-seven years until he succeeded his elder half-brother as king in 1851.

Some Western writers have implied or asserted that Rama III was a usurper, which is not true. While selection by the Accession Council of a lower-ranking prince to become king may have been unusual, it was not forbidden.

Rama III was a devout Buddhist. He completed the construction of Wat Arun and built at Wat Po a new building to house the huge reclining Buddha familiar to most Bangkok visitors. He strongly supported the work of his half-brother, Prince Mongkut, in the Sangha. Prince Mongkut became a great scholar while a monk and rose in rank in the Buddhist hierarchy. In 1837 Rama III appointed his half-brother to be abbot of Wat Bovoranives in Bangkok, and while serving as abbot of that wat, Prince Mongkut founded the Dhammayut sect of Buddhist monks, a smaller and more strict sect than the much larger Mahanikaya sect.

Rama III also took strong action during his reign to suppress crime in the capital city and the kingdom. He also tried, without complete success, to suppress the opium trade which was being promoted by some Chinese secret societies. These societies were beginning to appear in Thailand for the first time.

From the revolution in Ayudhya in 1688 until the reign of Rama III Thailand had few contacts with Westerners. During the reign of Rama II, the Portuguese in Macao had begun some trade again with the Thai, and in 1822 the Marquis of Hastings as Governor General of India sent John Crawfurd to establish new trade relations with Thailand for the English. Crawfurd, due to many reasons, did not win over the Thai and his mission had little success.

Contacts with the West increased, however, in the reign of Rama III. In the late 1820's the first Protestant missionaries, many of them Americans, began arriving. They had little success in converting Thai Buddhists to Christianity, but they had a strong nonreligious impact. Several of the missionaries were medical men and they introduced Western ideas of medicine and science into Thailand. One of their ablest pupils was the monk, Prince Mongkut. In 1835 the American missionaries introduced the first printing press into Thailand.

Early in his reign Rama III had trouble with revolts in some of the Malay states which were his vassals. The British had trading colonies at Penang and in Province Wellesley on the Malay Peninsula opposite Penang. The British were also undertaking their first war against the Burmese in 1824–26, and it was not unusual for the British to extend aid to Malay states in revolt against Thailand. On June 20, 1826, Thailand signed a treaty with Great Britain, the first treaty the Thai had signed with a Western power since the seventeenth century. Captain Henry Burney, who negotiated for the British, had been much more successful than his predecessor, John Crawfurd. The treaty provided that Thailand would not interfere with British trade in Malaya. Up to that time all foreign trade in the area under the control of the Thai kingdom was, theoretically at least, in the king's hands alone. Now the British were to be permitted to trade direct with certain vassal states of the Thai king. Thailand recognized the independence of Selangor and Perak states in Malaya and that Penang and Province Wellesley were British possessions. In return, the British recognized that the Malay states of Kedah, Kelantan, and Trengganu were under the suzerainty of Thailand. Some of these early territorial arrangements with Britain and later with France were to become matters of controversy again as late as World War II.

A few years later, in 1833, Edmund Roberts arrived in Thailand as an envoy of the United States. Before his departure he, too, was able to get a trade treaty between his country and Thailand. This was the beginning of a long history of friendly relations between the two nations.

During the reign of Rama III a historical incident occurred which created a new heroine for Thailand. In 1827, there was a revolt in the Lao provinces under Thai control. The Lao army marched across the Northeast region and captured Khorat, taking many men prisoners and killing many others. Among those killed was the governor of Khorat. The governor's wife organized other Thai women in a plot to lure the Lao troops into a drunken party. When the troops were thoroughly intoxicated the women freed the Thai prisoners, who then turned on the Lao troops, killing two thousand of them before rejoining the Thai armed forces. Eventually the Thai army stopped the revolt and destroyed Vientiane's military capability. A statue of the governor's wife can be seen in Khorat today.

The feeble contacts with the West during the reign of Rama II were increased by Rama III and greatly strengthened by Rama IV, who is better known as King Mongkut. When Rama III died the Accession Council called the prince-monk to the throne. He left the Sangha and ruled Thailand from

1851 to 1868. One of Thailand's greatest kings, Mongkut would stand high among the world's monarchs of any time.

During his twenty-seven years as a monk, King Mongkut had studied widely and diligently. He learned foreign languages, including English and French, from Christian missionaries. With these tools he read books on modern science and mathematics. He was an outstanding authority on the history and teachings of Buddhism and was an avid student of comparative religion. The Buddhist monastic order is a singular leveler of rank and as a monk the prince traveled widely among people at all social and economic levels, something he would not have been able to do if his life had been spent in the traditional manner of a royal prince. All that he learned and saw he brought to bear on his duties as king, and it is difficult to exaggerate the impact this man had on his country.

Just to list a few of his accomplishments will show the broad range of his interests. He restored the beautiful palace at Bang-Pa-In and constructed a new palace and astronomical observatory at Petchburi. He began the restoration of the great *chedi* or *stupa* at Nakorn Pathom. He introduced minted coins to the country. More canals were built for transportation and irrigation throughout the Central Plain on his orders. He began to reorganize the armed forces along modern European lines. He urged that women should be allowed to marry men of their own choice. He started to reduce the long-established corvée labor service. He restated the Thai belief in religious freedom and backed it up by giving financial support to all religions—and this from one of the most devout Buddhist kings the world has ever known. He built new roads outside the central city. Among them was Charoen Krung Road, known to foreigners to this day as New Road. He abolished for foreigners prostration in the king's presence, permitting them to behave before him as they would before their own sovereigns. And this is only a small list of his many innovations, for his concern for his country and his people extended to all aspects of Thai life.

In 1855 Sir John Bowring arrived in Bangkok as the representative of Queen Victoria. He negotiated a treaty with the Thai which was to have great importance for Thailand's relations with the West because it was to be used as a model for treaties with other Western nations in the years immediately following his visit. By this treaty Britain got the right to station a British consul in Bangkok with extraterritorial jurisdiction over all British subjects, both European and Asian. The treaty permitted rice to be exported, which previously had been forbidden, and permitted opium to be imported duty free from India. A limitation was placed on the duty which Thailand could put on imports, and the British were permitted to purchase land in Thailand under certain restrictions. Prior to that time foreigners could not purchase land. These were the major concessions gained by Bowring, and following similar

treaties with the United States, France, and other Western nations in 1856
and subsequent years, these patterns of relationships were to extend well into
the twentieth century.

Before becoming a monk in 1824 Prince Mongkut had married and had
two children. After becoming king in 1851 at the age of forty-seven, he followed the customary practice of having many wives and also had eighty more
children.

Throughout his adult life one of King Mongkut's personal interests was
astronomy. In 1868 he calculated and predicted the time for a total eclipse of
the sun. To observe it he organized a great party of Thai and foreign scientists
and other dignitaries to travel to a spot in Southern Thailand on the Malay
Peninsula, where a camp had been constructed for housing the guests as well
as numerous telescopes and other scientific equipment. On the day of the
eclipse the sky was clouded, but it cleared shortly before the predicted
time. To his great joy the king's scientific predictions turned out to be extremely accurate and the eclipse occurred when he said it would. Unfortunately, despite the precautions taken in this temporary camp, the king became
seriously ill with malaria after he returned to Bangkok, and in October he
died on his sixty-fourth birthday. This great king left behind him a country
which he had pushed far ahead into the modern world.

Frequently in the history of any country a great king is succeeded by a
mediocre or even a poor one, and this has happened at times in Thai history,
too. But it was not to happen to King Mongkut. He was succeeded by his son,
King Chulalongkorn (Rama V) who was to reign in Thailand for forty-two
years, from 1868 to 1910, and if anything, the son was greater than his father.
King Mongkut had launched his country on the way to modernization and
King Chulalongkorn guided it faster along that path.

With all the changes and innovations begun by these two kings in the six
decades they ruled Thailand, tradition was not totally lost. This was tragically
seen in an event in the king's own family in 1881. One of King Chulalongkorn's wives, Queen Sunanda, was traveling by boat on the Chao Phya River
to the palace at Bang-Pa-In. Near the palace the boat capsized and the twenty-
one-year-old queen and her children who were with her drowned in full view
of hundreds of people. None dared try to save her because the traditional laws
and customs of the country punished by death anyone who touched the royal
persons. Thus, at the very time the king was making dramatic revisions in the
laws and customs of the country, tradition persisted in some areas of life.

King Chulalongkorn was fifteen years old when his father died in 1868, and
during the first five years of his reign the country had a regent. But in 1873
the king's coronation was celebrated and he took full control of the kingdom.
He immediately began making changes both in customs and in laws. So many

changes were made during his long reign that only a few can be recited here. The practice of prostration by Thai before the monarch was abolished, although again traditions die hard. I saw prostration practiced in the 1960's. European-style uniforms were introduced for court and military officials which altered the appearance of the court to some extent.

Other changes had more widespread effects outside the immediate court. The king opened a model school for princes and the sons of high nobles in the Grand Palace. Outside of the palace he founded Suan Kularb College, a school for the sons of lower officials and prominent merchants. Suan Kularb College exists today as one of the finest secondary schools in Thailand.

Steps were taken to enlarge and modernize the army and the king began a navy with the purchase of a few gunboats. Government administration was improved and made more centralized. In this task the king was assisted by a remarkable group of senior princes, including some of his brothers and half-brothers. Notable among these were Prince Damrong, Prince Devawongse, and Prince Naris, who took leading positions in modernizing the administration of state affairs. King Chulalongkorn also made extensive use of foreign advisers, including Belgians, Danes, French, Germans, Britishers, and Americans to work in the military, foreign affairs, financial, medical, and agriculture departments of the government. A new postal and telegraph system was built. The construction of railroads leading out of Bangkok to the major regions of the country was started. New hospitals using Western as well as traditional medicine and medical practices were begun. The list of the king's reforms and innovations seems almost endless.

One of his most significant reforms was the abolition of slavery, which had been known in Thailand from its earliest days. As early as 1868 when King Chulalongkorn first became king it was decreed that all persons born during his reign would be free. Beginning in 1874 a series of steps was taken leading to the end of slavery. It was completely abolished in 1905.

King Chulalongkorn was faced with increasing pressures from external political forces. He had a keen interest in other countries and foreign affairs. While the country was still under a regent, the young king had traveled abroad, first to Malaya and Java, and later to India. Toward the end of his reign he made two major trips to Europe in 1897 and 1907. During much of his reign, however, he was involved in the delicate balancing of his relationships with Great Britain in Malaya and Burma on the one hand and with an increasingly aggressive France in Indo-China on the other.

France had taken control of Annam (Vietnam) and was moving against the Thai tributary provinces of Cambodia and Laos along the Mekong River. In 1886, Thailand signed a treaty with France, giving France all the Thai territory east of the Mekong River except that of the Lao state of Luang Prabang.

But France was not satisfied and continued to apply pressure to gain control over the Cambodian provinces west of the Mekong and the remaining Lao territory. In 1893 France sent a gunboat up the Chao Phya as far as Bangkok and on the way exchanged shots with a Thai shore battery. Demanding redress, France landed troops to occupy a part of southeast Thailand in Chantaburi Province. Thailand turned to Britain for help, but was advised to move cautiously while the two great European powers worked out their own rivalries throughout the world.

The dispute between France and Thailand dragged on until 1904 when French troops finally left Chantaburi, and to gain that objective Thailand had to cede Luang Prabang and Vientiane to France. At about the same time France and Britain agreed to guarantee Thailand's borders and King Chulalongkorn's kingdom became a buffer between the growing Asian empires of the two European powers. Three years later Thailand gave up to France the Cambodian provinces of Battembang, Siemrap, and Srisophon, in return for which France gave up extraterritorial rights over French Asian subjects, but not over European Frenchmen. Finally, in 1909, Thailand gave control of the Malay states of Kedah, Kelantan, Trengganu, and Perlis to Britain in return for which the British, too, gave up some extraterritorial rights which had been negotiated by Sir John Bowring fifty-four years earlier.

At the end of King Chulalongkorn's reign, therefore, Thailand was smaller than at the beginning, but of great importance then and in the future Thailand, unlike its neighbors in Indo-China, Burma, and Malaya, was still not under European control and the only country in Southeast Asia to remain fully independent. The central core of the long independent kingdom of the Thai remained intact under Thai control. The areas lost to the French and the British were fringe states, largely tributary in nature, which had changed hands in earlier Thai history at various times depending on the strength of particular Thai kings in relation to their Burmese, Khmer, and Lao contemporaries and rivals. Most Thai would agree, I am sure, that despite the loss of the outlying provinces, the foreign policies of King Mongkut and King Chulalongkorn had paid off handsomely.

King Chulalongkorn died on October 23, 1910, which is now a national holiday. He was succeeded by his son, King Vajiravudh (Rama VI), who ruled until 1925. King Vajiravudh had been educated in England and was one of Thailand's best-known writers. He was a poet and had a strong interest in the theater, for which he translated three of Shakespeare's plays into Thai and wrote or translated from French and English almost one hundred other plays.

During World War I Thailand was officially neutral at first, although the king personally, due to his years at school in England, was pro-English. After the United States entered the war in 1917 Thailand, too, joined the Allies and sent some troops to provide a transportation unit in Europe and a few pilots to be trained.

Near the end of the war King Vajiravudh's half-brother and cousin (their father was King Chulalongkorn and their mothers were sisters), Prince Mahidol, went abroad to study medicine. While studying in several countries during the next decade Prince Mahidol met and married a Thai nursing student and had three children who were born abroad. The eldest was Princess Galyani, born in London, and the next two were sons—Prince Ananda Mahidol (later King Rama VIII) born in Heidelberg in 1925, and Prince Bhumibol Adulyadej (the present King Rama IX) born in Cambridge, Massachusetts, in 1927.

King Vajiravudh is often remembered today as the promoter of education for in 1921 he enacted a law providing free and compulsory education for a minimum of four years for all children between seven and fourteen. In addition, he founded Chulalongkorn University, which he named after his father, and a Royal Page School, which is now one of Thailand's outstanding secondary schools, Vajiravudh College. He is also known as the founder of the Thai Boy Scout Organization.

King Vajiravudh is remembered, too, for having required his subjects to acquire last names. Prior to his reign each Thai had only one name by which he was known or else he was known by the title of the office which he held. In 1916 the king ordered everyone to adopt a last name and provided such names himself for lower members of royalty. Other citizens selected their own last names, often choosing names which were held by astrologers to be auspicious or which were related to Buddhism or good fortune. Many unrelated Thai chose the same last name so that today it is unwise to assume that persons with the same last name are in any way related. The Thai are still known to each other by their first names, preceded by any title they may have. For example, the present prime minister's full name is Marshal Thanom Kittakachorn, but he is regularly referred to as Marshal Thanom, and many Thai friends call me Mr. James even when they meet me in the United States.

King Vajiravudh did not marry until shortly before he died and did not leave any sons. When he died in 1925 the throne passed to his brother, King Prajadhipok (Rama VII) who reigned from 1925 to 1935.

There was an old myth in Thailand that during the reign of Rama I a prediction had been made that the Chakri dynasty would last 150 years. That time period had only seven years to go when this seventh ruler of the dynasty became king. He continued the policies of his predecessors in using senior princes to supervise the government ministries and created a Supreme Council of senior princes which acted as a kind of advisory cabinet for him. Thailand for some years had been sending young military officers and civil servants to Europe for education and training. Some of these young men had returned and resented the continued placement of princes in the top ministerial posts as their supervisors. Many of these young officials educated abroad had absorbed the ideas of democracy and constitutional rule which they had seen in the West. There were rumors that the king was considering granting a Constitution to the country, but no action was ever taken by him to do so.

At the end of the 1920's Thailand was affected—as was the rest of the world—by the enormous economic problems of the world-wide depression. The king had to initiate strong economies in his government in both the military and civil services, which added to the growing dissatisfaction among the junior officials.

On June 24, 1932, King Prajadhipok was in residence at his seaside palace at Hua Hin. Early that day the government in Bangkok was seized by a revolutionary group of both military and civilian government officials. Led by a group of twenty-seven who called themselves the "Promoters" the revolutionary group took over without any bloodshed and held all the senior princes, except Prince Purachatra, who managed to escape their net, as hostages while sending an ultimatum to the king demanding he become a constitutional monarch under the leadership of the Promoters. The Promoters were led by former students who had met in France. Among them were an army officer, Captain (soon to be Colonel) Luang Pibun Songgram, and a lawyer, Nai Pridi Phanomyong. Although the Promoters were increased to seventy in a short time, these two men, often rivals, were to dominate the government for the next two decades.

The king accepted the ultimatum. The princely hostages were released, but all had to resign their official posts in the government, and before the end of the month a provisional constitution had been proclaimed. The prediction of the end of the Chakri dynasty in 150 years had not proven entirely accurate, but the absolute monarchy under the Chakri kings had ended and was replaced by a constitutional monarchy of quite a different character.

2

Saffron Robes and Temple Bells

The temple and the saffron-robed monk are Thailand's two most visible signs —obvious to tourist and resident alike—of the country's reverence for Buddhism. An overwhelming majority of the people of Thailand are Buddhist. Of the total population an estimated 93 to 94 percent are Buddhist while the small remainder is divided among followers of Islam, Confucianism, Christianity, all other religions, or no religion at all.

For most Thai the royal Temple of the Emerald Buddha, Wat Phra Keo, is a magnet that draws them in crowds to visit the temple precincts on those days when the temple is open to the public, so that they may show respect for the revered image of the Buddha cut from green jasper stone. The image is not large as many Buddha images are; it is only about two feet tall, and set high on a lofty golden pedestal altar in the main chapel of the temple it looks very small indeed. Yet, it has had a dramatic history. Discovered in Chiengrai in the first half of the fifteenth century, it later was moved to Lampang and Chiengrai in northern Thailand. Still later it journeyed to several other Thai-Lao cities and was in Vientiane when Chao Phya Chakri captured that city in 1778 and brought the Emerald Buddha to Thonburi. After a few years in that city, it was moved, along with the Thai capital, across the river to Bangkok, where Rama I constructed his new palace and city.

Wat Phra Keo is one of a great many royal temples in Thailand, but it is especially significant because of its location inside the walls of the Grand Palace and because most major religious ceremonies and state ceremonies involving religion are celebrated by the king at this temple. Three times a year the king comes to the temple to change the gold and jeweled robes that are placed on the Emerald Buddha image. The robes are changed with the three main seasons—summer, rainy, and cool.

On entering the precincts of the Emerald Buddha Temple the visitor feels he is entering another world, a kind of fairyland. The temple has many buildings. This is typical, although not necessary, of most Thai temples. Some of the simpler rural temples may have only two or three small buildings while some of the larger temples cover many acres of land and have scores of buildings for one use or another.

One of the buildings will be built in an area around which will be found eight small stone markers embedded in the ground at the eight main points of the compass. In Thailand these markers often are in the shape of a wheel to symbolize the Buddhist wheel of the law. These stone markers, called *sima,* mark the limits of the consecrated ground of the temple. The amount of land included in this sacred area is not definitely set. It can be any size so long as it is large enough to hold at least twenty-one monks, the minimum number which is necessary to conduct certain functions of the monastic order. Usually, of course, the consecrated area is much larger than this minimum size. All land in the temples is, formally at least, owned by the government on behalf of the monastic order, and once ground is consecrated it can never be used for any other purpose even if the temple should be abandoned for some reason—unless the order takes the required action to deconsecrate it. This restriction applies only to that part of the temple's land which is within the markers. A large part of the land in most temples will not be within this consecrated area.

Within the sima-marked area there is a rectangular building which often has a portico at one or both ends or all the way around. This building is called a *bot* and usually houses the principal Buddha image of the temple. Within the bot will be held those ceremonies, especially those for the monastic order, which must be held on sacred ground. Among the services which monastic rules require to be held in this area are those in which a young man is ordained a novice or a monk.

A temple will usually have another similar building which also will hold one or more Buddha images, sometimes including the principal one, and which is the building used by lay worshipers as well as by monks. This building is called a *vihara.* Most of these buildings are relatively small especially when compared to the great cathedrals of the West and the giant mosques of the Middle East. Buddhism as practiced in Thailand and other Theravada Buddhist countries does not have the kind of ceremony that brings hundreds or thousands of persons together in one place at a prescribed time to pay homage to a god. Therefore, there is no need for a St. Paul's as in London or a St. Patrick's as in New York or a Sultanahmet Camii (Blue) Mosque as in Istanbul with their great open areas in which throngs of worshipers can gather. The vihara is often a smaller building than the bot, which itself need not be large.

A third building found in most Thai temples is a *stupa.* Originally in India the stupa was built to house the relics of the Lord Buddha after he died. His relics were distributed to several countries and stupas were built in each to house the relics. Now the stupa, which appears in the hundreds of thousands throughout the Buddhist world, houses objects other than the relics of the Buddha. The stupas are used today in Thailand and elsewhere to house other revered objects such as the relics of famous Buddhist monks and the relics and ashes of kings and other greatly honored leaders of the country and society.

The stupas in Thailand are found in many sizes. Some may be no more than a few feet high while others may be as much as two or three hundred feet high. The tallest of all is the great stupa at Nakorn Pathom, an old city about thirty-five miles west of Bangkok. At that quiet town the stupa, called Phra Pathom Chedi, is almost 380 feet high. Covered with gold-colored tiles from top to bottom this lofty temple building can be seen in all directions for many miles across the flat countryside.

In Thailand there are, from an architectural standpoint, two major kinds of stupas. One, the most common, is a bell-shaped building tapering to a tall thin spire at the top. This style is found throughout Thailand and is called a *chedi*. Small and large chedi can be found in the compounds of thousands of temples. Frequently, tiny bronze bells are hung high up on a chedi. The bells tinkle softly in the breeze and add a gentle note of music to the temple scene. The second type of stupa is a blunt tower, modeled on the tower commonly found in the Khmer style of architecture. This tower is often ridged vertically, covered with sculpture, and has almost no tapering from its pedestal to its top. It looks a little like a stone corncob stood on end. This type of stupa is called a *prang* and can best be seen in Bangkok at the famous Wat Arun, or Temple of the Dawn, on the riverbank in Thonburi almost directly across the river from the Grand Palace.

Wat Arun has a central prang, which rises almost 220 feet from its pedestal, and four smaller prangs in the four corners of the base of the temple. This temple is well known to tourists because it is visited on most river trips. Besides its awe-inspiring size and unusual architecture, Wat Arun is also noted for the broken table pottery with which it is covered. Plates, saucers, cups, and dishes of all kinds were broken into pieces and affixed to the stucco to make flower patterns of various sizes and shapes.

While most temples in Bangkok will have a bot and a vihara for housing Buddha images, and at least one stupa to contain sacred relics, there are other buildings often found in wats as well. Among these are the living quarters for the monks. In order to have a functioning monastery as part of a temple there must be a minimum of five monks and they must have a place to live. There are a few temples, such as Wat Phra Keo, which do not have resident monks, but most temples do. The average number of monks in a Thai temple is twelve, but some, such as the famous Wat Bovoranives in Bangkok, may have several hundred. In such a case, the living quarters take up a substantial part of the temple compound.

It is not unusual to find laymen living in a wat. Some of these may be temple boys who are there to assist the monks in return for religious instruction and a place to live. In Bangkok, however, many wats have permanent or semipermanent male residents. Sometimes these are students who are attending Bangkok universities and secondary schools. They come from all over Thailand and with little money can live inexpensively in a wat which may be headed by or have monks from their home area or monks who are relatives. The residents, however, are not limited to students, for on several occasions I met government staff employees who lived in Bangkok temples on a regular basis.

Other buildings which may be found on the temple grounds are libraries and school buildings, for many wats have religious schools and some still provide the facilities for government schools as well. One often finds open-sided buildings, or *salas*, which may be used for any of several purposes, including schools.

A Buddhist temple in Thailand, therefore, is much more than the single building place of worship with which the West is most familiar as a church, synagogue, or mosque. Wat Phra Keo, except for the absence of living quarters, represents the Thai temple of many buildings although it is much more lavishly and richly decorated in gold, colored tiles, painted walls, colored glass, statues of *kinnaris, garudas,* demons, and other mythical creatures, and other works of art in the grounds.

In the building housing the Emerald Buddha image the walls are covered with paintings based on the life and teachings of Buddha with some more recent scenes as well. Of particular grandeur in this temple is the covered cloister, or gallery, which runs completely around the edge of the whole temple grounds. This long gallery is one great wall mural stretching for hundreds of feet along the four sides of the compound. The mural depicts the story of the *Ramakien,* the Thai version of the Hindu epic, the *Ramayana,* written by the poet Valmiki many centuries ago. Although the mural, which was completed in the 1920's, is a comparatively new one, it needs restoring from time to time to keep its colors fresh and bright. If one is fortunate, he may see a Thai artist painstakingly working on one of the episodes of the epic, although most of the work is done when the temple is closed to the public.

Besides Wat Phra Keo and Wat Arun there are other noted temples in Bangkok which both Thai and foreigners frequently visit. Just across the street from the south wall of the Grand Palace at the far end of the palace compound from Wat Phra Keo is a temple well known to visitors, Wat Po. This large temple has many buildings, Buddha images, other statues, stupas of varying sizes, and many works of art. In one of the buildings of this temple is a giant reclining Buddha resting on its right side with its head supported by its right hand and elbow. This image is approximately 160 feet long and 40 feet high and seems to fill the large building in which it lies. Because of this one cannot stand back to view the whole image from a distance and appreciate its immensity. The image is brick covered with stucco which, in turn, has been completely covered with gold leaf. The flat soles of the feet, which are eight or ten feet long, are inlaid with mother-of-pearl to show a series of 108 scenes related to Buddhism and the Buddha's life.

The walls of Wat Po are covered from floor to ceiling with murals depicting information from every available branch of knowledge at the time they were painted. Included are scenes of astronomy, astrology, archeology, literature, medicine, military science, religion, and many other fields. These murals have often been referred to as the "first university" in Thailand. Unfortunately, these murals have deteriorated badly at the lower levels and it is difficult to stand back from the walls to see the upper levels. Moisture seeping up through the walls has streaked and in many places obliterated them. It is sad that the Thai government has not found the financial resources at home or abroad to preserve this important work in a major temple. Even more unfortunate was the sight in the spring of 1969, of huge sections of the reclining Buddha showing only stucco where the gold leaf had raggedly come off. This neglect, it is hoped, will be remedied soon. The Thai government is taking steps to repair and restore some of Bangkok's other major temples including Wat Arun, Wat Bovoranives, and Wat Sutat, and perhaps some work will be done on Wat Po, too.

Another temple well worth a visit in Bangkok is Wat Benchamabopitr, or the Marble Temple. It is made of white marble with gold multiple roofs and is a relatively new wat less than seventy-five years old. It has beautiful gardens and around a courtyard behind the bot is a gallery of Buddha images, either the originals or copies, of some of the most interesting and beautiful images gathered from all parts of the country. The images represent, also, the different poses in which the Buddha is depicted. The bot of the temple houses a magnificent golden image copied from the old original in Wat Phra Chinnaraj in Pitsanuloke in Northern Thailand. The original image is reputedly one of the most beautiful images in the world, and was so considered by King Chulalongkorn when he had it copied for his new temple in Bangkok.

At Wat Trimitr in Bangkok is a solid gold Buddha image which weighs five and a half tons and stands ten feet high. It is one of the few solid gold images of such a size in the world and was uncovered by accident. About thirty-five years ago the image, encased in plaster, was brought to Wat Trimitr from an abandoned temple on the Bangkok riverfront in a crowded port section of the city. The old temple grounds had been deconsecrated and were to be used for building new port facilities. There was no building at Wat Trimitr large enough for the image so it was placed in a shed for storage for the next two decades. In 1955, a new building to house the image was built. While the heavy image was being transferred from the shed to the new building it crashed to the ground from the crane carrying it. During that night rain fell. In the morning the abbot started to clean the mud and dirt from the image lying on the ground and noticed glittering metal through some cracks in the plaster. Other monks were called and they removed the plaster cover, discovering the solid gold image underneath. It is believed the image had been coated with plaster to protect it from invaders, probably the Burmese, at the time of an earlier attack. The origin of the image is unknown.

Two other temples of special interest in Bangkok are Wat Saket and Wat Sutat. One of the early Chakri kings wanted to construct an artificial mountain to house a temple to be called the Temple of the Golden Mount after one of the temples in the destroyed capital of Ayudhya. And so an artificial mountain was built and the Temple of the Golden Mount, or Wat Saket, was erected with its chedi on top of the mountain. In 1898 the British discovered an old stupa near the Nepal-India border, in the vicinity of the area where traditional history says the Buddha lived. In the old stupa were found relics dated prior to the rule in India of King Asoka, the great Buddhist king who ruled a couple of centuries after the death of the Lord Buddha. The inscription on the container for the relics has been variously interpreted to be either the relics of the Lord Buddha himself or of some of his relatives. The British distributed these relics to several Buddhist countries and those received by Thailand are now in Wat Saket. These may be the only authentic (or closest to authentic) relics of the Buddha in Thailand. Each November Wat Saket has a special fair when thousands of Buddhists visit the temple. At night the pathway leading to the top of the artificial mountain is brightly lighted and can be seen from all over the flat capital city.

Wat Sutat, another large temple, is remembered by many visitors because it is on the same plaza as the giant swing, a non-Buddhist symbol. Only the tall, red-painted teakwood pillars which supported the swing still can be seen in the square. Until early this century the swing, which could hold four men at a time, was used in certain Brahmanical festivals each year to honor the god Siva. The festival is no longer held. Wat Sutat adjoining the square has a long four-sided gallery around it similar to the one at Wat Phra Keo. But instead of murals in its gallery, the one at Wat Sutat has well over a hundred, bigger-than-life-size seated Buddhas which make an awesome impression.

With more than twenty thousand temples in Thailand not all, in fact not many, are as large and impressive as these. Even in Bangkok which has three or four hundred temples, many are smaller, neighborhood institutions. One of these I used to visit quite often because it was within walking distance of my home and had two special attractions for me. It was located on a main klong and had a tiny covered pavilion with two benches where one could sit quietly and watch the evening life on the klong. Many evenings I walked there and did exactly that. The second attraction was a big, live, black bear which the monks kept in a large cage. No one knew for certain where it came from, but both adults and children in the neighborhood never tired of watching the bear's antics. On my last visit to that wat, the pavilion with the benches was there, but the bear was gone.

In the villages of Thailand the wat is much more than a house of worship or a place for religious activities. In many ways it is the true center of community life for the villagers. It may house a school. If it has a library, it may collect more than religious books and thus serve as a community library. Travelers reaching the village who have no place to stay may spend the night in one of the open temple buildings, making the wat a temporary hotel. It is frequently the principal information center for and about the village. It may act as a village safe deposit vault for the villagers who give their valuables into the care of the monks. Often fairs and festivals are celebrated on temple grounds. Movies may be shown or plays performed. It may be used as a hospital, dispensary, home for the aged or for the psychotic, and as a welfare agency for villagers who may need help in an emergency. Villagers seeking advice on work may seek the employment counsel of a monk. His advice may be asked on scores of subjects that have nothing to do with religion. In every village and town the Buddhist monk is revered and respected as a leader of his community. He and the teacher, where there is one, will probably be the best-educated persons in the village. The monk's advice will be sought and his influence will often extend far beyond his role as a religious figure, and the temple itself will become the focus of village activities.

Like the temple, the ubiquitous, brightly clad monk is a visible symbol of Thailand's Buddhism. At any one time there are usually about 250,000 monks and novices living at the thousands of temples throughout the country. Unlike the more settled monastic orders known to Europe and America, the Buddhist order in Thailand is constantly in flux. It is relatively easy to become a monk and it is even easier to leave the order. Many enter for the traditional three-month period of the rainy season. Some stay for less time and others spend a lifetime in the order. I met one venerable abbot on a trip to Northeastern Thailand who, well past eighty years old, had been in the Sangha as a novice and a monk for more than seventy years, truly a life of great devotion and dedication to the Lord Buddha and his teachings.

I had the privilege to be invited to an upcountry ordination in a Northeastern province some distance off the main highway from Bangkok into the

Northeast. The young man who was to be ordained was a new government staff employee who was taking the three-month period which each male government employee is allowed so that he may enter the monastic order. Following the customary practice he was returning to his home village where his parents and many of his relatives still lived. He was to be ordained at the provincial capital, a few kilometers from his village. His own village was too small to have a temple of its own.

Two Thai friends made the journey by car with me. After driving a few hours, we turned off the main highway on to a secondary road headed almost straight north. Although there had been some rains earlier, a late June dry spell had once again dried out the region through which we were driving. The earlier rains had, however, softened the ground so that the buses and a few trucks which were almost the only vehicles that used this dirt road had deeply rutted it in parts. The ruts had now dried into cementlike ridges which made rough driving for the small passenger car I was using. In spots we found it easier to leave the road and drive across the still dry rice paddies. The little dikes which divide one field from another had been knocked down in places to permit other vehicles before us to use this route without too much difficulty. It, too, was rough, but in many places smoother than the roadway.

Early in the evening before the sun had set we arrived in the provincial capital, a small town of probably no more than two or three thousand people. It had a small new hotel and, after washing the road dust from ourselves, we were ready to drive the few kilometers to the village we were seeking outside of town.

We arrived at the village just at dusk. It was easy to find the right house. It was a wooden house of several rooms set high on stilts. A special generator had been brought to the house to provide the electric power for the colored lights strung in the trees of the yard and for a record player from which Thai songs blared loudly all night long.

On our arrival we climbed the outside stairs and entered a spotlessly clean room where we were greeted by the young man preparing to enter the Sangha, his parents, his grandmother, brothers, sisters, and numerous other relatives and friends who had gathered from the village and nearby town. A gay celebration for the eve of departure of the monk-to-be was in full swing. Although most of the persons present were seated on the floor chatting, eating, or preparing gifts to be taken to the wat the next day, chairs were brought for me and my companions. We were honored guests from Bangkok, and as the only foreigner present, I was especially honored. I also was conscious that everything I did was being watched by the old folks present to see if I behaved properly. I was relieved the next day to learn I had passed their silent inspection.

To refresh us we were given glasses of water to which something had been added to give it a light pink color and to indicate it had been purified for safety's sake. One Thai acquaintance once called this "cooking water" by which he meant boiled water. To chill our pink water, however, ice had been dropped into the glasses, and the ice was a dirty brown in color. One of the brothers of the man to be ordained quietly sent a boy running to a village store to bring back cold, unopened bottles of soda for the Bangkok guests. We were also served a delicious meal of curry and sticky rice. Eating with our fingers and using the sticky rice as a scoop we were soon pleasantly filled with the excellent curry topped off with fruits. Much of the evening I spent listening to some of the younger persons in the household, at first shy, but later patiently practicing their words and phrases of English learned at school. One of the problems of learning English in the upcountry schools of Thailand is the lack of native English speakers to whom the young students can listen and with whom they can practice. Each one of several teen-agers hesitantly, awkwardly asked the same few questions they had learned at school, and I repeated the same answers. Sometimes a young man would make an error which all the others recognized and there would be great laughter in which the man making the mistake would join heartily.

Here was a good example of the useful and in many ways wonderful Thai spirit of *mai pen rai* which is generally translated as "never mind" or "it doesn't matter." This common phrase is known and used throughout the country to ease many a situation which might be embarrassing to someone. A person makes a mistake; mai pen rai, it will be better next time. A person is caught telling a lie; mai pen rai, maybe his task would have been easier if he had got away with it, but now that he did not, he will do the best he can in the circumstances. A houseboy or maid breaks a dish. Rather than cause an embarrassing scene, the wise householder says mai pen rai; the dish can be repaired or replaced. A business appointment is missed; mai pen rai, a new one can be scheduled and no one need be upset. The phrase and the attitude it symbolizes can be frustrating to many foreigners, but in time most foreigners come to recognize its usefulness in eliminating the possibility of embarrassment in an awkward situation. The phrase is a soothing balm for troubled nerves.

One of the activities going on in the farmer's house that night especially interested me. Several young girls were making artificial flowers out of paper money. These flowers were to be part of the gifts carried to the temple the next day and were so delicately and artfully made they looked like real flowers.

Later that night as neighbors and friends continued to frolic while others settled down for the night, my Bangkok companions and I returned to the hotel in town. As we drove away we could still see the colored lights in the trees and hear the recorded music of the happy household anticipating the auspicious event of the next day.

Entering the monastic order is the most important way in which a young man can earn merit for his next incarnation. Part of this merit is shared with others. Usually the young man will enter the order before he marries. In that case, the merit is shared with his parents, whom he is honoring by this act. After he marries, such merit would be shared with his wife.

It is customary for a majority of Thai men to enter the monastic order for some short period of time. Until relatively recently almost every young Buddhist man did so. In many villages a man who did not enter the order was not considered a fully matured person and ready for marriage. Some young women would refuse to marry a man who had not already served a period of time as a monk. A young man gains respect and prestige by entering the order and even older persons will show him that respect. In more recent times the practice of entering the order has been declining, especially among young men in Bangkok and other large cities. But it is far from dying out and in the villages service in the order for some period of time is still considered an important obligation for most young Buddhist men.

The following morning we returned to the village farmhouse. A chapter of nine monks had come that morning to chant from the Buddhist writings. By the time we arrived their service of chanting was completed and the monks were being served a meal by the family and its friends.

The candidate had drawn apart from the subdued merrymakers and was quietly meditating on the course he was about to follow. His head had been completely shaved after a practice instigated by the Lord Buddha and symbolizing the rejection of the material world which the candidate was about to do. He was dressed in white robes as a sign of purity.

Shortly after midday when the monks at the wat would have completed their last meal of the day, a procession was formed to go from the village to the wat in town. Since I had the only automobile available and the family had neither a horse nor an elephant for the candidate to ride, I was asked to drive the candidate in the procession. I was greatly honored. The candidate, holding a candle and a single flower in his palms clasped together in meditation, got into the front seat with me and one of our mutual friends from Bangkok who would give me directions because the candidate had to remain silent. In the back seat sat the candidate's parents and grandmother. Behind us came a truck with many of the younger members of the family carrying their money flowers and other gifts. A local band, too, was aboard the truck and played for the procession. Others in the procession rode bicycles or climbed into *samlors*.

The samlor is a three-wheeled pedicab with the driver pedaling from a bicycle seat in front and a small carriage for passengers in back. The samlor is usually big enough for two small Thai men and women, but oversize and sometimes overweight foreigners are usually more comfortable one to a samlor. Samlor drivers, regardless of age, are usually thin and seem to be made of 100 percent muscle and sinews. Often dark brown from riding in the sun all day, they all wear caps, helmets, or straw hats to protect their heads against the heat of the glaring sun. Their well-worn shirts and shorts are probably best described as made of patches on patches.

Samlors were common in Bangkok until 1959, when their use was declared illegal in the capital city. They were replaced by small motorized vehicles with three scooter-sized wheels and canvas tops. The word samlor means three wheels and these new vehicles are called motorized samlors. The growing traffic in Bangkok in the 1950's had been impeded by the slow-moving pedaled samlors and by their annoying habit of making sudden sharp turns in front of motor vehicles. For that reason the police decided to outlaw pedaled samlors in Bangkok.

Outside the capital city the samlor is still a major means of transporting people in all cities and towns. Although the samlor has a top to put up to shield the passenger from the hot sun and sides that can be added in the event of a rainfall, it is often driven with sides and top down, and a slow samlor ride on a cool evening can be a special delight of an upcountry visit.

Behind the samlors and the bicycles in our procession to the temple many other friends and relatives walked. It was a joyous group as we proceeded slowly from the village along the main street of the nearby town to the wat.

Once at the wat everyone dismounted from his vehicle and formed a new procession on foot to circumambulate the wat in a clockwise direction keeping the right shoulder toward the bot because this was an auspicious occasion. Only on inauspicious occasions does one walk in the other direction with the left shoulder toward the building.

Leading the procession, quite unintentionally, was a samlor driver who, in celebrating, had drunk a little too much Mekong, a Thai whisky. In his happy condition he led the procession with his own version of the *ramwong*, a popular Thai dance of graceful gestures and circular movements. Behind him came the band and then the candidate riding on the shoulders of one of his elder brothers while another held an umbrella over his head to shield him from the sun. Behind them came the other members of his family and friends, many bearing their gifts for the wat or for the new monk.

Three times the procession marched around the bot and then we all entered into the building where a group of monks was already seated facing each other in two parallel lines on a low platform leading away from the main Buddha image. The abbot sat beneath the image and faced the two lines of monks. The laymen entering the bot divided—men on the left and women on the right.

One of the surprises to any Westerner when he first attends a Thai Buddhist service is the informality of the proceedings. The first service I attended was in the beautiful and dignified Wat Benchamabopitr in Bangkok and it was presided over by the Supreme Patriarch, the highest Buddhist monk in the nation. Still, talking among the laymen went on almost continuously during the service. Spittoons were placed throughout the room, especially on the ladies' side, to permit the old women to spit out their red betel juice. Halfway through, the ceremony was interrupted for a few minutes so everyone, including the monks, could take liquid refreshment. I could not see what the monks had, but among the laymen we received Pepsi Cola, Coca Cola, 7-Up, and Fanta Orange drink.

Upcountry, once everyone had entered the bot, the simple ordination ceremony began. The entire ceremony is conducted in the Pali language, the ancient religious language of Buddhism, so that most persons do not understand what is said, which may help to explain why the talking goes on. The candidate has usually spent sufficient time before the ceremony learning the questions and answers in Pali so that he can carry out his part of the ceremony properly.

The candidate approached the abbot who was presiding and who was authorized to ordain. Monks must have reached a certain grade before they receive this authority. Three times the candidate asked to be admitted to the Sangha. He then received instructions concerning the three refuges—the Buddha, the *Dharma* (the word or teachings of the Buddha), and the Sangha —and the precepts. These latter include the five precepts to be followed by all Buddhists, both lay and monk alike, namely, the prohibitions against killing, stealing, adultery, lying, and drinking intoxicants, plus other rules especially for monks such as the prohibitions against eating after midday and using bodily adornments. For monks, of course, the prohibition against adultery is a broader prohibition against all sexual activity.

After receiving these instructions the candidate was given his saffron robes and the bowl which he would use to gather food in his morning rounds. He retired with two monks who assisted him in changing from the white robes he had been wearing to his saffron robes. During this short interval the laymen took their first full break in the ceremony with everyone chatting until the candidate reappeared.

When the candidate came back he was taken aside by his preceptor, who had prepared him for his entry into the order. The preceptor, a monk, examined his pupil in a voice loud enough for all to hear and on completing this examination presented his pupil to the abbot and the other monks present for examination by the entire body. The questions are the same in both examinations. The candidate is asked if he is human, if he is male, and if he is over twenty years of age. Legend says that a sacred snake, or *naga,* took human form once and became a monk, but the Buddha found out, forced him to leave the order, and ruled that only humans could be monks.

The Buddha from the beginning limited his order to males. Near the end of his teaching years a disciple pointed out that women could follow the same path of the Buddha's teachings as men so he argued that they should be allowed to join the order. The Buddha saw the logic of this argument and permitted women to join an order, but not the same one as men and in a definitely secondary and subordinate position. Few women in any Buddhist country become nuns and generally they do not receive the same respect given to the monks.

A man cannot become a monk until he has reached the age of twenty. Travelers to Thailand often note that there are young boys in the order. These young boys are novices, not full-fledged monks. They may enter the order to receive special religious instruction, to attend Buddhist schools, or to fulfill a vow made by themselves or their parents, or to do honor to a parent or other relative who has died. They may serve a period as short as a few days and after reaching the age of twenty often will return to serve a period as a regular monk. Some boys spend several years as a novice in order to complete an education that they might not be able to get otherwise.

Other questions are also asked of the candidate. He is asked if he is a free man, if he is free of debt, if he is free of government service (the Sangha cannot be used as a military draft dodge), and if he has his parents' permission. He is also asked if he has leprosy, ringworm, tuberculosis, epilepsy, and certain other diseases which could exclude him. More questions are asked and finally he is asked the name in Pali which he is to use in the order. Upon satisfactorily completing the examination he receives further instructions on the rules applicable to the order and then the formal ordination ceremony is finished.

Generally the formal ceremony is followed by an informal period when friends and relatives of the new monk present him and other monks at the wat with gifts. In the ceremony I attended the money flowers were presented to the wat itself and other gifts were presented to the monks. Gifts to the new monk included books on the Buddha's teachings which he could study in his weeks ahead while he was confined to the wat during the rainy season of Buddhist Lent and such practical gifts as candles, soap, toilet paper, an umbrella, and similar minimum necessities which monks are permitted to have.

The new monk joins the life of the temple where he is to serve his period of time. The life he will lead is a simple yet active one. Each day he will rise before dawn and early-morning chants will be recited. As dawn breaks each monk, regardless of rank, takes his bowl and sets out to gather his food for the day. This is often referred to in the West as begging, but that is not correct. A monk does not beg in the sense of asking for his food or anything else. He walks along without approaching anyone, waiting for the layman to stop him and present him with rice or fruit, a little fish, and perhaps a flower or two. The early-rising tourist in Bangkok or any other town and village of Thailand will see the monks on their morning walks sometimes trailed by a temple boy who will assist the monk in carrying the food he receives. The monk does not thank the giver, for the giver is making the gift voluntarily to earn merit, and to thank him, or more often her, would be to decrease the merit gained by the donation. The giver instead thanks the monk for accepting the gift and act of merit.

Temple boys are a common sight in Thailand. Usually they live at the temple and share the quarters of the monk whom they serve. The temple boy will assist the monk to carry the food and other donations he receives on his morning rounds. The boy will also keep the monk's quarters clean and do other tasks in return for instruction in religious and other subjects and a share of the monk's food.

After completing his morning rounds the monk returns to the temple for his first meal. This is followed by a worship service and then a period of study. For the monk this study period is an important time for him to learn the teachings of the Buddha and of Buddhism. The second and final meal of the day is usually taken between eleven and eleven thirty; in any event, it must be finished before noon. In the afternoon the monk spends more time in study or relaxation or receiving instruction from a senior monk. In the evening there is a second worship service followed by more study or relaxation until the time for retiring. The routine may be altered, of course, by special ceremonies, such as an ordination, or by special duties or functions that some monks have such as those concerned with the administration of the wat.

Laymen may come to the temple at any time to join in the services or to seek counsel from the monks or just to meet friends and chat. Each lunar month has four special holy days, called *wan phra*, when laymen make special efforts to attend a wat service. These special days are the new moon day, the eighth day of the waxing moon, the full moon day, and the eighth day of the waning moon. These days can fall on any day of the week so that Buddhists do not have any one set day of the week for worship as do Christians on Sunday, Jews on Saturday, and Muslims on Friday.

More than twenty thousand wats in Thailand and a quarter of a million men make a huge organization. The individual local temple with five or more monks is the basic unit of the Buddhist organization in Thailand. The local wat, headed by an abbot appointed by superiors in the hierarchy, has considerable independence in what it does within a community. The abbot has administrative, custodial, and some disciplinary authority over his wat and the monks living there.

Above the local wat in the Buddhist organization there are head monks for a province. In some cases, large districts in a province may have an additional level of leadership between the local wat and the provincial headquarters. In Thailand there are two principal sects of monks so that in provinces where both sects function there will be head monks for each sect. These head monks are assisted in their duties by provincial or district councils with responsibilities on their own geographical levels similar to the national ecclesiastical cabinet.

The national organization of the Sangha, or monastic order, is similar in several ways to the organization of the national government. At the head of the Sangha, including both sects, is a Supreme Patriarch with the short title of Somdech Phra Sangharaj. (His full title is much longer.) He is assisted by an ecclesiastical cabinet headed by an ecclesiastical prime minister with the title of Sanghanayok. By custom the Sangharaj is usually from one sect and the Sanghanayok from the other although which holds which post is not firmly set. The cabinet has nine members including the heads of departments of administration, education, propagation, and public works. The national organization also has a General Assembly of not more than forty-five members chosen from among monks senior in rank and service. The assembly and the cabinet are the chief policy-making and administrative bodies for the Sangha, which also has its own judiciary. The Sangharaj is appointed by the king and the Sangharaj in turn appoints the cabinet. Each level of authority appoints those immediately below it down to the level of the abbot of the local wat. The whole religious organization is closely related to the government of the country through a Department of Religious Affairs in the Ministry of Education. This department provides government-supporting services when necessary for the Sangha. For an infraction of Sangha rules discipline is handled by the Sangha's own judicial system. For an infraction of a law, a monk must first be defrocked before he can be arrested and tried by the civil authorities.

Because a large number of men are continually entering and leaving the Sangha, the ceremony for leaving the order is even simpler than for entering. If a man is only a novice, all he need do is declare he is leaving the order and put aside his robes. If he is a monk, there is a slightly longer ceremony including his reaffirmation of his intentions to follow the teachings of the Buddha as a layman. Although the leave-taking ceremony is simple and thousands do leave every year, there are other thousands who remain monks for many years, and some who devote their lifetime services to the Lord Buddha. Many of these last become outstanding religious scholars and have great influence among the people as a whole and in the councils of leadership of the country.

The monk is basically seeking to achieve Buddhist aims for himself through a life dedicated to learning, discovery, and meditation. In the process he may undertake a great many works beneficial to others. In no sense, however, is he a priest of the kind familiar to the West. He cannot give absolution for sins and he cannot act as an intercessor for other persons. In Theravada Buddhism, which is the main form of Buddhism in Thailand, each individual is responsible for his own acts and no other person can interrupt his *karma,* the inevitable working out of the consequences. In a country which is more than 90 percent Buddhist, some understanding of the beliefs of the religion will be useful in order to understand the country's people and their behavior.

The religious literature of Buddhism comes to many hundreds of volumes. One-volume condensations attempting to describe Buddhism are but skeletons of this rich and complicated literature, so that the few paragraphs here included are no more than a shadow of a skeleton from which some of the main bones may be missing.

Thai Buddhism comprises several elements some of which are not essentially Buddhist. For example, the teachings of Buddha do not include detailed unique ceremonies for such personal events as birth, death, and marriage. Nor does Buddhism include religious ceremonies for public events such as coronations and other state celebrations. The failure to have such ceremonies carefully defined has left the way open for the use of Brahmanic or other local ceremonies to celebrate these events. When King Mongkut became ruler of Thailand a little over a century ago after his long career as a religious scholar and monk, he had Buddhist chants added to several of the existing Brahmanic ceremonies in order to provide some relationship between Buddhism and the ancient rites. It was a wedding of convenience to both parties.

Recognizing the time (roughly the sixth century B.C.) and the place (northeastern India) of the birth of Buddhism, one can easily understand how Buddhism and Brahmanism or Hinduism became intertwined almost from the birth of the former. Both Buddhism and Brahmanism have certain features in common, although I can only suggest one or two of them here. For example, the idea of karma, that everything that a person does is part of a long chain of events extending in cause before the person is born and in effect beyond the death of the person in his present form, is part of both religions. The doctrine of continuous reincarnation in one form or another is incorporated in both. The idea that the individual can be released from this continuous process of reincarnation only by following certain beliefs and practices of meditation and spiritual discipline is a common one. Likewise, both believe that each individual must work out his own karma.

The two religions differ in many ways as well. Brahmanism includes a large pantheon of gods at several levels of authority which are not included in formal Buddhism, although the gods may often be incorporated in one form or another into the popular Buddhism which the people believe and follow. A difference also exists in the steps to be taken to break the chain of reincarnation, and, of course, there are a vast number of differences in details of belief and practice between the two religions.

To these brief introductory general comments should be added the fact that within each religion, Buddhism and Brahmanism, there are a great many schools which differ widely in their teachings. These schools often differ as much among themselves as do the different religions. The variations in the interpretations of their own religions among the different schools lead to differences with some group somewhere on almost every point of belief and practice within and between Buddhism and Brahmanism.

Some of the facts concerning the last life on this earth of the Lord Buddha are themselves in doubt. Much that is known about him and his teachings was written centuries after his death. Prior to that time it had been transmitted orally and errors could have easily entered. The early Indians, unlike the Chinese at that time and present-day Westerners, were not much concerned with exact dates in the histories of their religions, but were more concerned with the teachings and the truths appearing in them as illustrated by human experiences as then known. Thus, there is some doubt about the exact period of Buddha's life on this earth. The dates I have most often encountered are 563–483 B.C. All authorities seem to accept the fact that he lived for eighty years, but the Thai and Burmese among others do not accept these dates.

The year A.D. 1969 in Thailand is the year B.E. 2512 (Buddhist Era). In 1957 huge celebrations were held in Thailand for the twenty-five-hundredth year of the Buddhist Era, the midpoint in the current era which is supposed to last five thousand years before the next Buddha appears to live on earth. Since the years of this era began their count with the death of the Buddha and his entrance thereby into nirvana, that event according to Thai calculations would be placed in 543 B.C. and his birth eighty years earlier would be in 623 B.C. It might be noted that some Chinese Buddhists use dates altogether different by a few hundred years.

Putting aside the confusion of dates, it can be reported that a son was born to a woman named Maya in Lumbini Grove near the present Indian-Nepal border. (Lumpini Park in Bangkok is named after the Buddha's birthplace.) The woman died seven days after giving birth to the boy. His father, named Suddhodana, was the ruler or raja of a small kingdom in northeastern India. The family name was Gautama, and the new son was named Siddhartha. The son was reared in all the comfort and luxury that his father could provide and was educated as a prince. At the age of sixteen he married a girl named Yasodhara, and in time, had a son, named Rahula.

Legend says that Siddhartha was reared under closely protected circumstances so that he would not see evil or any signs of it in the world. But as an adult he managed to slip out of his palace accompanied only by his charioteer. On four of these secret trips he saw four signs which were to change his life. He saw an old man, a sick man, a religious beggar or mendicant, and a corpse, and for the first time he learned that all men suffer from age, sickness, sorrow, and death. At the age of twenty-nine, the prince left his palace, his wife, and son to devote himself to learning how to overcome this suffering and how to develop man's spirit to its highest level.

For several years he wandered about searching for the answers. He attempted to discipline his physical senses by submitting his body and life to rigid austerities. In time he gathered a handful of followers. But at the end of six years he had not achieved the goals for which he had set out on his wanderings and he went back to eating regularly and otherwise living a normal life while continuing his search. His followers deserted him. He reached in his travels the place called Bodhgaya and, sitting under a Bo tree, he entered a mental condition which was probably a trance and dwelled upon what he had learned and what he was seeking to achieve. Legend adds to the story by reporting that while in this condition, *Mara,* or evil, appeared to the prince and attacked and tempted him in all sorts of ways in an effort to make him give up his quest. But calling on Earth to be his witness Gautama defeated all of Mara's efforts. When at the end of a day Gautama awoke from the trance, he had learned the way for man to end his suffering. He had achieved Enlightenment. He was no longer the Prince Siddhartha, but he was the Buddha, the one who is enlightened.

For the next forty-five years he wandered throughout northeastern India teaching what he had learned. His first sermon was delivered at Sarnath, near Benares, and he was soon a successful teacher and gained many followers including those earlier ones who had deserted him. Years later during the Buddha's life as a teacher one of his wealthy followers provided a garden plot of land and the Buddha made that his headquarters from which he went out to teach. On a journey at the age of eighty he became ill. Some stories report it as a form of food poisoning. He died of the illness while at Kusinara, now revered as the place where the Buddha entered nirvana, that special existence for the fully enlightened who are finally able to break the chain of continuous suffering and reincarnation. Lumbini Grove, Bodhgaya, Benares, and Kusinara are still the four main holy sites of Buddhism even though Buddhism later declined in India almost to the point of disappearance, being replaced by Hinduism.

The Buddha taught that each man creates his own karma. Man's acts and even intentions cause certain effects which inevitably follow. There is no god to create these causes and effects and there is no god which can change the effects once man has created certain causes. Wrongdoing cannot be forgiven, it must reap its own punishment. Right doing, in the same way, must reap its due rewards. The rich, powerful, honored man, therefore, has his position because he has done right and the poor and suffering man has his status because he has done wrong. (This belief has had a great effect on the acceptance by the Thai of whatever leadership is in power in their country.) Each man accumulates his own karma, which in turn determines his position in his next reincarnation.

The Thai Buddhist in contemporary Thailand accepts this belief in karma and strives to perform personal acts that may help him accumulate a favorable karma and merit for his next incarnation. There are many ways, it is believed, to earn merit. The most important way for a man is to enter the monastic order for at least a short period during his lifetime. For all persons there are other, simpler everyday activities that can help them accrue merit. They may help build or repair a wat with service or with money. They may give food or other necessities to monks for their use. They may help other persons in any one of numerous charitable ways. They may present candles or flowers or incense to a Buddha image or attach a square of gold leaf to an image. They may participate in services or religious activities at a wat. They may adhere strictly to the five main precepts. They may free captured birds and other animals or fish. This last act has led to a practice that seems strange, if not ludicrous, to many non-Buddhists. Birds are deliberately captured and placed in cages to be sold at the market and outside temples to devout Buddhists who then free them as an act of merit. It is important to note that all acts of merit are voluntary decisions on the individual's part. He is not enjoined or coerced in any way. Unlike the Christian and certain other religions, doing good to and for other people is not necessarily an essential part of the religious belief for Buddhists. They may do so, but there are other, seemingly more selfish, but still acceptable, ways for the Buddhist to earn merit. Each man can create his own actions, his own karma for himself.

The Buddha taught the Four Noble Truths which he had learned when he became enlightened: all life is suffering; all suffering has a cause in cravings or desire; the suffering can be overcome by eliminating the desire; and the way to do this is to follow the Eightfold Path of (1) right view, (2) right intention, (3) right speech, (4) right action, (5) right livelihood, (6) right effort, (7) right mindfulness, and (8) right concentration. One and two concern motivation; three, four, and five concern moral conduct; and six, seven, and eight concern the control of man's mind for right ends. By recognizing these truths and following these paths one may in time destroy the cravings and desire, break the chain of reincarnation, receive Enlightenment, and enter the state of nirvana.

This is a gross oversimplification of what the Buddha taught although it contains the essence of it. But the Four Noble Truths and the Eightfold Path are no more complete Buddhism than the Ten Commandments are complete

Judaism and the Sermon on the Mount is complete Christianity. They all are, however, important guideposts for their respective religions.

In the centuries that followed the Buddha's death his teachings were explained, modified, expanded, reinterpreted, and mixed with other teachings until a vast body of literature on Buddhism was collected. To the layman and sometimes to the Buddhist scholar parts of this body of work appear, as do those for many other religions, to be internally contradictory. Part of this apparent contradiction is due to the fact that the Buddha did not write down his teachings and we must rely on his followers and interpreters. Many of his teachings were not written until long after his death and by then changes had probably seeped in. Many of the interpretations of Buddhist teachings that exist today are also due to the natural evolution that any religion has over a history of many centuries.

Increasing in numbers of adherents in northeastern India at first, the religion soon spread to other parts of India and the rest of the Eastern world. Over the years new experiences were integrated into the teachings and new scholars brought different insights and interpretations to the original teachings. In time, two major schools of Buddhism developed. One of these is called Mahayana (the Greater Vehicle); it spread to China, Korea, Japan, and Vietnam. Tibetan Buddhism, while related to Mahayana, is a separate development. Mahayana Buddhism sprouted many sects of its own. One of the best known Mahayana offspring is Zen Buddhism, which recently has had much popularity in the West.

The other major school of Buddhism is Hinayana (the Lesser Vehicle); the name was given to the school naturally by the Mahayana Buddhists. This school is more properly called Theravada Buddhism (the Doctrine of the Elders). Theravada Buddhists claim to be more closely aligned to the original teachings of Buddha and tend to look at Mahayana Buddhism as a distortion of the true teachings. Mahayana Buddhists, on the other hand, recognize the Theravada followers as Buddhists, but believe their teachings to be a simpler form of Buddhism than Mahayanist Buddhism which is more advanced, more developed, and a more mature form of Buddhism. Theravada Buddhism is the prevalent form today in Ceylon, Burma, Laos, Cambodia, and Thailand and has far fewer sects than do the Mahayanists.

Exactly how or when Buddhism reached Thailand is not definitely known. The Thai who moved from Yunnan south to the Chao Phya River valley were probably mainly animists although they may have already had contact with Mahayana Buddhists in China, where Buddhism had already existed for several centuries. When the Thai reached present-day Thailand in the thirteenth century, however, they encountered people who were Theravada Buddhists.

King Asoka, the great Indian ruler who reigned two centuries after the

Buddha's death, had made major efforts to spread Buddhism by sending missionaries in all directions out of his kingdom. Those he sent east went to present-day Burma, and some scholars believe they may have gone as far east as the area around Nakorn Pathom in Thailand which is only about thirty-five miles west of Bangkok. If Asoka's missionaries did not reach that far, the Mon people did, and they brought Theravada Buddhism with them from southern Burma.

In later centuries Mahayana Buddhism spread south as well as north. It reached Sumatra from where the kingdom of Srivijaya extended its teachings up the Malay Peninsula and across the sea to the Khmer empire in Cambodia. In the Khmer area there developed a mixture of Brahmanism and Mahayana Buddhism. The Cambodians shifted to Theravada Buddhism later after contact with the Mons and Thai. The great temples at Angkor are mainly Brahman or Hindu. Farther north in present-day Thailand, the Burmese brought Theravada Buddhism to the area of Lopburi, where the Mon-Dvaravati kingdom was located. Later the Burmese also brought their Buddhist beliefs to the far northern regions of the kingdom of Lanna Thai around Chiengmai.

Regardless of what the exact path of Buddhism to Thailand was, the first Thai kingdom of Sukhothai adopted Theravada Buddhism. With the decline of Buddhism in India, Ceylon had become the most important Theravada Buddhist country. The early kings of Sukhothai sent for Ceylonese monks from their southern Mon territories and from Nakornsrithammarat to come to Sukhothai. Eventually monks came all the way from Ceylon as well. The famous stone inscription of King Ramkamheng from A.D. 1292 includes the statement that "King Ramkamheng, sovereign of Muang Sukhothai, and also the princes and princesses, men as well as women, nobles and chiefs, all without exception, without distinction of rank or sex, devoutly practice the religion of the Buddha and observe the special precepts for the rainy season."

Since that time Thailand has remained a Theravada Buddhist country. In the eighteenth century when Ceylon had some difficulties maintaining its Buddhism after some internal upheavals, the earlier process of help was reversed. Ceylon requested Ayudhya to send monks to Ceylon to ordain new Ceylonese monks and to revive the Buddhist religion. The Thai king of Ayudhya acceded to the request.

Buddhism is probably the most tolerant of all religions. The kings of Thailand must be Buddhist, yet they have always tolerated other religious practices on their soil. Over many years the kings have even given financial support to other religious groups, both Christian and Muslim, as well as to the Buddhist religion.

During the twenty-seven years that King Mongkut served as a monk before becoming king, he became a great Buddhist scholar. He saw that many of the customs and practices carried out by both the people and monks, such as astrological predictions, fortunetelling, and similar endeavors had drifted far from the teachings of Buddha. The monk-prince decided to do what he could to reform the order by adhering more strictly to the teachings of the Buddha and following only those practices that could definitely be found supported in the Dharma. After Rama III made his half-brother abbot of Wat Bovoranives in Bangkok, Prince Mongkut was able to carry out his reforms. The result of his reform movement was the formation of a new Thai Buddhist sect called the Dhammayut sect. It has remained a comparatively small, strict group, but its reforms have had some impact on the much larger, older Mahanikaya sect as well.

It might be noted that each Thai sect has opened a university for monks to undertake advanced Buddhist studies as well as to study foreign languages, comparative religion, and science. The Dhammayut sect operates Mahamakut University at Wat Bovoranives and the Mahanikaya have Mahachulalongkorn University at Wat Mahadhat. Both universities are in Bangkok and were opened in the first two years after World War II. The location of both Buddhist universities in the capital city has one disadvantage. Well-educated monks tend to remain in Bangkok, where study and research resources and fellow scholars, both monks and laymen, are located. Many of these educated monks are needed in the upcountry towns and villages where their influence is often great and where they could apply what they have learned to the immediate benefit of the Thai people. The Sangha leadership is trying to accomplish this end, but the pressures it can bring are limited. If a young monk does not want to return upcountry, he can always leave the order and find other uses in the city for his education.

Popular Buddhism—what the people actually do and believe—as distinct from the formal Buddhism taught by the Buddha and his successors, is compounded of several elements. Many of the Brahman beliefs and gods have found niches within the Buddhist temple. Astrology, too, plays an important part in the popular beliefs and some monks, as well as Brahmans and others, are astrologers. No significant event from state ceremonies to weddings to opening new places of business would be scheduled without first consulting an astrologer to select an auspicious time. This often results in strange invitations, such as one I received inviting me to the dedication of a new business office at 7:21 A.M.

Perhaps the most important and widespread daily influence on the Buddhism of the people in Thailand is the remnants of animism in Thai society. Spirits are omnipresent. On one occasion some years ago I arrived at my office early in the morning and saw a taxicab in the driveway ahead of me. The driveway passed under a second floor porch of the house to which our office was annexed. Beyond the porch the driveway continued to a parking lot and place to turn around. The taxi was parked directly under the porch and there was no way to get around it to the parking lot. The driver had already discharged his passenger, one of our young Thai lady employees, and I waited for him to pull ahead to the turnaround. But he did not budge. After waiting several minutes I got out and, walking over to the taxi, asked the driver to move his car. He said something in Thai which I did not understand and then sat there grimly determined not to move. I called the lady employee back to ask her to tell the driver to move, but he would say nothing to her and still refused to move. We tried repeatedly to coax him to drive on with no success whatsoever. Finally, another car pulled in behind me and its driver, a Thai male employee of our office, came to see what could be done. After several minutes of conversation with the driver, my colleague stepped back and looked at the porch overhead. On it the lady of the house was having breakfast served by a maid. My colleague asked the two ladies to step back into the house off the porch. When they did so, the taxi driver drove ahead, turned around, and after we drove the other cars to the parking lot he left the compound. Later it was explained to me that a spirit curse had been placed on the taxi driver to the effect that he would be harmed if any women were above his head and, therefore, the two women on the porch above were a serious threat, if he had to drive with them there. He would say nothing to our Thai lady employee because standing beside the car, talking to him seated, she was actually above him. Only when they all moved was it safe for him to drive on.

The general word for spirits is *phi* (pronounced pee). The phi are found to dwell everywhere and can have strong effects on Thai believers. Some weeks after the taxi incident a police officer from the local precinct came to ask me to have some branches of a tree on our property cut because they were hanging dangerously into the yard of a neighbor who had complained. I asked the gardener and his cousin visiting him, both from Northeastern Thailand, to cut down the offending branches, which they promptly did. I forgot the matter until later in the day when I searched for the gardener and could not find him. I found his cousin, who reported the gardener was seriously ill. That was a surprise because he had been quite well earlier when I gave him the tree-cutting assignment.

I found the gardener in his quarters and there was no doubt he was ill. He was too weak to stand. On inquiry I learned that he had forgotten to ask the phi of the tree for permission to cut some branches and the phi had taken its revenge by making the gardener ill. There was only one remedy. A doctor would be of no use. I sent the cousin to buy some candles, incense, and flowers. When he returned I presented them to the gardener, who then crawled on his hands and knees, because he could not stand, from his quarters to the tree, where he presented the gifts at the foot of the tree as an offering to the tree's phi. Apparently the phi accepted the offering as satisfactory because when I saw the gardener a few hours later he had completely recovered his health.

Perhaps the most common phi familiar to visitors to Thailand is the spirit guarding the land. In rural areas offerings to this phi are made at different times during the rice-growing season. In the city, one commonly sees a small spirit house in the corner of the property for each residence or other building. The spirit house is set on a pole at about eye level and is located on the property in a place where the building's shadow will never fall on it. Some of these spirit houses are very simple while others are so elaborate they look like Buddhist temples the size of a birdhouse. Each piece of property has a guardian spirit who takes up residence in the spirit house from which it controls fortune, good and bad, on its property. Before taking up residence on the property or before leaving it the Thai believer will ask the phi's permission. At various appropriate times the phi will be given offerings of flowers, candles, incense, and rice to insure that it is satisfied and happy.

Once when I was living in a Bangkok apartment house I witnessed the serious manner in which one Thai regarded the phi for the property. The Thai was a porter who worked in the apartment house and lived on the property with his wife, who was pregnant. For about two weeks before the baby was born the man each day presented an offering to the phi in the spirit house. A fine, handsome baby boy was born and for several days thereafter the man continued to present daily offerings in thanksgiving to the spirit of the property which had so happily welcomed the new arrival.

The sophisticated, educated Thai, especially when talking to a Westerner, may well play down this belief in spirits in a Buddhist country. At the same time he may continue to pay homage to the phi himself following the rule that the spirits might exist, and if they do, it might help to honor them in traditional ways. If they do not exist, no harm is done by merely carrying out traditional observances. Buddhism does not prohibit the propitiation of spirits, therefore doing so does no injury to the individual's belief in Buddhism either.

One small incident I witnessed demonstrated the versatility and adaptability of the Thai when it comes to their beliefs, be they Buddhist or animistic. They are easily able to combine traditional beliefs with modern practical technology. Driving to a beach resort one weekend my driver and I passed along a broad sweeping curve in the highway. At midpoint in the curve a spirit house was set up on the outside of the curve. My driver, following the practice that sometimes frightens foreigners the first time they see it, took both hands off the wheel without slowing down on the curve and made a *wai* as we passed the spirit house. He explained to me that before the spirit house was erected at that spot there had been many accidents. He claimed that hundreds of people had been killed or horribly maimed. Then the spirit house was put up, the spirit moved in, and was pacified. Now when a driver passed and showed respect with a wai there was no chance of an accident. He said there had not been one fatal accident on that curve since the phi had been given a proper residence.

I found that quite remarkable and said so. At the same time I asked if anything else had been done to prevent accidents there. After thinking a few moments he replied matter-of-factly that the highway department had widened the curve considerably and regraded the roadway. But he assured me that while the changes in the roadbed might have helped, the real cause for the change from a death curve to a safe curve was the propitiation of the guardian spirit of that stretch of the highway. And more important, he firmly believed what he said.

In one common practice today popular Buddhism and animism are brought face to face, not in conflict, but in cooperation. In order to ward off dangers from the numerous bad spirits many Thai wear amulets and charms on gold chains around their necks. It is a rare Thai man who does not have at least one of these, and it is one of his most valuable possessions. An employee of a hotel at which I stayed in Bangkok told me he had paid 1,500 baht (U.S. $75) for the gold chain on which he hung his amulets. The chain was the most expensive personal item he had ever bought. It cost more than any clothes, shoes, radio, or watch that he owned. He felt the large expenditure to be completely appropriate because of the importance of the charms that hung on it. Usually these charms are Buddhist medals or tiny Buddhas kept in small metal containers to protect them. These Buddhist charms are effective against snakebite, witches, gunshots, bad phi, accidents, and evils of all kinds. This practice, of course, is one they share with peoples of other religions all over the world.

Aside from the believers in Buddhism, Thailand does have citizens who belong to other world religions. Of the total Thai population slightly less than 4 percent are Muslim, which is the second largest religious group in Thailand. Although much smaller in number than the Buddhist group, the uneven distribution of the Muslims makes them a potent group in the area where they are heavily concentrated. Muslims will be found in many parts of the kingdom and mosques can be seen in the Bangkok-Thonburi area as well as in other more northern cities, but the greatest concentration of Muslim people is in the southern part of the Malay Peninsula region of Thailand. In the southernmost provinces of Naradhivas, Pattani, Setul, Yala, and Songkhla, the Muslim population is larger than the Buddhist population. The religious and ethical differences between the Southern Thai-Malays and the Central, Northern, and Northeastern Thai have created potential and real problems for the government of Thailand.

Confucianism and other Chinese-related religions account for less than 2 percent of the total population, and despite a long history of missionary work,

Christianity trails with probably less than one-half of 1 percent of the total Thai population. Christian missionaries from Catholic countries came early in the seventeenth century accompanying the Portuguese and later the French traders. While they were given freedom to work in Thailand they made few converts. Protestant missionaries arrived much later, in the second quarter of the nineteenth century. They made almost no inroads among the Thai Buddhists and have had little success up to the present date. Much of what little success they have had, as can be seen if one looks at the languages used in Bangkok Christian churches, has been among the Chinese some of whom may have first learned of Christianity in China before coming to Thailand. Some conversions have also been made among the non-Thai hill tribes in the north of Thailand. Religiously, the Christian missionaries have had little success, but they made significant contributions in education, medicine, printing, and science.

3

Images and Shadows

Silpakorn University (the University of Fine Arts) is one of several "cultural" institutions which are situated close together in the small area between the Phra Mane Ground and the Chao Phya River. Indeed, if any one area of the country can be called the cultural center of Thailand, this must be it, for in this small part of Bangkok are the Silpakorn University, the Fine Arts Department of the government, the National Library, Thammasat University (the University of Moral and Political Sciences, one of two general universities in Bangkok), the National Museum (in the former palace of the second king), and the new National Theater.

During the cool season Silpakorn University provides a major artistic treat for Thai and visitor alike. Performances of a classical dance-drama based on sections of the *Ramakien,* the Thai version of the *Ramayana* are given regularly. In recent years there has been a tendency to shorten the *Ramakien* portion of each performance to one scene and, for the benefit of tourists, add short dances representing other dance styles and regions of the country.

At one of the first classical dance-dramas I attended two spectacular stage bits occurred which have stayed in my memory as two of the most unusual feats of theater magic I have ever seen. In one battle scene of the *Ramakien* a leader of the demon army is fighting from the back of an elephant which is able to fly through the air. The elephant is attacked by one of the monkey generals who severs the elephant's head from its body. When this scene was played an artificial elephant, which appeared to the audience to be full size, flew across the stage in the battle and when the head fell from the body stage blood made the scene extremely vivid and effective.

The second short scene was even more effective. Again a battle was being fought. This time between Rama and a demon general who was able to divide himself into several replicas of himself so as to confuse Rama. The fight was underway between Rama and the masked demon in his colorful green costume. Suddenly the stage was darkened for what seemed only a fraction of a second and when it was relighted the full grown demon had disappeared and in his place were ten little boys in masks and green costumes identical to those of the demon. The boys were scattered at several places around the stage at different levels to confuse Rama further.

In the classical theatrical art of Thailand dancing and acting are so intertwined that they must be treated as one rather than as separate arts. Traditional Thai art includes several types of Thai drama. One of these is called the *khon*. In the khon the performers, originally all men, all wear masks, and the masks, costumes, and music themes are used to identify the characters and the action as much as does the acting of the characters themselves. Because the masks are full head masks it is difficult for the wearer to talk. Consequently, the actors on the stage do not speak. Their lines are read and sung by an offstage chorus and soloists who recite the story, speak the dialogue, and generally describe what is happening on the stage. The orchestra, too, performs a major role in a khon performance, for the orchestra must set the mood of the play and the specific action, accompany the dancers on the stage, and accompany the offstage singers. There is no such thing as incidental music in a Thai classical dance-drama presentation. Music, acting, dancing, singing are all essential parts of the whole. Without any one of them the khon cannot be performed.

A second type of Thai drama is the *lakhon*. Like the khon, the lakhon is usually based upon the stories from the *Ramayana* or *Ramakien,* although other classic tales are also told. It differs from khon, however, in some major ways. For one thing, lakhon dancers are mostly women who dance both male and female roles. Sometimes, at least in recent years, both men and women appear in lakhon, in which case women usually portray the heroes and heroines while men portray the demons and monkeys. Masks are not worn by all the characters in the lakhon. Usually the nonhuman characters wear masks while the human characters do not. The latter keep their faces expressionless and allow their postures and gestures to indicate their actions and feelings. Although some of the characters do not wear masks, none of the characters speaks his own lines. Again, as in khon, all lines are said or sung by offstage singers.

Thai dance performers in both khon and lakhon must go through a long period of rigorous training to maintain disciplined and flexible bodies to perform and hold the positions needed to depict the various characters in the drama and their actions. The dancers who portray monkeys must also be skilled at acrobatics for performing a monkey role calls for unusual agility. The monkeys are often the spectators' favorite characters because of their acrobatics and general liveliness. Even if the spectator cannot identify the monkeys from their costumes and masks, he can always tell who they are because the monkeys constantly scratch themselves in an easily observable, stylized way to rid themselves of persistent itching monkey fleas.

The basic positions for all Thai classical dancers, called the "alphabet of dancing," must be learned early in the dancer's career. There are actually two alphabets, a short one of nineteen positions and a long one, incorporating the short one, of sixty-four positions. These positions have charming descriptive names. In the short alphabet are such positions as the stag walking in the forest, the bee caressing the flower, and wedded love. The longer alphabet adds others such as the blades of the windmill in motion, walking gracefully, lascivious dancing, the Chinese disembowels himself, and the lion plays with its tail. If a member of the audience has learned all the positions, he is better able to follow the story; but few outside the profession are in that enviable position, and it is not essential to an understanding of the play.

Both khon and lakhon are based on stories mainly drawn from the *Ramayana*. This Hindu epic poem in its Thai version, the *Ramakien*, is important to many fields of Thai art and is well known to most Thai. The visitor will find scenes from it used in paintings, woodcarvings, lacquer work, nielloware, and other Thai decorative art. If a visitor to Thailand has some knowledge of this old and impressive story, he will have a much easier and more satisfying time in understanding the Thai art which he sees. The story has gone through many versions in India, Indonesia, Thailand, and other countries since it was first written by the Indian poet Valmiki many centuries ago.

The central story begins when Brahma, creator of the world, is approached by many celestial beings who are troubled by a demon king named Ravana (in the Thai version he is called Thosakan) who lives in Lanka, an island kingdom which is usually identified with Ceylon. Because of past events before the central story begins, Ravana cannot be killed by any god or other celestial being, but only by a human being. After some thought and discussion Brahma decides to send Vishnu (Narayana or Narai in Thai) to earth reincarnated as a human prince named Rama who will have the task to destroy the demon. At the same time, Vishnu's consort, Lakshmi, is to be reincarnated as the human princess Sita.

Rama is born to one of the wives of the king of Ayodhya, and Sita, who is not really born, springs from a plowed furrow as the daughter of another Indian raja. Rama grows to be a great prince. He learns everything there is to know and masters all the virtues which guide him in his daily life. Of him it was said, for example, that he remembered a single kindness while forgetting a hundred injuries. In time, Sita's father holds a contest to see who can bend a magic bow; whoever does so will win Sita for a bride. Of course, Rama is the only one who does and so he marries Sita and also gains the magic bow for his weapon.

Rama is so loved by almost everyone that his father decides to name him heir to the kingdom. But one of the king's other wives is jealous of Rama's mother and Rama's special position. In an earlier episode this queen had saved the king's life and he had promised her a boon whenever she might claim it. Now she claims it by asking the king to banish Rama to live as a hermit in the forest for fourteen years and to name her son, Bharata, heir instead. Greatly grieved, the king tries to find a way out of his dilemma, but is not able to do so. He must adhere to his promised word and carry out the jealous queen's wishes. Rama accepts the inevitable and with Sita and his younger brother, Lakshman, he goes to live in the forest. Incidentally, Bharata is very angry with his mother. He also loves Rama, like most other people in Ayodhya, and asks Rama to return. When Rama replies that he must stay in the forest for fourteen years as their father has instructed him, Bharata pledges to rule only as a viceroy for Rama when the time comes to succeed their father.

While the three royal refugees are living in the forest, Ravana's sister visits them. She tries to seduce Rama away from Sita. When the sister fails in this effort, she then tries to entice Lakshman away, but fails there, too. In fact, Lakshman attacks her with his sword and cuts her face and body. The sister returns to Lanka and her brother Ravana; together they plot revenge.

Ravana wants Sita for himself. He persuades a magician to take the shape of a golden deer and pass near the hermitage of the three refugees. Sita sees the deer and cajoles the reluctant Rama to go after it for her. He finally does and the deer lures him deep into the forest. When he does not return soon, Lakshman, who is guarding Sita on Rama's orders while the latter is away, and Sita become worried. Then they hear Rama's voice (actually an imitation by the same magician) calling for help. Sita begs Lakshman to go to help his brother, but Lakshman refuses. Finally Sita accuses him of wanting her for himself, and to protect his honor Lakshman must obey her and disobey Rama. He goes in search of his brother. Lakshman is barely gone, of course, when Ravana, the demon king, appears in disguise as a religious mendicant. Sita, compassionate and unsuspecting, invites him into the lodge and he tries to persuade her to go with him to Lanka. When she refuses, he returns to his ten-headed demon shape and seizing Sita carries her off to his kingdom.

When Rama and Lakshman return they begin a long search for Sita. They learn from an ancient friendly vulture, who had tried to save Sita but failed when his aging strength faltered, that she has been kidnapped by Ravana. The two brothers set out to rescue her, but they have no army. On the way they meet some monkey leaders, including Sugriva and Hanuman. Sugriva has been exiled by his brother who has usurped the monkey king's throne from Sugriva. Rama uses his magic weapons to help Sugriva recover his kingdom and, in turn, Sugriva calls forth a huge monkey army to help Rama rescue Sita.

Hanuman is a special monkey. He is actually the son of the wind and can never die because he is always revived whenever a wind blows. Furthermore, as son of the wind he can fly anywhere. He does fly around and finds Sita a prisoner in Lanka. He informs her of Rama's plans to rescue her and then leaves to return to Rama with his news of Sita. Before going back to Rama, however, Hanuman flies around Lanka causing damage and gets captured. After explaining truthfully who he is and why he is there, Hanuman is punished by Ravana. The punishment is to have his tail set on fire. Hanuman escapes and flies around setting fire with his tail to half the city before he douses the fire in his tail and returns to Rama.

Ravana's brother Vibhishana (Bhibek in Thai), a great astrologer and wizard, cautions the demon king and urges him to return Sita to Rama. Ravana curses his brother, who flees Lanka and joins Rama's forces. The Ocean gives Rama and his monkeys permission to build a bridge across the water to Lanka. After the bridge is built and the army crosses there are a great many battles with Ravana calling on all his relatives to help him. Rama and many of his forces are wounded, but they are healed by celestial intervention which comes by the Garuda (part man, part bird) and through other sources. At one point impatient Hanuman dashes off to the Himalayas to find some healing herbs. When it takes him too long to find the herbs, he uproots a whole mountain and carries it back.

Finally, Ravana, who usually has tried to hide his ten heads from the beautiful Sita, brings all his heads to concentrate on the battles. He sends his son, Indrajit, into the battle and the son is killed by Lakshman. Then Ravana enters the battle himself and after much fighting is killed by Rama.

The task which was set for Vishnu in his Rama reincarnation is completed. Rama and Sita are reunited, but Rama renounces her because he suspects she may have submitted to Ravana. She proves her purity by undergoing an ordeal by fire. (Interestingly in the Thai version, Rama does not renounce Sita, but she initiates the ordeal to prove her purity in case Rama has any doubts.) After fourteen years of this long epic, Rama, Sita, and Lakshman return to Ayodhya where all welcome them and Bharata happily turns the throne back to Rama.

This is an appropriate place to end, but the *Ramayana* does not do so. Later Rama suspects Sita again and sends Sita back to the forest alone. There she gives birth to his twin sons and rears them to young manhood. In time, Rama learns of his sons and forgives Sita. She returns and swears to her innocence, but instead of resuming life she returns to the earth from which she had sprung. Later Rama as Vishnu returns to the celestial world with all his family and monkey followers. Presumably he is reunited with Sita, as Lakshmi, there. One version has Sita returning from the forest and living happily with Rama, which seems more likely if she were really his celestial consort. In any case, the reader can choose his own ending. They both are happy ones eventually.

With a story of this complexity one can easily see the immense possibilities for unusual variations available to the imaginative artist. It seems almost needless to say that the *Ramayana* as drama is never performed in its entirety. Usually a few scenes are done, and sometimes a general condensation using the main scenes is performed. That in itself can often take several hours. One traditional rule governing the length of any particular performance is that it can never end in tragedy for the hero. That means whenever Rama or Lakshman is wounded in one of the many battles the performance must continue until the hero or his brother is healed and heading his forces again.

In adapting the drama to Thailand, not only have names of persons and the setting been changed, but episodes have been added and subtracted. Thai costumes, masks, and music have been provided and Rama has been identified as a future Buddha. The text most often used in Thailand is a version made by King Rama II, although the most complete version of the whole *Ramayana* is the one made by King Rama I. The reader can see in Thailand the great influence of this epic on the names of places (e.g., the old capital of Ayudhya is a version of Ayodhya) and the names of real persons today, including the general title of Rama given to the Chakri kings.

Another form of Thai drama often based on the *Ramayana* is the *nang*, or shadow play. Like the khon, the nang is less often seen, except in the south of Thailand, than are the performances of the lakhon. The nang probably originated in India and reached Thailand by a circuitous route through Sumatra and the Malay Peninsula when both were part of the Srivijaya empire. Similar shadow-play theater is more common in Malaysia and Indonesia than it is in Thailand.

The nang theater uses figures of the characters in the drama projected as shadows against a white screen. The figures used to make the shadows are cut from cow hides which have been soaked in water, dried and smoothed in the sun and then polished by a gourd. On these prepared hides artists draw the necessary figures and the parts between the lines are cut out. A large number of these figures is needed to project any scene from the *Ramayana* on the screen. The figures may be cut to represent individuals, two figures interacting, or groups of three or more figures. The hide figures are usually mounted on two sticks with which the manipulator holds the figures above his head. A trained manipulator will assume the attitudes and positions of the figure characters he manipulates and by so doing adds to the authenticity of the performance.

Historically, khon, lakhon, and nang troupes were supported mainly for performance at court or in the palaces and villas of royalty, nobles, and other wealthy persons. Today such performances in Bangkok are largely limited to those given by Silpakorn University and a few other groups. A more popular form of theater often performed at village festivals and temple fairs is *likay*. I first saw a likay group perform at a temple fair some years ago in Hua Hin, a popular resort and fishing town on the west coast of the Gulf of Thailand. A few years later I attended another fair at the same wat and found the likay performance had been replaced by a motion picture which seemed to attract almost half the town's population.

One of the big differences between likay and the other dramatic forms is the absence in likay of gods and demon characters. All the likay characters are human and the actors do their own speaking and singing. The plays loosely follow a plot drawn from historical romances and adventure stories based on Sanskrit and Chinese literature with some more recent Thai tales especially based on history used as well. These plays are most often presented in short scenes following one another in rapid succession. Usually comedies, and often bawdy, the plays emphasize characters and action more than the plot itself. The performing group will select a particular story to tell and the actors will all be familiar with the plot line. The dialogue will then be improvised by the skilled actors. This improvisation of the dialogue based on a standard story means no two provincial towns will see the same play because no two performances are identical. The actors often work comments and humor about the local scene into their dialogue.

If a festival or fair runs several nights, the likay group may decide to expand one play rather than to perform different ones each night. If a single play is expanded to cover performances on several nights, each evening's show takes on some of the characteristics of the old-fashioned movie serial with each nightly episode ending in a way calculated to hold the audience in suspense until the next evening so that it will return to see the next performance. Likay is a widespread theater form and many troupes travel out of Bangkok throughout the country.

One other form of theater, which is especially popular in the Northeastern region of Thailand, should be mentioned. Now so many Northeasterners live permanently or temporarily in Bangkok, regular radio and live performances of *mohlam* singers are available in the capital city. Each New Year's Day my room boy, a young man from the Northeast, spent most of the afternoon and evening at one of the capital's boxing stadiums where, with thousands of other Northeasterners, the holiday was celebrated by listening to one mohlam singer after another. A mohlam singer is a kind of traveling minstrel, sometimes traveling alone, but more often with a small group of singers from village to village. Accompanied by a musician playing a reed instrument called a *khaen*, the mohlam singer, who may be either a man or a woman, sings his stories in the Thai-Lao language. These stories, always well-known and appreciated no matter how many times heard, are usually bawdy, erotic, and humorous.

An unusual feature of the mohlam performance is the material which the singer weaves into his song. He may include fragments of classic stories or the tales of Rama. Current news and local village gossip may be included. Before radios and in the absence of newspapers outside Bangkok and a few major towns, the mohlam singer was eagerly awaited in the village to bring news of the outside world. Even today he can be a source of local news and gossip that is never carried by radio stations and sometimes the singer is aware of major news before it is known to the wider news media. This special feature of mohlam performances has led in the last decade or so to an unusual use of this form of theater. Both the government of Thailand, with assistance from its allies, and the pro-Communist forces in Northeastern Thailand, supported by similar groups in Laos, have used or attempted to use mohlam singers for po-litical purposes by paying them to incorporate propaganda for their respective causes into the songs and tales the singers perform as they wander from village to village. Fortunately for the preservation of an art form, most mohlam sing-ers have adhered to their traditional folk and historical tales and not incorpo-rated large hunks of Cold War political propaganda into their work.

The khaen used for musical accompaniment has a haunting sound. It sounds like a cross between a mouth organ and an accordion. Since it is played while both inhaling and exhaling it has a continuous, uninterrupted flow of tone which adds to the eerie beauty of the music. Most khaen today are roughly twenty to forty inches in length, but some have been made as long as six feet or more. A khaen consists of fourteen pieces of cane pipe or bamboo about the size of a man's finger in diameter. They are arranged in two parallel rows of seven pairs. Each pair decreases in size except for the two longest pair which are the same length. The mouthpiece, shaped a little like a small, hol-low hardwood barrel, has a rectangular hole through it on the long sides. Through this rectangular hole the pipes are fitted. Metal reeds are inserted near the bottom of the pipes and finger holes are made in the pipes just above the mouthpiece. The holes are cut all the way through the pipes and when the instrument is played by blowing through the mouthpiece, both hands are needed to cover the holes on the pipes.

To the Northeastern Thai the khaen has a function similar to the guitar in Spanish-speaking countries. It is an instrument of courting. The first time I heard one played was on a visit to a small town in the Northeast. I was lying in bed waiting for sleep in the quiet night when I heard the gentle continuous sound of a khaen being played in the distance somewhere. It was the only sound I could hear as the whole town seemed to rest from its labors to relax and listen to a young man playing his song for the girl he was wooing. When the first player stopped, another from a different direction began, and I finally fell asleep to the soothing enchantment of a distant khaen.

Visitors to Bangkok may not have the opportunity to witness a performance of any of the major theatrical forms, but they will always have the chance to see representative selections of Thai dance. Several hotels present short nightly performances of a few Thai dances which, however, are often modified to fit the tourist audience and the setting of a dining room or a night club.

There are two institutions which do provide regular theatrical performances of Thai dance. These are the Silpakorn Theater and the Phakavali Institute of Dance and Music. The first is the government-supported theater and the second is a small private music and dance institute known to the West from its tour of America and Europe in 1962 and 1963 and America again in 1970. The Phakavali has also appeared in several Asian nations. Both of these institutions present performances of several short classical and Thai folk dances representative of several regions of the country.

Among the dances most often seen and photographed by tourists is the fingernail dance which originated in Northern Thailand. Unusually long fingernails are a sign of leisure, or wealth enough to support a life of leisure. And in the northern part of the country around Chiengmai long fingernails on women are a traditional sign of beauty. (One often sees some workingmen in Thailand—servants, taxi drivers, hotel porters, etc.—who as a status sign allow the nail on the little finger of one hand to grow to great length.) In the fingernail dance the beautiful Thai girls attach long metal nails, several inches of gold or bronze curving back slightly toward the wrist, to all their fingers except the thumbs. These elongated fingers add to the beauty and grace of the many hand and finger movements in the dance. At night a dance using similar hand movements substituting candles held in the hands for the long fingernails may be performed. In the dark the candles weave an intricate pattern of light as the hands move with the dance.

Closely allied to the dance are the preliminary warm-up movements used by ritualistic fighters with sword, staves, and shields. Similar movements, though shorter and less elaborate, are used by modern-day Thai boxers before a bout. Both dance theaters include in their regular shows a performance of the ritualistic dance invocations used by fighters to honor their gods, their teachers, and the Lord Buddha. After the preliminary dance, the fighters will perform a real sword or stave fight.

In Thai dance and Thai classical theater the orchestra is an important part of the whole. A Thai-instrument orchestra is called a *piphat* band and consists mostly of woodwind and percussion instruments, although string instruments are sometimes included. The woodwind instrument, called a *pi nai*, is made of rosewood and has six finger holes. It looks and sounds something like an oboe.

Percussion instruments, which form the majority of instruments in a piphat band, are divided into those which provide the melody and those which provide rhythm. One group of the melody instruments looks like xylophones or marimbas built without legs. The player sits on the floor and strikes the bars with mallets. These instruments are called *ranad* and there are several varieties of them. The different kinds are determined by the pitch, the material out of which they are made, and the shape. Some have wooden bars and others have metal bars. Some fit in a frame shaped like a boat curved up at both ends while others are on a frame that makes them appear more like a flat box.

A second group of percussion melody instruments is a family of gong instruments in which the disklike gongs are suspended horizontally from a circular rattan frame only a few inches high. The circular frame is not closed and the player sits inside the circle on the floor with the gongs around him on all sides except at his back. He strikes the gongs with mallets. The size of the disks determines the pitch, and when there are two or more of these instruments they are usually set at different octaves. Each instrument has sixteen or eighteen disk gongs suspended on its frame. The most important of these instruments is called the *gong wong yai*; it provides the principal melody for the orchestra.

The rhythmic percussion instruments include drums of various sizes played on one or both ends and beaten by hands or sticks. This group of instruments also includes gongs and cymbals. The gongs are usually the single, vertically suspended gongs familiar to the West. They give different tones depending on the size and are usually struck with padded sticks. The cymbals, too, are of different sizes and are played by striking them together. One kind of cymbal, called a *ching,* is especially important. This is a small, thick, cup-shaped cymbal in which the two halves are linked together by a cord. This small, high-pitched cymbal is used to beat the tempo for the band. Thai piphat bands do not have conductors and the ching takes over part of the conductor's function in indicating the beat.

The Thai musical scale has an octave like that of Western music, but there is one significant difference. The tones of the Thai scale are full tone intervals apart; there are no half notes as in the Western musical scale. This means that a Thai musical score for the ranad, for example, cannot be transferred direct to the Western xylophone, a similar instrument, without making a considerable adjustment in the score. Nor can Western music be played direct by a piphat band. Little music has yet been transposed to play by the other.

Records, radio, television, and motion pictures have all contributed to interest in Western music, especially Western popular music, in Thailand. A decade ago there were two Western-style classical orchestras, one at Silpakorn University and one in the Thai navy; they performed annual concerts. There were also a great many popular dance bands playing for night clubs and students' social affairs. The main characteristic of the dance bands is their volume. They played loudly, but as they were not used to hearing the Western scales, they were frequently not in tune and sometimes different parts of the band were not even in the same key. A decade later, partly as a result, I assume, of the great influx of American servicemen as well as just general improvement, the dance bands of Bangkok and other major cities are first-rate and some of the night clubs present singers and bands performing both Thai and Western popular music as well played as much of that heard in the West.

Thailand has introduced to the world a popular dance which is now done in many countries in Asia. It is a social dance which in Thailand is called the *ramwong*. Much Thai popular music is written for the strong rhythm of the ramwong. Customarily in many Asian countries men and women do not show affection by touching in public and the ramwong is well suited to this custom. In this dance the couples form a wide circle and while the woman moves around the circle with small steps and hand and arm gestures similar to those used in the classical dance, the man weaves a pattern around her, approaching her with intricate and delicate hand gestures. He often comes close to his partner, but he never touches her. I have often seen this dance done at parties, university dances, and other social affairs, but I must admit I have not yet seen a Westerner who could do it with the grace and beauty of a Thai. When the Thai do it, it is not only a popular dance, but a modern expression of an old, well-loved dance heritage.

On a visit some years ago to the central prison for long-term criminals, near Bangkok, I was with a group being entertained during lunch by an *angkalung* orchestra. The angkalung is not a Thai instrument, but was imported, I believe, from Malaysia or Indonesia. It is an instrument made of three short sections of bamboo of different lengths and different thicknesses. The middle section is loose and when the instrument is shaken it strikes a note against the other sections. Each instrument produces only one note, and each musician usually holds one instrument in each hand. He must know precisely where in the melody, as it is being played, he is to shake his right hand or left hand to make the proper note. The sound reminded me of a soft, rather high-pitched marimba, yet that is an inadequate description. Each of the prison instruments was topped by a long peacock feather so that shaking the instruments provided not only a sound but a sight of waving peacock plumes which added to an altogether pleasing performance.

Most of the literature in Thailand before the nineteenth century was in the form of poetry. Without the printing presses which were introduced by the missionaries in that century, Thai literary works had to be written or printed by hand and many were simply transmitted orally. In this latter process the stories were often expanded or changed to suit particular times and places so that it is difficult to attribute classics of Thai literature to any one known author.

Much of this early Thai literature was based on religion and history, both real and mythological. Some of these tales were drawn from Thai experiences while others, such as the *Ramayana,* can be traced back to Indian and Chinese sources. The *Jataka* tales, stories of the 547 previous Buddha births, are, like the *Ramayana* epic, well known in many countries. Many of the early stories in Thailand, such as the famous romantic story of northern Thai kings and princesses, entitled *Phra Law,* at the beginning were mainly written and recited in the language of Thai royalty and the nobility. Other stories, such as the equally famous story named *Khun Chang, Khun Phaen,* about two men with those names who were rivals for the love of the same woman, were written in the everyday speech of ordinary men and women. Such stories were widespread and had much popularity.

Another series of tales popular in classic Thai literature and sometimes used as the basis for classical Thai dance-drama is the *Inao.* Like the *Ramakien,* adapted from an Indian epic, the *Inao* is a Thai adaptation of the Indonesian *Panji* tales about a famous king and hero from Java.

Thailand has had the good fortune, especially during the Bangkok period of its history, of having several kings who themselves were talented and well-known authors. Earlier Ayudhyan kings such as King Trailok (1448–1488) and King Narai (1657–1688) gathered poets and artists at their courts and encouraged their work. But among the more recent kings both Rama I and Rama II were outstanding poets in their own right, producing in collaboration with other poets at their courts new versions of the *Ramakien* and the *Inao* tales. In the twentieth century King Vajiravudh was a noted playwright and poet who translated several works for the theater from the West as well as writing plays of his own.

All of these kings as well as others of the Chakri dynasty have encouraged the development of Thai literature and art. During the first half of the nineteenth century one of Thailand's greatest poets, Sunthorn Bhu (1786–1855), lived and worked at the court of Rama II. Unfortunately, the great poet sometimes got into arguments about poetry with members of the court who held grudges. One of those with whom he argued was Prince Chesda, himself a poet. When the prince became King Rama III, the poet Sunthorn Bhu was banished from the court and he spent part of that reign wandering around the country and part of it as a monk. When King Mongkut began his rule in 1851, Sunthorn Bhu was welcomed back for the last few years of his life as a court poet.

Sunthorn Bhu was a talented poet, whose love lyrics were immensely popular. He also wrote a famous fantasy in which the heroes roamed around the world having adventures on the seas and in many countries. One of his short poems, *Swasdi Raksa,* considered by many as a masterpiece of Thai literature, is written as instructions of a practical nature to two Thai princes as well as to explain various superstitions to them and tell them which ones to obey.

Little is known about contemporary Thai literature in the West and almost none of it has been translated into Western languages. A visit to any Thai bookstore will show, however, a large stock of modern novels and adventure stories as well as a good selection of children's literature. Some of these volumes are translations or local copies of popular Western literary works, while others have been written by Thai poets and novelists.

Since its founding in 1933 by the Fine Arts Department as the School of Fine Arts, Silpakorn University has been at the center of artistic developments in Thailand. It became a university in 1943 and has faculties of Painting and Sculpture, Architecture, Archeology, and Interior Decoration, as well as programs for music and drama. While its emphasis has been on traditional Thai art, it has found a place for some contemporary Thai painting and sculpture as well.

Much of the university's interest in the field of modern art can be traced to the influence of an unusual man, the late Professor Silpa Bhirasri, a sculptor credited with some of Bangkok's major monuments. He was dean of the Faculty of Painting and Sculpture for many years until his death in 1962. He was Italian by birth. His name was Carlo Feroci when he was born in Florence in 1892. After he graduated from the Royal Academy of Fine Arts in Florence, he went to Thailand and entered Thai government service in the Fine Arts Department in 1924. From then until his death he devoted himself to his adopted country, its art, and to training its young artists. In this dedication he became a Thai citizen and was given a Thai name. At his death he left some major statues in several parts of Bangkok and a national annual art exhibit which shows many of Thailand's young as well as mature artists of both traditional and modern schools.

Until recently a major earmark of Thai art was its limited subject matter. Modern art was and is largely unknown throughout the country. Traditional art ruled in architecture, painting, sculpture, and the performing arts. By traditional art in Thailand I mean art related closely to the Buddhist religion or to the myths and stories that stemmed from or sprung up around the history and teachings of religion and the established ways of depicting them. Only in recent years have the Thai begun to see limited inroads by other styles and subjects into the vast area of the arts controlled by tradition. Except for motion pictures, modern drama and dance familiar to the West and to such Asian nations as the Philippines and Japan have failed to catch hold of the imagination of the Thai people.

Thai traditional art, however, is a rich and beautiful art of which every Thai is justly proud. It finds its best expression in architecture, sculpture, painting, and the classical dance-drama.

Thai art is usually divided into historical periods related not only to time, but to distinct cultural groups that were dominant in sections of Southeast Asia, including what is now Thailand, during each particular period of several centuries. The most general historical division is that between the pre-Thai periods of art and those periods after the Thai arrived in and then dominated the part of the peninsula which is present-day Thailand. There is considerable agreement on the general outline of Thai art history, but much disagreement among authorities on the specifics such as the beginning and ending centuries of any particular period of art. The dates I give are approximate, based on several sources.

The pre-Thai periods of Thailand's art history are the Dvaravati, or Mon, about sixth to the eleventh centuries A.D., the Srivijaya in the southern peninsular part of Thailand and the Lopburi or Khmer period in Central, Northern, and Northeastern Thailand, both from about the eighth to the thirteenth centuries.

All of these early pre-Thai periods were heavily influenced by Indian cultural developments. The Dvaravati civilization, consisting of a Mon-speaking people with a religion mixing both Brahmanism and Theravada Buddhism, was probably centered on Nakorn Pathom, where today exists the tallest chedi in Thailand. This chedi, or stupa, built to its present height only about a century ago, is one of the greatest reliquary monuments in the entire Buddhist world. When the Thai moved southward into the Chao Phya valley they encountered the Mon people who by that time, however, had been influenced culturally as well as politically by the Khmer empire which had spread westward from Cambodia. Descendants of these early Mon peoples can still be found in scattered communities around Bangkok and elsewhere in Thailand.

The Khmers had moved into Central Thailand after the Mons and brought with them the distinctive architecture which reached its peak in the magnificent temples and palaces of their capital city of Angkor Thom and its nearby temple of Angkor Wat. Similar architecture to Angkor can be seen in Thai ruins at Lopburi and Sukhothai and is especially notable at Pimai in Northeastern Thailand not far from Khorat. But there are Khmer ruins at scattered sites throughout Northeastern Thailand. The art of the Khmers is heavily influenced in its subject matter by its Hindu religion of the Brahmans and by Mahayana Buddhism which Angkor had probably received via the Srivijaya kingdoms in the southern part of the Malay Peninsula and the large islands which today make up part of Indonesia. Theravada Buddhism did not become part of the Cambodian religious beliefs until late in the Khmer history after the Khmers had been in contact with the Mons and still later the Thai. These contacts were many years after the main buildings of Angkor had been designed and constructed reflecting the earlier religious beliefs of the Khmers.

The Srivijaya kingdom is generally believed to have had its capital on Sumatra, although some scholars have argued for a capital somewhere on the Malay Peninsula. In any event, the Srivijayans were believers in Mahayana Buddhism, which provided a broader range of subject matter for their sculpture. At one time, it is believed, the Srivijayans extended their kingdom, their religion, and their artistic influences on the Malay Peninsula as far north as Nakornsrithammarat and the Bay of Bandon in what is today Thailand.

The styles and periods of Thai art history starting in the thirteenth century after the Thai moved down in increasing numbers from Yunnan in China are usually divided into five major eras: (1) the Chieng Sen or Northern Thai period from the eleventh to the sixteenth centuries; (2) the Sukhothai from the thirteenth to the fifteenth centuries; (3) the U Tong, farther south geographically, but at approximately the same time as the Sukhothai; (4) the Ayudhya period from the fourteenth to the eighteenth centuries; and (5) the Bangkok period from the eighteenth century to the present.

The Northern Thai or Chieng Sen style was partly influenced by Theravada Buddhism brought in from Burma and by some remnants of Chinese styles carried down from the north. The Sukhothai and U Tong styles farther to the south were influenced by the contacts with the Mons and even more importantly, the Khmers. Many authorities consider the Buddhas made in the Sukhothai style with their slender, graceful, almost effeminate bodies to be the most beautiful of all Thai Buddhas. The Ayudhya period later developed a synthesis of all the others and a kind of "national" style of sculpture and architecture emerged. By the time of the destruction of Ayudhya in 1767, art generally and sculpture particularly had begun a decline in its simple beauty as the clean, relatively unadorned lines of the Buddha statues of earlier times, especially the Sukhothai ones, evolved into images which were sometimes ornamented excessively and almost garishly, so that the viewer of the image was distracted from the serenity of the Buddha by the costume and decoration. During the Bangkok period Buddhist traditional art continued to decline in simple splendor, and with the acquiring of new art styles from contacts with the West in the nineteenth century traditional art seemed to become stagnant. There have been few developments of any consequence in traditional art in recent decades.

One late nineteenth-century building, however, made a major and lasting contribution to art in Thailand. That building is Wat Benchamabopitr, the

Marble Temple. The building of almost pure white marble with its multiple-tiered golden roofs, perfectly symmetrical in its proportions, and set among lovely landscaped gardens near the palace where the present king lives has been compared favorably to some of the most beautiful buildings in the world.

Of the main buildings in the Thai temple compound the bot and the vihara housing the Buddha images are frequently similar in architectural style. The building is usually rectangular, constructed of brick and stucco, with sloping, slightly concave, many-tiered roofs of colored, glazed tiles. The outer walls of the building are most often painted white and the roofs may be of gold, blue, green, orange, or bright yellow tiles in one color or in simple geometric patterns of two or more colors. These colored roofs and white walls make the temples more cheerful and gay in appearance than the churches and other religious buildings in the West. At the peaks of the ridges of the roofs are finials hornlike in shape or in the shape of the sacred naga, or snake, which give a distinctive characteristic to the ridge ends of the temple's roof.

These main temple buildings often have porches in the front with the roofs supported by pillars. At times they have pillars completely surrounding the buildings and a careful look at these exterior pillars will show that they usually slant slightly inward rather than stand straight. The specific reason for this peculiar trait seems obscure. Frequently, the wall area of the porches above the doors and windows will be elaborately decorated with carvings, gilt-painted designs, lacquer work, or bits of glass. The wooden doors and window shutters are also usually colorfully decorated in carvings, lacquer, or gilt paintings of guardian demons, angels, and other celestial beings from Buddhist mythology.

Inside the main temple buildings one finds the principal Buddha image at the end opposite the door. The main image is often surrounded by other Buddha images or statues of other Buddhist leaders and sometimes Thai nonreligious leaders as well. The walls and interior pillars may be covered with murals showing scenes from the Buddha's life and teachings as well as many other religious and secular subjects. One temple in Bangkok has paintings of Mount Vernon, the Virginia residence of George Washington. Often the wooden beams and the ceiling are painted red with gold stars to depict the heavens. The amount of interior decoration varies greatly from the elaborate and intricate paintings of some large royal temples to almost nothing except plain walls and ceilings in some of the smaller temples of the towns and villages. There may be other variations in the bot and vihara as well, such as the material from which the building is constructed, but this short description is typical of many wats throughout the country.

We have also noted that many wats have one or more stupas or reliquary monuments. These, too, vary in architecture, but the two most common types are the chedi and the prang. They may be any size from a few feet to the 380 feet of the great chedi at Nakorn Pathom. This great chedi was built in the nineteenth century in its present form and is believed to cover earlier, smaller chedi which are encased in this great pagoda covered with golden porcelain tiles imported from China.

The typical chedi has a base or plinth, a bell-like dome, and a tall graceful spire which tapers to a very narrow point. Often there is little or no decoration on the chedi. Along the spire may be found the umbrellas symbolic of royalty and the Buddha in the same material as the chedi, and a small orb may be located near the top of the spire. While the most common chedi are round, there are square ones and a few with more than four sides. Near the base, of the larger chedi at least, there are usually four niches, one on each side. One of these usually gives entrance to the interior and the others contain Buddha images. The second style of stupa, the prang, is modeled on the Khmer tower with its blunter shape and top and is often covered with sculpture or other decoration for its full height.

A fundamental trait of all Thai Buddhist sculpture based on religious writings is its imitativeness, not imitative of other nations, but of earlier religious artists of the same country. In theory, all Buddha images are copies of an ideal Buddha image based on legendary portraits made of the Buddha during his lifetime. No portraits are known to exist of the Prince Siddhartha, so the ideal image is supposedly based on descriptions of the Buddha in the Pali texts of the Buddhist canon. Copying these descriptions has resulted in the creation of statues quite different from the Greek and Italian traditions with which the West is familiar. There are no bones, muscles, or tendons usually shown in Buddha images. Instead one sees a head covered with spiral curls and a protuberance on top, ears with lobes which are distended to great length, unusually long arms, flat footsoles, fingers all the same length in some styles, eyebrows that are roundly arched rather than straight so that they appear "like drawn bows," and many other features not common to men as we know them.

The sculptor of the Buddha image is not expected to be experimental or original. Actually, of course, there are differences in detail—the shape of the body and the head, the nature of the protuberance on the head, the dress, posture, and material of the image—and it is these differences, along with the approximate year of creation and the geographical location from which the image comes, that determine the style or period into which an image is classified. The Thai were master craftsmen in bronze casting and many of their finest images are cast in that metal. Other metals, such as gold, have also been used, and images were often made in stone, especially in the earlier periods of Thai history. At one time or another images in Thailand have also been made in wood, stucco, terra cotta, glass, jade, and other precious stones and metals so that most materials known to sculptors have been used.

The posture of the Buddha images is limited to four positions traditionally. All images are either standing, sitting, reclining, or walking. In the sitting position the Buddha is usually on a pedestal of a coiled snake or a lotus flower and his legs are bent under him either crossed or one on top of the other. Occasionally a seated Buddha will be found in the European style sitting on a throne. Reclining Buddhas are often found, like the one at Wat Po, on their right sides with their heads resting on their right hand with the right arm bent at the elbow.

Buddha images also have a limited number of gestures all of which have meanings. Perhaps the most common is the seated Buddha with his right hand over the right leg, palm turned in and fingers pointing down, and with his left hand resting palm up on his crossed legs. This is the position known as "Calling the Earth to Witness" the truth of the Buddha's Enlightenment.

Other common gestures include a standing Buddha with one hand raised, fingers straight up, palm out. This is called the gesture of dispelling fear. In Thailand it is said that the Buddha is forbidding his relatives to argue. When a standing Buddha has both hands raised, fingers up and palms out, he is subduing the violence of the ocean which symbolizes the mastery of the individual's cravings and desires. In similar standing positions when the thumb and forefinger are held together, this is the gesture of giving instruction and preaching. There are a few other permitted gestures as well, but these are the most common.

With these limitations on posture and gesture one does not find in Thai Buddhist sculpture the wide range of expressed attitudes that are seen in Hindu sculpture with its many gods and their avatars. Mahayana sculpture which includes images of many Bodhisattvas (persons who have achieved the last stage before nirvana) as well as of the Lord Buddha also is able to cover a much broader range of form, shape, and gesture.

Traditional Thai painting has a much wider range of subject matter than does Thai sculpture. It includes paintings of the Buddha and scenes from his life, of other gods, of some kings and their courts, and sometimes scenes based on the daily lives of the common farmers and townspeople. A rich resource for the subject of Thai painting was the literary tradition of Buddhism and Hinduism. Both the 547 *Jataka* tales and the Hindu epic, the *Ramayana*, provided many delightful scenes for the artist to paint.

Most of Thai traditional painting is closely allied to the wat and usually found on wat premises. Often it was painted by anonymous monks some of whom were more ambitious than talented. Their art often took the form of murals in the bot or vihara buildings and such murals were often there to instruct and guide the worshipers not only in the teachings of Buddhism but in other aspects of life as well. The murals were lessons as well as decoration.

The murals at Wat Po in Bangkok are sometimes referred to as the "first university in Thailand" because of their inclusion of many subjects including science, medicine, mythology, and anatomy as well as religion. Unfortunately, most of the oldest murals in Thailand have disappeared or have deteriorated so badly that little is left of them. In a tropical country with heavy rains, dampness is a menace to murals painted on stucco walls. Even murals done in the Bangkok period suffer and most older period ones are already gone, although a few from the Ayudhya period exist in bad condition.

Probably the most famous mural for visitors in Bangkok is the one on the walls of the rectangular gallery around the Temple of the Emerald Buddha. The present murals which retell the *Ramayana* story are not the first painted on those walls. The earliest murals were often restored, and at the end of the 1920's the murals were completely redone in preparation for the one hundred and fiftieth anniversary in 1932 of the founding of the Chakri dynasty and the construction of the Grand Palace with its Royal Chapel of the Emerald Buddha. These murals, therefore, are quite new but still need regular refurbishing at the present time.

In addition to the mural paintings other traditional paintings were done on banners used for various ceremonies and on doors and window shutters of the wats. These last were usually guardian figures to protect the wat. Early Thai paintings also were used to illustrate manuscripts. A typical old Thai manuscript opens like an accordion and may have its text illustrated with paintings in the middle of an open leaf or at either end. Many of these art works can be seen in the National Museum which itself is a fine example of Thai architecture during the early Bangkok period.

During the reign of Rama III in the nineteenth century contacts between Thailand and the countries of Europe and America once more began to increase in number after a long period of limited relations. Later King Chulalongkorn and his successors sent many Thai abroad for their education, and many of these Thai students saw Western art. In time the Thai artist learned new techniques of painting and sculpture from Western artists and was bound to be affected by the apparently unlimited scope of subject matter which the Western artist used in his paintings and other artwork. Thai artists of the twentieth century began to feel the need to break away from traditional art in technique, in style, and in subjects.

Turning away from traditional art in any society is a long, difficult process, and Thai artists have had only limited success so far. Student artists at both Silpakorn University and the School of Arts and Crafts are studying modern art of the whole world and trying to apply its lessons to their own work. But their teachers, mainly trained in more traditional art forms, are able to give little instruction and encouragement, and what is worse, there are almost no patrons of modern artists in Thailand. In recent years there has been a little encouragement for modern artists working in areas other than the traditional ones, but that little encouragement has often come from foreigners. Thai art patrons willingly support traditional Buddhist art as a way to earn merit, but they see no way of earning merit from supporting a modern abstract artist whose work they cannot understand or appreciate because it is too far removed from their own experience.

The failure so far of Thai leadership at almost all levels in society to support modern Thai art has resulted in at least two disadvantages for the development of art in Thailand in recent years. First, many young artists working in new styles and media must work at other jobs to earn a living or else spend their time painting what could be called "tourist" art, mediocre paintings of temples, rice fields, buffaloes, and similar subjects done over and over again. Commercial galleries displaying these works can be found on some of the lanes in Bangkapi, the section of Bangkok where most foreigners live, and in most tourist hotels. The young artist engaged in these activities no longer has time to experiment with new techniques and styles.

Secondly, several of Thailand's leading, younger artists not working in traditional fields, but experimenting with new media and new styles are spending long periods of study and work abroad. They do not leave their home because they especially wish to live abroad, but it is only in other countries that they are able to find the support and sales for their paintings and sculpture and the opportunity to keep in close touch with other artists of the modern schools. Fortunately, most or perhaps all of these younger artists expect to return to Thailand at some time in the future, but without a gallery or museum in which to show their works and with little patronage to support them, there will not be much incentive, other than their own artistic integrity, for them to continue.

When I first went to Thailand a young artist, popular and well known for his paintings and woodblock prints of Thai subjects in his own unique style, was Damrong Wong-Uparaj. Since then he has studied in England and in the United States where he experimented with new styles as he developed into an outstanding and mature artist. Between his periods of study abroad he taught at the Northeastern Technical Institute at Khorat and helped to bring new concepts and new ideas of art to students outside the two major art schools in Bangkok.

Another Thai artist well known for his woodblock and masonite block prints is Praphan Srisouta, who studied in Germany and has now returned to Bangkok where he, too, is experimenting with new abstract styles in painting. Among others currently studying abroad are the painters Mr. Pricha Arjunka, Mr. Banchong Kosalawat, and Mr. Panom Suwanath, and the painter-sculptor who is now concentrating on the latter, Mr. Inson Wongsam. All have broken from traditional Thai art styles and subject matter and are searching for new ways to express themselves and their conceptions of the world and life within it. These artists are only a few of those from Thailand who have recently studied abroad and are bringing recognition and honor in the art world to their homeland. Several of these young men have won bronze and silver medals in the annual national art exhibits in Bangkok, and it is hoped that a permanent gallery of modern art can be erected soon to add their works and the works of other Thai artists to its collection for permanent viewing.

In a pamphlet on contemporary art in 1960, Professor Silpa Bhirasri, who encouraged many of Thailand's younger artists in their first shy steps toward breaking tradition, wrote: "No sculptures obtained by iron bars and sheet welding have yet been made by our artists, the principal reason being that there is not yet a demand or appreciation for such artistic expression." In the decade since he wrote that, the first part of the statement has been changed by developments. A Thai sculptor, Mr. Inson Wongsam, has had two shows in New York of wire and metal-welded sculpture, and perhaps other Thai artists are working in these media elsewhere. The second part of Professor Bhirasri's statement, however, is still a correct diagnosis of the demand and appreciation for such work in Bangkok.

In time, of course, conditions in Thailand for the encouragement of modern art will probably change for the better. It is hoped that these changes will come sooner rather than later so that the present generation of modern artists will find an honorable position of demand and appreciation beside the rich traditional art of Thailand. Unless the artist deliberately and consciously copies the work of another, he will always reflect in his own work his racial, ethnic, and national background. They are part of both his conscious and unconscious experience which make him the particular artist that he is. The modern Thai artist is as much Thai as the traditional artist, and his work, like the work of the traditional Buddhist sculptor and painter, is an expression in contemporary terms of the rich heritage he has received as a particular Thai living and learning in a particular time.

4
Yawarat Road

Opposite the Grand Palace, between the road and the Chao Phya River, is a small green park adjoining the royal landing stage on the riverbank. From there one can watch the exciting activities of the constantly changing river scene.

Across the river are the glittering, broken-pottery-covered towers of Wat Arun. The Naval Academy is to the left of the wat, and just beyond the Academy, at a point of junction between a major klong and the river, is the remnant of an old fort built to prevent marauding vessels from sailing up the river to attack or plunder Bangkok or Ayudhya farther upstream. Anchored closely together in the middle of the river are three small, blue-gray naval vessels, their guns shrouded but still reminders of Thailand's proud, valiant, and politically important military forces.

Scudding around the bows and the tails of the low, sleek but aging naval vessels are numerous small boats of teak with inboard motors and canopies of canvas or wood. These ferry boats crowded with shoppers and office workers flit back and forth between the landings on both sides of the river. Long, narrow, yellow and red wooden boats flash by with their noses out of the water and their tails held down by a motor with a long shaft and a tiny propeller at the end of it which whirls frantically, pushing these water taxis at great speed on their river course. The slower, more sluggish ferries crawl along ignoring the flashy taxis except perhaps for a wave of greetings between the two masters of the tiny craft.

Down the middle of the river come great teakwood barges, some empty, some filled with rice and other products. The barges, tied together in a long line, move slowly but determinedly toward their destinations. Each barge has a man and his wife and a quota of children who live on these barges which are home and job in one. Small boats laden with fruits and vegetables move

83

slowly. Each one is poled by one man or woman walking on a narrow platform at one end and along one side of the boat. Piers along the banks of the river have ocean-going freighters tied up loading cargoes of rice and maize and kenaf and tapioca or unloading machinery, chemicals, mineral fuels, and manufactured goods needed for Thailand's economy.

The Chao Phya, less glamorous and often garbage-strewn when one looks close, has been the center of life in Bangkok and Thonburi since the time many people lived in boats on the river or in raft houses anchored to its banks to the present time when it is continuously bustling with the activities of a growing city and country. One could stand all day watching the fascinating, ever-changing river scene and learn something new about the country at each glance.

Southeast of the Grand Palace and across a klong there is a district which is even busier and more crowded than life on the river. Two-story or three-story row buildings of brick and stucco on both sides of the street are painted a bright yellow which has become streaked with rain and grime. Each row is divided into a score or more of rectangular cubicles, all of which appear to be laid out exactly the same. On the ground floor front is a retail store or restaurant or a machine shop. Behind it one can see family living quarters and a cooking area. Above it are the sleeping rooms on one or two floors. A couple of teen-age boys and a girl or two are leaning on the counters or waiting on a customer, if one is there.

In the rear a woman seated on a wooden platform plays with a tiny baby. From time to time she says a few words in a hasty excited voice. A man, probably her husband and father of the baby, sits in his undershirt in a straight chair in a corner reading a newspaper. On one side in an old adjustable canvas chair flattened out almost to the horizontal position and tucked behind a counter is an ancient man sound asleep. His thin hair is gray. His shirt is opened, and without an undershirt covering his body we can see his ribs through the rough, wrinkled, tough skin of his chest. From the wide-legged short pants which he wears and which seem much too big for him, two thin bony legs stick out over the end of his chair.

Cubicle after cubicle repeats the same scene with variations only in detail. Some of the rooms are ten feet long and others are longer or wider. Some sell toothpaste and others sell buttons or jewelry or shoes or food or any of hundreds of other items. Some have more people and some have fewer.

There are some narrow breaks in the row buildings and through these alleyways can be seen still more buildings jammed into the crowded space behind the street front shops. The rear buildings are made of wood. Squeezed into one of the narrow alleys is the stand of a noodle vendor. In another is a seller of Thai sweets. In still another is an old woman crouching under a wide straw hat selling sandals.

A wider alley is flanked on one side by a kiosk selling magazines and candy and on the other by a booth at which the eternally hopeful buy lottery tickets in the national drawing held three times a month. Lining both sides of the alleyway are stalls of flower sellers and at the back end of the alley there is a large open market for fruit, vegetables, meat, fish, and rice. Crowds of men and women come and go with bags and baskets on their arms. Hustling around the street entrance to the market eagerly waiting for customers to hire them are many of the three-wheeled blue-and-yellow motor samlors, not much larger than a motor scooter with a seat for the driver in front and a seat for two riders in back.

Many of the women with their gray hair pulled back tightly into a bun are wearing light blue, short-sleeved blouses, almost like men's shirts, which hang down over black cotton or rayon wide-legged pants which are known in Thailand as Chinese pants and are worn by both men and women. Many of the store signs in this area are not only in Thai, but also in Chinese and some in English, and Chinese is spoken as often or more often than Thai. This is the Sampeng district of Bangkok, the center of Bangkok's large Chinese commercial population.

When King Rama I moved his capital from Thonburi to Bangkok across the river, he moved some Chinese from along the river at the site where he proposed to build his inner city and palace to an area farther southeast along the bending river. This new area for the Chinese was called Sampeng and it is still the center of Bangkok's Chinese community. Center it is, but it is not a Chinese ghetto. Far from it. There is no Chinese ghetto in Bangkok, for the large Chinese population, which has at several times in Bangkok's history been more than half the total population of the city, can be found living and working in all parts of the metropolitan area.

Although there is still a Sampeng Lane in this central Chinese district, the main street is Yawarat Road running from the large movie houses on Maha Chai Road at one end to Charoen Krung (New Road) at the other. Along this wide street, choked with every conceivable form of vehicular and pedestrian traffic, can be found large retail stores, cinemas, banks, and business buildings of all kinds. Even the short-term visitor to Bangkok soon comes to recognize the important role of the Chinese in Thailand's business community.

In Thailand, as in most other Southeast Asian countries, one hears frequent comments about the Chinese problem. Usually the Chinese problem is a complex set of relationships, some of which are problems and some of which are not, between a large ethnic minority group of Chinese and the majority in the country, the Thai in this case. The problem is often considered to have two major facets. One is the economic side, for the Chinese have an unusually important economic role way out of proportion to their segment of the population. The second is the security side. This has gained in importance since the end of World War II and the Chinese civil war which ended in two opposing governments claiming the loyalties of and rights over Chinese citizens in Thailand and other Southeast Asian nations. Since one of these Chinese governments, the People's Republic of China, has spoken openly about its plans to expand its domination, if not its actual control, over certain countries throughout Southeast Asia, large Chinese minorities in these countries which might be loyal to Communist China constitute potential security threats to the countries that harbor them.

In the case of Thailand probably the greatest Chinese "problem" is to identify who is a Chinese and, therefore, part of the problem. While this is especially confusing to most Westerners who recall that the Thai came to Thailand from a part of present-day China, who remember that a major Thai hero against the Burmese was a half-Chinese general who later became King Taksin, who realize that various Chakri kings had Chinese consorts so that there is Chinese blood in the royal family, and who learn that several major Thai leaders in the twentieth century (including some who were strongly anti-Chinese) have had Chinese ancestors, it is also a cloudy area of knowledge and understanding to many Thai.

Clearly those residents of Thailand born in China of Chinese parents, who have never become naturalized Thai citizens, and who still claim Chinese citizenship *are* Chinese. There are others who may not have been born in China, but have Chinese parents and claim Chinese citizenship; these, too, are Chinese. These groups claiming Chinese citizenship are aliens and their total number in Thailand is probably less than half a million or somewhere between 1 and 2 percent of the total population. They are, however, the largest alien group in Thailand. The Chinese aliens probably account for 90 percent or more of all alien residents in Thailand. When Thailand passes any law restricting alien activities in any way, the burden of that law is felt almost entirely by the Chinese.

When Thai or others talk about the "Chinese" or "the Chinese problem," they are usually concerned with a much larger group than the 1 or 2 percent of the total population who are Chinese aliens. They are including a large number of persons of Chinese origin who are now Thai citizens either by birth or naturalization. Why should one group of Thai citizens be a problem? To answer that question it is necessary to look at the particular group, its size, and its history.

The special group concerned includes that portion of Sino-Thai citizens who have not been completely assimilated into the Thai population. Although a Thai citizen, this "Chinese" person is still Chinese in language, dress, and culture and, probably most important of all, regardless of the legal facts of his status, he thinks of himself as Chinese rather than as Thai. These "ethnic"

Chinese rather than "legal" Chinese may add two or three million to the group ordinarily lumped together as the Chinese population of Thailand making a total of two and a half to three and a half million Chinese or approximately 8 to 10 percent of the total population of Thailand. (These figures are all estimates because not even the experts, either Thai or foreign, can agree precisely on these numbers. But these figures are approximations based on the best available estimates.) An ethnic minority of nearly 10 percent of the total population of any country is significant, but when that minority has a disproportionately large economic role, then it becomes unusually important both to the economic and to the political development of the nation.

Much of what little is known about the history of Southeast Asia before the arrival of the Thai is known from Chinese writers, and the Thai, from the beginning of their independent kingdom at Sukhothai, have had a history intertwined with the Chinese. Until about a century ago the Thai paid nominal tribute periodically to the Chinese emperor as overlord of all Southeast Asia, although the emperor never exercised any direct control over the area which is Thailand as he did for almost a thousand years in Vietnam. Thai leaders did not consult the Chinese emperor on what they wanted to do in ruling their country, nor did they pay much attention to him apart from their nominal tributary payments. Traditional history says the great Thai king of Sukhothai, Ramkamheng, made one or two trips to the emperor's court and brought back from China potters who helped establish the famous pottery works at Swankaloke, a town a little north of Sukhothai. Whenever there was a new Thai ruler and especially if there was a change in the dynasty, the new king usually sought the emperor's recognition of his legitimate status as king. This step was taken by the Thonburi and Chakri dynasties at their beginning as well as by earlier kings.

While this tributary relationship was largely a nominal one, a real and much more important relationship between Thailand and China developed through trade. Chinese traders were well known in Ayudhya and in many of the trading ports such as Pattani, Songkhla, and Nakornsrithammarat on the Gulf of Thailand coast of the Malay Peninsula. It was easy for the Chinese traders to make this long journey because they could sail the entire distance without ever being out of sight of land.

Several events close together in time during the second half of the nineteenth century caused an increase in the number of Chinese leaving China for overseas work in the nations of Southeast Asia. In Thailand, the renewed commercial contacts with the West after the Bowring Treaty of 1855 with England and the treaties with the United States and several European countries in the subsequent years stimulated trade between Thailand and the West. This new and increased trade received a further stimulus with the opening of the Suez Canal in 1869, and the European demand grew for Thailand's tin, tobacco, teak, and—later—rubber. More workers were needed for the mines and the plantations, and the owners often found it difficult to lure Thai farmers from their rice farms to work in these new trade and commercial farm jobs. The owners turned to the importation of laborers, mostly from China, to meet the mine and plantation needs. A similar situation was developing in other Southeast Asian nations, but the Burmese were to import many workers from India instead of China. At about the same time steamships were introduced into the sea trade between China and Southeast Asia, and with their coming transportation overseas became both safer and cheaper for Chinese workers who traveled to the new jobs waiting for them in Southeast Asia.

Most of the early Chinese arrivals were men, and many of them left families in China. Most intended to return to China after they had acquired some wealth. Over a number of years probably half of these early Chinese laborers did return to China and in some years the number returning to China exceeded the number coming to Thailand.

By the end of the nineteenth century and the start of the first decade of the twentieth Thailand was building its railroads outward to the north, south, east, and northeast. Many Chinese followed the railroad construction to provide the necessary labor. Later many decided to stay in the towns along the lines and set up their own businesses. In that way new Chinese residents were a familiar sight in many upcountry towns. The Chinese trader and businessman were soon living in all parts of the country, not just in the major trading ports as they had been in earlier centuries.

Recently in the lobby of a hotel in a north central town along the railroad line I counted eight Thai reading. One was reading a Thai magazine and seven were reading Chinese-language newspapers, a sight which is not uncommon in many larger Thai towns. Because foreigners generally travel to the larger towns where they are most apt to see Chinese businessmen and travelers, the foreigner must take care that he does not overestimate from incidents such as this the number and power of the Chinese in the country.

During the nineteenth century many Chinese going to Thailand entered into trade and commerce following the paths of the earlier Chinese traders active in the country for centuries. As foreigners the Chinese were never Thai slaves nor were they subject to the corvée system. Being free of obligations under these compulsory labor systems, the Chinese could devote all their time to their own business interests and were free to travel in the country. They did so as traders. Furthermore, the Thai, traditionally independent, preferred such occupations as farming and fishing. In recent years they have added government service to the occupations in which they as Thai are willing to work because government service gives higher status than any commercial enterprise. The Chinese went to Thailand with different motives and values. They wanted to make money, to save it, and to return to China, if possible.

The Thai had no such compulsion to save. The result was an accumulation of savings by the Chinese and the absence of such savings, necessary to business investment, among the Thai. When new businesses were organized the Chinese had the funds, the Thai did not. It was not many decades before the thrifty, hard-working Chinese dominated the retail trade, finance, the middleman's role for upcountry trading, mining, wage labor, and what little industry existed in Thailand.

The Chinese, with the great increase in their numbers in the second half of the nineteenth century, naturally sought out other Chinese who had arrived before them. Most of the Chinese who went to Thailand were from South China along the coast, principally Fukien and Kwangtung provinces. The largest language group was the Teochiu which came from the Han River delta-Swatow area of China. This is still the largest Chinese-language group in Thailand. As Chinese with similar backgrounds came together in Thailand organizations were established. At first these were secret societies which were sometimes very angry rivals competing violently for the available jobs. Occasionally there were "shoot-outs" on the streets of Bangkok between rival groups reminiscent of the American West. In time, the secret societies were suppressed and new organizations formed.

Unlike Thai society which tends not to be organization-minded, the Chinese society in Thailand is highly organized. There are associations based on the Chinese dialect spoken, on a common regional home in China, on common surnames (at a time when the Thai did not even have surnames), on common occupations and businesses, and on common support for particular charities. All of these associations acted to give assistance of many kinds to their members and, from a more critical viewpoint, kept their members apart from the general society in Thailand. Most of the associations provided various benefits, including hospitals, schools, clinics, temples, and cemeteries for their members. In so doing, they kept their members tied together for their common good. Frequently, the associations mediated disputes among their members. This permitted them to keep their members out of Thai courts and away from government administrative agencies and thereby separated from that part of Thai society as much as possible. The associations also helped new arrivals get started and gave financial assistance to poor members of their group or those who might suffer in some emergency such as a fire. The stereotype of every Chinese being prosperous is a myth. Within Chinese society there is a full range of economic levels much as there is in the society as a whole.

If Chinese associations had been largely limited to welfare programs there probably would have been less criticism and less talk about a Chinese problem. But the business associations came in for attack from non-Chinese Thai, that is, the majority of the population. The associations were accused of engaging in monopolistic practices, of restricting apprenticeship programs to Chinese so that Thai could not enter into that restricted business, and of conducting their correspondence and keeping books in Chinese so that Thai were excluded from working on them or checking on them for that matter. These practices became an irritation to the Thai government and in time to wider segments of Thai society. A minority group had become the dominant group in the retail trade, in the processing, retailing, and exporting of rice and rubber, and a major force in the teak and tin industries, all of which were vital parts of the Thai economy. Not only was a minority group in control, but it acted in a way to exclude the majority group from ever getting a foothold in these major Thai industries. This appeared to be a clear case of the minority discriminating against the majority.

More than sixty years ago, soon after the beginning of the present century, several Chinese business groups joined to establish the Chinese Chamber of Commerce. Its purpose was to promote Chinese business interests by cutting across all divisions of the various associations, and in so doing to present a united front of Chinese businessmen against any encroachments on their spheres of interest from Western or Thai business groups. In a few years the Chinese Chamber of Commerce, because it did incorporate the interests of all other associations, became the chief spokesman for Chinese economic and political interests in Thailand. The Chamber continues in that role today.

Looking back to the early years of this century and observing developments within the Thai-Chinese community, it seems almost inevitable that an unfavorable Thai reaction to Chinese exclusionism would set in. And it did. The Chinese as aliens had long had a favorable tax position in Thailand. In 1910, their taxes were raised to equal those imposed on Thai citizens. The Chinese called a three-day strike which almost paralyzed business in Bangkok. Rice, the staple food for most Thai, became scarce and the people began to suffer. (If one wants to see the effects of the closing of Chinese businesses in Bangkok today, one need only be in the city any year at the time of the Chinese New Year's festival in late January or early February. Row after row of retail establishments are closed for one to three days. Since the time of this celebration is known ahead of time, it causes no hardship because everyone stocks up on necessary supplies beforehand. But one can imagine if a general strike of Chinese were ordered today without advance notice what difficulties would ensue for the ordinary Thai citizen.) The strike of 1910 failed and the Thai government adhered to its tax decision, but the strike undoubtedly contributed to the rising anti-Chinese feeling.

At the time of the strike the long reign of King Chulalongkorn ended and King Vajiravudh came to the throne. King Vajiravudh was a strongly nationalist king and promoted Thai nationalism during his reign. With this attitude toward Thai society the king, of course, resented the apparent economic power of the Chinese whom he regarded as alien. The king was an able writer and often wrote popular articles and pamphlets under pen names. One, he allegedly wrote, was entitled *The Jews of the East,* in which the author summed up all the anti-Chinese arguments then current among the Thai. The author charged the Chinese with being unassimilable, opportunistic, without civic virtues, worshipers of money, and economic parasites who were draining Thailand of its rightful funds by sending large sums back to China. There was no doubt that the Thai were reacting against the dominant Chinese position in the economy.

Far away in China events were also happening that were to have an effect in making the Chinese in Thailand seem even more unassimilable. The Chinese revolution to overthrow the empire and to establish a republic occurred in 1911. Prior to that time few Chinese women had come to Thailand. But after the revolution the number of Chinese women emigrating to Southeast Asia increased enormously. Before the women came most Chinese single men either waited to marry until they returned to China or married Thai women. In the latter case they often gave up ideas of returning to China and settled down to raising a Thai family. They learned Thai and became more closely associated with Thai society in general. Once the number of Chinese women increased in Thailand, however, many Chinese men married them and established an overseas family that was Chinese in all ways except geography. The part-Chinese, part-Thai families began to disappear and there was less assimilation than before.

Despite the strong nationalism of King Vajiravudh, Chinese society within Thailand generally flourished during the reigns of the last two Thai absolute monarchs. In those years Chinese schools which gave instruction in the Chinese language and taught Chinese history and culture became one of the strongest props for maintaining a separate Chinese society. The Chinese children who attended Thai schools rather than Chinese schools and learned the Thai language, history, and culture tended to be more easily assimilated into Thai general society than those children who went to Chinese schools.

The 1920's also saw the rise of a division within Chinese society in Thailand, which was a forerunner of the split that was to tear across all Chinese associations after World War II. The fight in China between the Kuomintang and the Communists found both sides with supporters in Thailand among the Chinese press and groups within the various associations.

In 1932, the absolute monarchy was overthrown in Thailand and replaced by a military-civilian oligarchy under a constitutional monarch. Although the Chinese community as such took no part in the revolution, the change in government was to have a deep effect on Chinese society. The new government was strongly nationalist and determined to promote assimilation of the Chinese subsociety into the general Thai society and to reduce what it regarded as the Chinese stranglehold on the Thai economy.

By the 1930's a great many Thai with some Chinese ancestors had become Thai in the full cultural, social, and political sense. Assimilated into Thai society they no longer considered themselves Chinese in any sense; they were Thai like any other Thai citizen. If this fact is understood, the knowledge that some of the revolutionary leaders, such as Phraya Phahon Phalaphayu, Luang Vichit Vathakarn, and Nai Pridi Phanomyong, all had one Chinese parent and still supported action restricting the Chinese becomes less difficult to comprehend.

When Luang Pibun Songgram became prime minister late in 1938, the restrictions on Chinese society increased. These restrictions took several forms. In the economic area several Chinese concessions (for example, the concession on the sale of edible birds' nests used to make a delicious soup) which gave the concession holder a monopoly on the particular item were ended, and Thai citizens were encouraged to form competing businesses. At the other end of the spectrum, certain businesses were reserved exclusively for Thai citizens and the Chinese were prohibited from entering into these businesses. The effects of the exclusion varied considerably, however. There were some businesses in which the Thai were just not interested and the Chinese continued working in them by default. But the government entered business more widely than before. The manufacturing of tobacco products and slaughtering became government monopolies, and in the major field of rice milling and selling, a Thai rice company was established with the government owning 51 percent. The government did not hesitate to use its licensing powers to see that Thai-owned businesses were favored over Chinese businesses.

In the area of education restrictions were placed on the number of hours in which teaching could be done in the Chinese language. Several Chinese schools were closed and others were carefully watched. Restrictions were also placed on the Chinese-language press and some newspapers found that their doors were closed by the government, too.

During World War II and the Japanese occupation additional restrictions were placed on the Chinese in Thailand. Chinese citizens were technically enemies of the Japanese and their Thai allies, and many Chinese, still loyal to China, tried in several ways available to them to hamper the Japanese forces in Thailand. In 1943, the Thai government denied the right of any alien to purchase land. While this law applied equally to all aliens, the effects of this law were felt mainly by the Chinese, who constituted the overwhelming majority of aliens resident in the country. Several provinces, including Khorat, Chiengmai, Lamphun, and Lampang, where substantial numbers of Chinese resided, were declared out of bounds to aliens, and all resident aliens, again mostly Chinese, were forced to move out. Some exceptions were permitted, but in other cases overzealous Thai government officials gave the Chinese such short notice that they suffered hardship and losses in the rush to move. This particular restriction was lifted as soon as the war was over. Many Chinese were recruited in Thailand as well as in Malaya and Singapore to work on the Thai-Burmese "death railway" and along with thousands of war prisoners, many Chinese died in that monstrous waste of human lives.

The war was hardly over when Thailand faced a major ethnic riot in Bangkok. For nine days in September 1945 the Yawarat area was torn by looting, robbery, and gunfire from both the Chinese civilians and the Thai military forces. The causes were many and the frictions had been building for years. The whole Yawarat district was sealed off by troops and only after the violence had run its course was peace restored to this Chinese center of Bangkok.

Although Thailand had been tributary to China for centuries and the number of Chinese citizens moving back and forth between China and Thailand in the last century had reached into the millions, the two countries had never had formal diplomatic relations. Because Thailand allied itself with Japan during World War II, it had to meet certain conditions before it was admitted to the postwar United Nations organization. One of these conditions insisted upon by China was to grant formal diplomatic relationships to the Republic of China in return for which China agreed not to veto Thailand's admission to the United Nations. So for the first time, postwar Thailand and China exchanged ambassadors and Chinese citizens in Thailand could turn to the representative of their homeland for support against harassment by Thai authorities. The Chinese ambassador began to intercede with the Thai government to lift some of the restrictions on the Chinese or to limit the effects of those restrictions which could not be removed.

In 1949, the government of mainland China changed and within a few months the Communist Chinese government was indicating that it had an interest to protect all overseas Chinese, including those in Thailand. Thus, the Thai government, which continued to recognize the Nationalist Chinese government in Taiwan, was confronted by two Chinese governments claiming the right to protect the Chinese aliens in Thailand. One of the new postwar regulations in Thailand was to restrict the number of aliens from all countries who were permitted to immigrate to Thailand in any year. At first, due to pressure from the Chinese community and the Chinese ambassador, the Chinese quota was much larger than that set for other countries, but eventually all countries had an identical quota set at two hundred each. The result of this restriction will in time drastically reduce the number of Chinese aliens in Thailand, although it will have a slower effect on the ethnic Chinese group.

The division of China into two strongly opposed governments had direct effects on the Chinese community in Thailand. Both sides in the conflict had supporters in all the Chinese organizations, and the associations were often split into factions with either the pro-Communist or pro-Nationalist faction gaining ascendancy at one time or another. The split zigzagged sharply through the press and schools as well. Two sets of textbooks were available for Chinese schools. One set came from a Nationalist-supported publisher in Hong Kong and one from a Communist-supported publisher through Singapore. The slashes made in the Chinese community in the 1950's have not yet healed despite the rising and falling of the fortunes of both sides.

At the time of the Communist Chinese victory on the mainland, later when it attacked India and, in the belief of many overseas Chinese, almost defeated and humbled an arrogant India, when the Communists built up their technology even to the stage of developing nuclear weapons—at these times the prestige of Communist China was high. On the other hand, attempts of the Communists to extort money from overseas Chinese by threatening harm to relatives on the mainland of China and desecration of traditional Chinese culture have seriously decreased support for the Communists among Thailand's Chinese.

The Nationalist Chinese, too, have actively sought support within Thailand's Chinese community. Negatively, the Nationalists have sponsored propaganda against the mainland Communists. Positively, they have encouraged the exchange of athletes and entertainers; they have brought Chinese from Thailand to Taiwan to see the economic developments there and the preservation of traditional Chinese culture; and they have promoted investment in Taiwan by overseas Chinese. On the road from the Taipei airport in Taiwan into the city is a new large luxury tourist hotel which has supposedly been built by a Chinese investor from Bangkok.

Another change in Thailand's traditional policies in the early 1950's contributed to the way the Thai government reacted toward its Chinese community. Abandoning its long-term foreign policy of balancing off various interests, Thailand became committed to support the West against Communist forces in Asia. The Thai sent troops to assist United Nations forces in Korea in 1950, and in 1954 joined the Southeast Asia Treaty Organizationt (SEATO), which established its headquarters in Bangkok and whose first secretary general was a Thai.

With these first steps toward Thai support of anti-Communist nations on the international scene, the split in the Chinese community made the pro-Communist supporters a potential threat to the national security of Thailand. Using this potential threat as an excuse, anti-Chinese leaders in the second Pibun Songgram government of the early 1950's took restrictive measures against all Chinese, not just those identified as or thought to be Communists.

After World War II all Chinese secondary schools had been kept closed. This action was followed by new restrictions on books and teachers in the elementary schools. All had to have Thai principals and the schools were fre-

quently examined not only by the Private Schools Division of the Ministry
of Education, but by the Police Department from the Ministry of Interior as
well. The Chinese had developed several methods for getting around earlier
education regulations. Special night schools were held which were only loosely
regulated by the government, if at all. Classes with less than eight students
were considered tutorial groups and not subject to school regulations; many
Chinese put their children into these tutorial groups. For many years Chinese
who could afford to do so sent their children abroad to Chinese schools. Some
still do. Recently on a visit to a southern city in Thailand, I was taken on an
auto tour of the city by a hotel owner's son, who spoke some English. I
learned he was home on vacation from his Chinese secondary school in
Penang, Malaysia. By going to school in Penang, a heavily Chinese city, he
was still able to get a fully traditional form of Chinese education. While some
of these methods for bypassing Thai government regulations are still practiced
in the first half of the 1950's the government began to pay closer attention to
these methods for circumventing the ban on Chinese-language education, and
regulations were more strictly enforced and new ones established when considered necessary.

Politically, the Thai government banned the Communist Party in Thailand,
and in 1952 passed an Un-Thai Activities Act which permitted the government to take all kinds of actions against alleged Communist activities among
the Chinese. The administration of the law was often abused by anti-Chinese
police officers and both the Nationalist Chinese Embassy and the Chinese
Chamber of Commerce took steps whenever they could to protect legitimate
Chinese business, political, and social interests. Economically, the Thai government continued to foster policies to promote the entrance of more Thai
citizens into the business arena and to restrict the activities of the Chinese.
The specific laws tended to follow the patterns of the first Pibun government
in the 1930's.

The Chinese business community found and began to use an unusual and
effective technique to protect its interests. With the steadily increasing
number of regulations covering even such business details as the awnings in
front of shops and the size of the Chinese lettering on signs, the Chinese
businessman often found himself violating one or another of these regulations,
sometimes unwittingly. Corrupt police officials, government inspectors, and
tax officials found violations that did not exist and were not averse to extorting
money from alien Chinese businessmen to overlook real or imagined violations. Many Chinese businesses soon found that the inclusion among their
directors of members of the Thai ruling elite would bring their firms a measure of protection against harassment from lower officials. The higher the military or civilian official in the elite the better he could serve to protect the
firm. Such powerful figures as the late Police General Phao Siyanond, head

of all the police forces in Thailand in Pibun Songgram's second government, served with a good salary on twenty or more boards of directors of major firms whose principal owners were Chinese. It was a simple favor-for-favor relationship. The government officials got rich and the Chinese firms got protection. And so grew up a pattern of interlocking directorships and relationships between the Thai governing elite and the Chinese business elite. It should be noted that not all government officials and not all Chinese firms engaged in these relationships, but certainly a great number of both did.

The practice of government officials serving on private business boards has not ended. The 1968 *Annual Report* of the Bangkok Bank Ltd., Thailand's largest commercial bank, lists the deputy prime minister and minister of interior as chairman of the board of directors, and two other generals and, most interesting of all, the finance minister as members of the board. The principle of "conflict of interest" which is so important in the United States and other Western nations, where senior government appointees must sever all private relationships which might in any way conflict with the proper exercise of their public duties, has no tradition or place in current Thai business and political society.

For the last decade, since the revolutionary government of Marshal Sarit replaced Marshal Pibun and General Phao and installed a new government, there has been a relaxation of some of the stringent anti-Chinese measures which had been put into effect during the first half of the 1950's. At the very end of Pibun's regime, after he had returned from his 1955 tour abroad, he had already taken some steps to relax the controls on the Chinese community, but it was the new government, greatly interested in using Chinese economic interests for the development of the country, which took the more important steps.

The current official policy appears to be the promotion of full assimilation of the ethnic Chinese into Thai society and to limit the growth of a separated minority as much as possible. To these ends immigration of Chinese to Thailand is controlled and most of the restrictions on Chinese schools are continued. By promoting a Thai education among the Chinese in Thailand and by limiting the number of new arrivals, the goal of assimilation is fostered. In the economic area, the Thai and Chinese leaders have worked out several mutually beneficial arrangements, and at the same time, the government promotes greater Thai participation in business and commerce by giving special concessions to Thai businessmen, by reserving certain occupations to Thai only, and by enacting other measures favorable to Thai citizens. This policy appears to be having some success. Of the newly registered companies and partnerships in 1966, 84 percent were classified as Thai and accounted for 88 percent of the paid-in capital; 12 percent were Chinese with 8 percent of the capital; and 4 percent were "others" with 4 percent of the capital. (The statistics in this chapter are from *Thailand, Facts and Figures, 1966,* published

in 1967 by the Department of Technical and Economic Cooperation in the
Thai Ministry of National Development, *Thailand, A Seminar on Economic
Development and Investment Opportunities,* and *Annual Report, 1968,* both
published by the Bangkok Bank Ltd., in 1968 and 1969 respectively.)

Since we do not know how these nationality classifications were determined,
it is always possible that some of the Thai companies were fronts for Chinese
business interests. On the record, however, and probably in reality, it appears
that Thai interests in new businesses are substantially increasing.

Thailand probably has had more success in assimilating its ethnic Chinese
population into its general society than any other country in Southeast Asia.
Many factors have contributed to this. One factor has been government policy
to encourage assimilation. A second has been the relative ethnic and cultural
homogeneity of the great majority of the Thai population. The country is not
faced with minorities almost as large as the major social group such as one
finds in Burma, Malaysia, and Laos; therefore, the majority Thai have no fear
of being absorbed into the minority. Thirdly, Buddhism in Thailand is tolerant of the Chinese religions and welcomes them whereas Islam in Malaysia
and Indonesia and Christianity among the ruling elite in the Philippines and
French Indo-China were obstacles to easy assimilation. Fourthly, Thailand
never has had a European governing elite. There was little racial difference
between the Chinese immigrants and the rulers. In all other neighboring lands
the Chinese immigrants coming in droves in the nineteenth century were,
like the local indigenous population, excluded under colonial administrations
from top government posts. In Thailand, a Chinese who adopted the Thai
culture and language, as many did, could rise in government circles as high
as any other Thai, and many top government officials today number Chinese
among their recent ancestors. As a result of these several factors and probably
others as well, there are thousands and thousands of Chinese of second, third,
and later generations who have been completely assimilated. They have Thai
names, speak only the Thai language, and in all other ways are indistinguish-
able from those Thai who descend from the earliest Thai settlers of Sukhothai, the Khmers, the Mons, and other ethnic groups which have intermixed
to make the contemporary Thai people. The Thai may continue to consider
unassimilated Chinese as a potential or real problem, but a majority of Thai
who think of it at all see it as a problem that can and will be solved on the
paths already laid out.

To the visitor to Thailand the most apparent of Chinese economic interests
is in the retail trade. The Chinese are also important in banking, insurance,
industry (including rice milling, sawmills, sugar refineries, and many kinds
of consumer goods), import and export, including the export of rice, and in
the professions. In all these fields they share their interests to some degree at
least with Thai and in many of them with other foreign business interests,

also. For example, out of twenty-nine commercial banks in Thailand in 1966, thirteen were foreign banks.

From an occupational standpoint the Thai economy is still mainly an agricultural economy. Out of a total labor force of approximately 16 million persons, about 80 percent are employed in agriculture and fishing, 7 percent in commerce, 5.5 percent in services, 4.7 percent in manufacturing, and 2.8 percent in all other fields. The overwhelming majority of farmers and other agricultural workers are Thai and the Thai farmer has long been the backbone of Thai society as well as the Thai economy.

Of the total land area in Thailand of about 128.5 million acres, 66 million, or more than half, are in forests. About 28 million acres are cultivated farmland of which approximately 5 million are under irrigation, which is of special importance in a wet rice-growing economy. Unfortunately, the irrigation projects have not been evenly distributed over the country. About 45 percent of the total cultivated land in the rich rice areas of Central Thailand is under irrigation, but in the dry, poorer Northeast where irrigation is more needed only about 7 percent of the land is under irrigation. More of the Northeast will receive irrigation as the new dams along the Mekong River and its tributaries are built in the 1970's. At the present time the average size of a Thai farm is about ten acres, although this varies considerably from region to region, and approximately 80 to 85 percent of all farms are owner-occupied. The problem of vast tracts of land owned by absentee landlords common in many developing countries is almost unknown in Thailand. Absentee landlords are more apt to own urban property than rural. Most of the rural land farmed by tenants can be found in a few districts close to Bangkok and Thonburi.

While agriculture accounts for 80 percent of the employment, it contributes only 32 percent to the gross national product. All forms of industry contribute 28 percent, commerce 27 percent, services 9 percent, and government 5 percent. With the small number of ethnic Chinese concentrated in industry and commerce and the large number of Thai in agriculture, it is easy to see how the minority plays a much greater role in the economy than one might ordinarily assume.

From the time of the 1958 revolution through the first half of the 1960's, the Thai economy expanded rapidly. Gross national product grew at an average 7 to 8 percent a year, and by 1966 had reached approximately U.S. $4 billion in value. In the latter half of the decade there has been a slowing down and the gross national product for 1967 was only about U.S. $4.16 billion, an increase of 4 percent or a little more. Estimates for 1968 were that the percentage of growth had started upward again, but had not yet reached the goals set in the current five-year plan (1967–1971). In the first plan

(1961–1966), the goals were exceeded, so perhaps in enthusiasm the goals were set too high for the second plan. One factor in the slowing growth has been the slower-than-anticipated growth in industry. The Thai government has taken several steps to encourage industrial growth in Thailand and is vigorously promoting new investments from abroad, but the gains have not been as great as hoped for.

Another factor in the slowing down has been the fall of rice production largely due to drought conditions in the late 1960's. With its most important crop heavily dependent on large amounts of water at the proper time, the need for irrigation and water control becomes of paramount importance. Thailand has long been a rice-exporting country and these exports have been the major source of its foreign income. In 1965, almost 1.9 million tons of rice were exported. In 1966, this dropped to 1.5 million; in 1967, 1.48 million, and in 1968 another big drop to 1.08 million tons.

This drop in rice exports has been the major factor in decreasing the Thai favorable balance of payments. Thailand has had a trade deficit for several years, but this deficit has been offset by other foreign income from tourists, investments, loans, government assistance, and so on, so that its balance of payments remained favorable until 1969. As the trade deficit increases, as it has for the last few years especially when rice exports are low, the margin of safety in the balance of payments decreases. For many years Thailand's favorable balance of payments has permitted it to accumulate foreign reserves of close to U.S. $1 billion and to stabilize its currency. For more than a decade the baht has fluctuated very little, generally hovering around 20.8 to the United States dollar. The baht continues to be one of the most stable currencies in Asia and the world. Once the drought is passed and Thailand irrigates more land so that it will not need to rely entirely on nature to provide water when needed, the rice exports should again increase and the trade deficit decrease.

In order to maintain the favorable economic and financial position the country has enjoyed in the last decade, the Thai government is encouraging new industry and diversification of agriculture. Maize, kenaf and jute, and tapioca products exported have all risen greatly in value. Between 1960 and 1968 the value of maize exports increased almost five times, kenaf and jute almost three times, and tapioca products about two and a half times.

The trade picture is not all favorable, however, as we have seen in the case of rice. Certain forest products, long a part of Thailand's exports, have substantially decreased in value often due as much to world price fluctuations as to decreases in volume. The value of rubber exports in 1968 was down about 30 percent from 1960, and teak was less than half of what it was in the earlier year.

In 1968, Thailand's main exports in order of value were rice, rubber, maize, tin, tapioca products, kenaf and jute, frozen shrimp, and teak. In the 1960's Japan has been Thailand's most important trading partner both for exports and imports. Other places to which Thailand sends major exports are Malaysia, Hong Kong, the United States of America, Singapore, and West Germany. Countries besides Japan from which Thailand receives its major imports of machinery, chemicals, manufactured goods, lubricants, and others are the United States, West Germany, the United Kingdom, the Netherlands, and Hong Kong. The heavy imports are necessary for Thailand's industrial and agricultural development, and despite their heavy costs, they are necessary, for without them the pace of development would be considerably slowed.

The growth of the total Thai economy has meant a growth in per capita income, but how much the latter has grown is not precisely known and there are many differing estimates. Part of these differences are due to the lack of statistics of a precise nature on population size and growth. The last census was taken in 1960, and at that time some groups such as the hill tribes were not counted. The annual growth of the population is variously estimated at 3 to 3.4 percent and the total population is now probably getting close to 35 million persons.

An amusing sidelight on the reliability of the census can be seen in the reports of ages of the population in many areas of Thailand. Obviously, many people do not know their exact age so that it was not unusual to see an age distribution looking something like this: Age 30—5,000 persons, Age 31—200, Age 32—100, Age 33—150, Age 34—150, Age 35— 4,000 persons. They were guessing their ages and tended to guess what they thought was the closest five-year multiple.

At the beginning of the 1960's annual per capita income was believed to be around U.S. $95–100. The most reasonable current estimates would place per capita income at U.S. $120–125, although estimates have ranged from U.S. $105 as high as U.S. $140. When the next census is taken a more accurate figure can be reported. In any case, using this low per capita figure of U.S. $120 to compare with other nations would still put Thailand among the poorer developing nations in cash income despite the major gains of recent years.

The statistical figure of per capita income does not, of course, indicate all there is to know about the income of the individual. Because of the abundance of rice in Thailand few, if any, Thai suffer from starvation despite low cash income. The general per capita figure does not indicate regional or individual differences. Some sources have estimated per capita income for Bangkok and Thonburi at U.S. $250, for Central Thailand and the Southern Peninsula at U.S. $150, and for the Northeast and mountain areas in the North at U.S. $100 or less, and for the hill tribes at U.S. $50 or less. Thus, there is considerable variation within the country itself.

In the years immediately following World War II, the Thai government permitted the organization of labor unions. Most of these early labor organizations became political tools as much or more than representatives of labor to secure better wages and working conditions for members. Some became instruments of Communist influence. Others were little more than organizations to promote the interests of particular military or civilian leaders of the Thai ruling elite. At the end of 1958, the new government abolished all labor organizations, and what labor protection there was provided for workers was given by a Department of Labor in the Ministry of Interior. The department's protection extended only to workers in the Bangkok-Thonburi area by the late 1960's, although plans were made to extend its activities to other parts of the nation. Early in 1969, the Thai government under the new constitution accepted in principle again the right of laborers to form unions and join in collective bargaining. What will result from this decision remains to be seen.

At the beginning of the 1970's Thailand has a growing economy, with a growing industrial base and a diversifying agriculture base, a stable currency, and a sound financial position. It is still a poor country on the whole although its standard of living is rising and, as in the past, its abundance of rice, fish, and fruit means there is food for all. While almost everyone has enough to eat, many are now seeking to satisfy other needs as well. It is to the satisfaction of these needs and to the solution of other economic problems, such as the disproportionate control of some segments of the economy by a relatively small minority of the population, the corruption on the part of some government officials in government-owned corporations and in administering regulations of all business, and traditions which assign certain ethnic groups to some businesses and prevent the free movement of economic skills and talents, that the Thai government and people must turn their attention in the decades ahead.

5
Along the Klongs and Roadways

For much of the first century of its existence as the capital city of Thailand, Bangkok's life was centered on the Chao Phya River and the numerous klongs. The klongs spread outward in all directions to make a network of water transportation through the low plain on which Bangkok and Thonburi were built. Many persons lived in boats on the waterways or in raft houses tied to the banks, and since roads were little known and the few existing ones poorly built and maintained, almost all travel was by boat on the river and the canals.

Only in the second half of the nineteenth century after King Mongkut's treaties with the Western nations brought new foreign residents to live in Bangkok and the advent of broadened trade relations brought new merchants, traders, shippers, and workers into Bangkok did the need for new roads grow. The increased population meant the expansion of the number of business and residence buildings built landward from the banks of the waterways. Until the end of World War II both klongs and roadways played major roles in the city's transportation network. Since then the emphasis has shifted to the roads, and while several major klongs continue to serve as important transportation arteries (more in Thonburi than in Bangkok), many klongs are being filled in to provide space for wider roads to carry the new flood of motorized vehicles. Trucks, buses, taxis, private automobiles, motorized samlors, bicycles, and pushcarts crawl slowly through the massive traffic jams of narrow streets in the older sections of Bangkok. Emerging into wider streets the crawling vehicles are suddenly transformed into a stampede of speeding glass-and-steel beasts. Like big cities everywhere Bangkok has become a traffic nightmare.

When I first lived in Bangkok my home was a lovely, large wooden house built about sixty years earlier. It differed from many Bangkok houses because it was painted. It was a stately old house with a veranda across the second

102

floor almost a hundred feet long and varying in width from about fifteen to thirty feet. Some of the rooms were of equally gargantuan proportions and appeared even larger than they were because of the sparse furnishings. I lived in this large house alone except for a laundry *amah* and her granddaughter who by agreement went with the house whether or not the occupant employed them. I did employ the wash amah and she was excellent. The woman and her granddaughter occupied a tiny room behind the serving kitchen on the first floor. This old house was one of several similar old sprawling houses in that old residential area of Bangkok off Sathorn Road. All the large houses in that area, as far as I knew, were occupied either by foreigners or by offices and businesses. Sathorn Road was an impressive street with a wide klong dividing traffic going in opposite directions. The klong was no longer used for boats, but the banks on both sides were well tended and made a pleasant place to walk.

My old house, much too large for one person, was set in an attractive compound of two or three acres well maintained by a gardener from the Northeast who spent a few weeks each year in his home village helping with the rice harvest, a custom quite common among upcountry men who work in the city. The gardener lived in a room in a small building behind the main house, where he shared a row of rooms with the cook, two maids, and their families. Altogether fourteen people besides myself lived on the property, three of us in the main house and twelve in the row of rooms behind it, admittedly a strange imbalance in housing assignments.

Only one room in the main house was air conditioned and that was the principal bedroom. Disliking air conditioning when I sleep, I did not use the conditioner at first, but soon found it was useful for another purpose. Bangkok is home to thousands of stray dogs. As Buddhists who do not believe in killing any animals, the Bangkok residents allow the dogs to wander about scavenging for food. Many of the dogs are poor, miserable wretches, so emaciated that their ribs protrude, and their bodies are often covered with open, running sores. Every night, almost on a regular schedule at ten or thereabouts, one of these dogs would begin to howl, and soon he would be answered by scores of others until the whole neighborhood was a howling uproar which lasted for an hour or more. I found that by closing all my bedroom windows and turning on the air conditioner I could shut out most of the howling and fall asleep to the steady, hypnotizing drone of the conditioner. From time to time the Bangkok municipal government holds drives to collect the stray dogs, but the dogs seem to survive, and the government must do a lot of explaining to justify its violation of religious precepts, if the dogs are killed.

I had been living in my big house for about six weeks when I experienced one night a special welcome from an unauthorized visitor, a member of a group found working throughout that neighborhood of many foreigners. I awakened that night to what I distinctly thought or instinctively felt was the squeak of my bedroom door. I stared hard at the closed door, but could see nothing in the darkness. In alarm I strained to listen for any strange sounds, but nothing could be heard. Then I saw a shadow move against a window and I shouted "Who's there?" The door squeaked loudly as it was jerked open and the shadow passed through it quickly silhouetted against the opening. I jumped out of bed shouting and fumbling for a light switch which, as luck would have it, turned nothing on. Searching for my glasses, I stumbled over the furniture, and within seconds was frantically pushing the buzzer which was supposed to call the servants. But there was no response from any of those fourteen people on the premises. Finally finding my glasses and turning on light after light that did work as I raced from the room shouting for servants, I managed to rouse them from their sleep after much effort since it was, after all, four in the morning.

All the doors and shutters of the house were still locked and only after a thorough search of the house did we find the means of access used by the *kamoy,* as these burglars are called. Another bedroom had once had an air conditioner which had been removed, leaving a small rectangular hole in the wall. The kamoy had been able to reach the hole from an outside staircase and had come in and gone out that way.

The next morning the police told me that my shouts had apparently frightened the kamoy away. The officer said that there was a gang regularly robbing the homes of foreigners in that area. The burglars usually fled if anyone awoke and started shouting. They never injured the householders provided the householder did not struggle with them or get between the burglar and his way of escape. The officer then entertained me with harrowing tales of foreigners who had been murdered when they tried to stop the kamoy from getting away. I never learned if the tales were true or not. That same morning I had the gardener board up the hole from the inside. Still, my successor in the house was robbed a few weeks after he moved in so the kamoys must have found another way of entering.

Many homes and offices employ night watchmen. These guards are always Indians. Although there is some doubt about the effectiveness of all of them, the Indian night watchman with a little table or other bundle carried on his head and wearing a white, often soiled *dhoti,* can still be seen walking each evening to his place of work to guard the premises of his employer.

The large house was too expensive for me to maintain with several servants, and after the kamoy's visit I started looking for a smaller place. Eventually I moved into a modern apartment house, one of the first in Bangkok, which now has many of them. All my needs in the apartment were taken care of by one able houseboy. Again he was from the Northeast, like so many servants in Bangkok, and he took off a couple of weeks at rice planting and rice harvesting time to go home to help his parents.

About the distance of a long city block behind my apartment house was one of the largest and busiest klongs in the city. Frequently, in the early evenings, I would walk down to the klong for refreshment or to eat at a small klongside restaurant at the end of the lane on which I lived. Sitting there I could watch the water taxis filled with passengers going home from work speeding along the canal. Often they passed the slower boats carrying charcoal, water jars, food, and other items; these slower boats were propelled by a weary, hard-working Thai man or woman with a single pole.

I visited the little store and restaurant with its friendly porch extending over the water so often that the owner, his family, and the families next door and across the klong soon came to expect to see me early in the evening. All these families had teen-age children studying English at school and between their little English and my limited Thai, plus a great many gestures, we were able to carry on extensive conversations. At the very beginning I found myself answering questions which I was to be asked repeatedly by almost every Thai I met at our first meeting. The questions always included, Are you married? If not, why not? How old are you? How much money do you make? And often, Have you had a bath today?

To the Westerner these seemed to be unusually personal questions which we ordinarily do not ask, at least not on first meeting a person. I was asked these and similar questions so often that I finally requested an explanation from Thai friends. I was told that asking personal questions is not a matter of prying, but is a way of showing genuine interest in the well-being of a friend or acquaintance. In a hot country, for example, one of the most refreshing things to do is to take a bath, so to ask a friend if he has had a bath is an indirect way of asking if he is cool, comfortable, and well. The person questioned does not have to give a correct answer unless he wants to, and no one will be insulted if he lies. I must have reported my salary in at least a hundred different amounts, a different answer for each questioner, and none of them was correct. No one expressed any doubt or dismay and all seemed to accept what I said. If they did not, they still did not repeat the question. Even after hearing the explanation of the reasons for the questions from Thai friends, I still suspected that the questions were sometimes asked solely out of nosy curiosity.

Any perceptive foreigner soon learns that most Thai are extremely well mannered, and a foreigner does well to adopt some of these good manners in his own behavior toward the Thai. Respect is always shown to elders, monks, and persons higher in status. When presenting anything direct to a person whom one respects, one presents it with both hands, whether it be a gift to a friend or a report to a superior at work. Often this is done simply, especially if the item is a small one, by holding the item to be presented in the right hand and grasping lightly the right forearm or elbow with the left hand when the presentation is made.

Most Thai are extremely sensitive about their heads and do not like them touched by any person unnecessarily. It is unwise for a foreigner to pat a Thai child on the head as he might casually do in the West. The reason is simple. Each person possesses a spirit called a *khwan* which resides in the head (not in the heart as believed by many Westerners). If the khwan should leave the person he may become ill or even die, if the khwan is not able to get back into the person after temporarily leaving for any reason. The khwan may flee from the head, if it is frightened, and a blow to the head can easily frighten the khwan. Whether or not the individual Thai still believes in spirits, most Thai resent anyone trying to touch their heads especially in a careless or joking way.

The sole of the foot, however, is considered a degraded part of the body because it is in touch with the soil and in violation of Buddhist teachings may unknowingly have killed insects and other life by stepping on them. To point the sole of the foot at a Thai is equivalent to insulting him openly. For this reason most foreigners have to learn not to cross their legs at the knees, if they want to behave properly because crossing the legs in such a manner shows the sole of the foot. On the one hand, the Thai because of their innate courtesy and desire not to embarrass a guest, will probably say nothing if he violates their rules of etiquette, unless a flagrant violation should occur in the presence of their majesties or other high-ranking members of royalty. On the other hand, the foreigner who takes time to follow a few simple rules of Thai etiquette will find himself warmly welcomed and appreciated by his Thai friends.

Seated on the klongside porch of my neighborhood restaurant and coffee house, I witnessed a scene that I had seen before only in old silent movies. A Thai dressed in a suit, white shirt, and tie, obviously going out somewhere special for the evening, came to the opposite bank of the klong where there was a small boat pulled up on the bank. He pushed it into the water and, noticing some water in the bottom of the boat, took off his shoes and socks and rolled up his pants legs a few inches. His activities took several minutes during which time he apparently failed to notice that the water level in the boat was getting deeper. Except for a few glances no one on either bank paid much attention to him until he got a few yards from shore when he suddenly began paddling frantically trying to reach our side.

We all looked then and saw the tiny boat was sinking fast underneath him. By the time he was in the middle of the klong the water inside the boat was three-quarters of the way to the gunwales. The more full of water the boat became the harder it was for the man to make it move with all his hard paddling. In a few more yards the water inside had reached the gunwales and was creeping up his trouser legs. His expression changed from one of desperation to one of absolute dumbfoundedness as he grabbed his shoes and socks and stood there erect in what was probably his best suit and watched the boat sink beneath him. As he stood there without moving the water came up to his knees, his thighs, his waist, and finally his chest before he struck out swimming for the bank from which he had started his perilous voyage. He emerged from the water clutching his shoes in one hand and his socks in the other, his suit clinging to his body, and a big sheepish grin on his face as the children and adults on both banks laughed with great amusement. He shrugged his shoulders as if to say "mai pen rai" (it doesn't matter) and started down the path from which he had come.

The klongs, as any visitor to Thailand who takes the tourist trip through the klongs of Thonburi to the floating market can see, are used for much more than boats and fishing. For the residents of the houses on its banks the klong is a front yard in which the children can swim, a laundry, and a bathroom for the whole family. It is not unusual to see one person scooping klong water up for brushing his teeth while a few yards away a young lady will be shampooing her hair and a little farther away a child will be urinating into the canal. The klong is regularly used by both men and women to take a bath, and the ability of the Thai to take a complete bath in public without ever becoming completely unclothed has often been commented on. The woman wears a long sarong fastened right under the armpits and the man wears a short saronglike garment called a *pakoma* around his waist while bathing. On completion each will put on dry clothes over the wet garments which are then permitted to fall to the ground from under the clean, dry garments. In a society where modesty is important and privacy almost nonexistent, the ability to bathe in this manner is a great asset.

The pakoma must be one of the most useful items of men's clothing found anywhere in the world. A rectangular piece of cotton cloth two and a half feet wide and six feet long, it is often a bright plaid. (In one province I visited recently plain bright red must have been the favorite color of the year for pakomas. Fully half the men I saw wearing pakomas were wearing red ones, and many more red pakomas could be seen drying on porch rails in front of houses.) The pakoma can be used as a bathing or swimming costume when it is wrapped around the waist, the ends pulled up tight between the legs and tucked in the waistband at the back to make a kind of shorts, or it may be worn as a short simple sarong. It can also be wrapped around the head as a turban, drapped around the neck to protect the neck and shoulders from the sun, or wrapped around the waist rolled as a belt. It can also be carried as a bag to hold rice or some other item, and in an emergency it can be used as a rope to lead oxen home. There are probably other uses, but these are the only ones I have seen.

The owner of the klongside restaurant was a Sino-Thai who spoke Thai and a few words of English to most of his customers, but spoke only Chinese with the members of his family. Beside his store was a small wooden house whose owner (guessing from his occupation) was also probably a Sino-Thai, but who never spoke Chinese that I heard, not even to members of his family. The house owner was quite proud of the fact that he spoke some English and after seeing me at the restaurant a few times, he invited me to visit his home so that he could practice his English.

The man was a stevedore foreman, and though he worked only when ships were in port, about half of each month, he was paid relatively well. His family lived simply but comfortably for a working-class Thai family and was even able to go to the sea for a few days each year for a vacation, provided they were able to find a friend with a house they could live in rent free at or near the beach. The stevedore had a tiny wife, who did all the work around the house, and two teen-age sons, who were both in upper-level secondary schools, the level called pre-university school at that time. The sons, too, spoke some English as I learned when their father was not home and they could speak freely to me. When the father was home, custom demanded that he speak to the guest for the whole family.

Their house was so close to the restaurant that there was no more than two feet between the walls of the two buildings, and the house on the other side was still closer. In front of the houses ran a ditch which was often filled with water backed up from the klong. The ditch was right in front of the house door so that an unwary individual might step from the doorway right into the water. The stevedore had placed two rough planks from the door across the ditch to the lane on the other side.

Most of the houses I had seen in Bangkok up to that time were the old rambling houses set in the big compounds such as the one in which I had first lived, or the large modern, open houses occupied by foreigners and a few upper-class Chinese and Thai who had invited me to their homes. I had learned soon after arriving in Thailand that most Thai entertain in restaurants so that it is often difficult to find an opportunity to visit them in their homes. For that reason I was especially pleased to be invited to the home of a workingman in Bangkok.

The house of the stevedore was built of wood and, typically, was unpainted. It had two stories. The ground floor was divided into three tiny rooms. The largest was about nine by ten feet and served as the family living room and a bedroom for one of the sons. The furniture included a narrow wooden bed covered only with a mat, one straight chair, a small table piled high with magazines, a little cupboard with some drinking glasses, a table radio, and a television set. At night many of the children from the neighborhood crowded into the room to watch the TV programs. The room generally and the floor in particular were spotlessly clean. Whenever I visited we all sat on the floor. Only rarely did my host sit in the one chair.

The second room in back was still smaller, about four by six feet, and had a concrete floor. It was used as the kitchen and was equipped with a portable charcoal burner, dishes, cooking pots, bottles of sauces, a rice sack half empty, and other items of food. Everything stood on the floor for there was no furniture. All the food preparation was done in pots and pans on the floor. At one side of the kitchen was a narrow stairway leading to the upstairs which was divided into a larger bedroom for the parents and a smaller bedroom for the other son. None of these rooms had closets or storage chests for clothes. Instead clothes were neatly hung on pegs in the walls.

Beside the kitchen was a small bathroom which contained a squat toilet and a large, fifty-gallon jar filled with clean water which was used for cooking, bathing, and flushing the toilet. The water is dipped out with a scoop and poured over the body for bathing. Most of the members of this family, however, bathed in the nearby klong. Both the kitchen and the bathroom had holes in the concrete floor at one side and any water spilled on the floor could run out the hole.

Later on I was privileged to visit other Thai homes both in the city and upcountry. They ranged all the way from thatch huts of fishermen to large modern villas which were the homes of members of Thai royalty. It would be difficult to label any of these as a typical Thai home. Yet of the houses of workingmen and students I saw in Bangkok, the stevedore's house would probably be as typical as any.

The stevedore's sons were ambitious and hoped to improve their economic status in the future by becoming government officials. The path they saw to achieving their goals was through education. Thailand has had a compulsory education law for almost fifty years and is justifiably proud that its 1960 census reported 70 percent of its population over the age of ten was literate. This figure puts Thailand way above most Asian countries; in fact, Thailand is ahead of countries in many other parts of the world as well. The reported figure should probably be accepted with some reservations. The base of the figure is probably determined from the percentage of the population completing the four-year primary schools. The great shortage of written materials of all kinds, including newspapers, in the upcountry areas means that many adults who have no need to read or write lose that ability, except for writing their names, once they have been out of school for several years. While they may be considered literate in the simplest meaning of the term, many are functionally illiterate in that they cannot use reading and writing as part of their everyday tools. Even with this qualification, however, there is no doubt that Thailand has achieved one of the highest rates of literacy in Asia and in the developing world as a whole.

The earliest known education in Thailand was the practical education the child learned at home. This was followed early in the country's history by education for boys in the Buddhist wats. Taught by monks, these early classes were first concerned with religious subjects exclusively, but later secular subjects were added as well. Today there are still two forms of schools found in many wats—one is the religious school for monks and the other is the secular school, either government or private, for all students.

King Mongkut in the middle of the nineteenth century, much interested in education for his children, employed tutors both from the foreign colony in Bangkok and from abroad to teach in the palace. In 1871, his son, King Chulalongkorn, established the first school in the Grand Palace for the sons of princes and other high ranks of the nobility to study and train for work in the government's service. Less than twenty years later, in 1887, the king established a Department (later a Ministry) of Education and the responsibility for an educational system in the country became the duty of the central government. Under the leadership of Prince Damrong, one of King Chulalongkorn's brothers and one of Thailand's most outstanding leaders in the last hundred years, the department near the end of the nineteenth century made a study of both the English and the Japanese school systems. The new Thai system of schools which emerged at the beginning of this century modeled its curriculum and organization on what the study had learned from the British schools, but added character training as the Thai had seen it in the Japanese schools.

In 1921, King Vajiravudh issued a compulsory education law calling for all children between ages seven and fourteen to attend school at least until they had passed the examinations at the end of the fourth elementary grade. At that time the school system consisted of four elementary grades, six secondary grades, and two pre-university grades. The compulsory education law was not strictly enforced because facilities were not available for schools in many areas of the country. Only after the revolutionary government took over in 1932 were stronger steps taken to enforce the law. That new government had an added reason to push education because the number of members elected, instead of appointed, to the National Assembly was tied to the achievement of education in the country.

In 1960, the education law was changed to require compulsory attendance through seven grades instead of four. Again, the complete enforcement depends on the availability of facilities not yet built as well as on some changes of attitude among the more remote and isolated farmers who sometimes keep their children home from school. The new law provides for an elementary level of seven grades and a secondary level of five including the old pre-university level. The secondary education may be either academic or vocational.

Beyond the twelfth grade is the higher education system which includes both higher vocational education and universities plus a few specialized professional schools such as those established for teacher training. Thailand has eight secular universities and two Buddhist universities. The latter (Mahamakut and Mahachulalongkorn) are both in Bangkok and provide to Buddhist monks higher religious education combined with other subjects.

Five of the eight secular universities are in Bangkok or its suburbs. The oldest university is Chulalongkorn University, founded in 1917. It is a general university with several faculties in the humanities, sciences, social sciences, commerce, and engineering. The other large general university is Thammasat University which has emphasized public administration, economics, social welfare, and law to prepare many of its graduates for work in the Thai civil service. In addition to these two general universities, there is a University of Fine Arts (Silpakorn), a University of Agricultural Sciences (Kasetsart), and a University of Medical Sciences with teaching units at Chulalongkorn Hospital in Bangkok, Siriraj Hospital in Thonburi, and the Chiengmai Medical School in Chiengmai.

Outside of Bangkok three new general universities were started in the 1960's. One is in Chiengmai in the North, one in Khon Kaen in the Northeast, and one in Songkhla and Haadyai in the South. A second campus of the Fine Arts University is opening in Nakorn Pathom. These institutions of higher education are especially important because they can be centers for training people needed in the developing areas where their skills and talents can be directly used. They should also change the traditional pattern of young persons attending the universities in Bangkok and staying there rather than spreading throughout the country once they have completed their education.

Thai students below the university level wear uniforms to school. For the boys the uniform consists of a white shirt without a tie and either blue or tan shorts. Many of the older boys in their late teens seem slightly embarrassed to be found wearing shorts that clearly mark them as students and change to long pants as soon as they reach home. I have seen some older boys at sports events change from shorts to long pants in the stands. The pakoma is a handy item to preserve one's modesty while changing clothes in public. For girls the uniform is a white blouse and blue skirt. Each morning and afternoon the streets of Bangkok are filled with uniform-clad boys and girls on their way to and from their elementary and secondary schools.

Clothing worn by residents of Bangkok nowadays is almost always Western in style. For a woman outside her home this is usually a skirt and blouse or a dress. Some wear a Thai-style dress which tends to be tight around the legs and shows a beautiful figure to great advantage. Many women in Bangkok, especially those from upcountry who come to live and work in the city, wear the *pasin* skirt with a blouse. This long skirt, wrapped around the waist and often worn with a gold belt, originated in Northern Thailand, but is now worn all over the country. The skirts usually are of solid colors, but have an unusually beautiful border several inches wide embroidered, often in gold, around the bottom. Much less often in Bangkok does one see the *phanung,* the traditional lower garment worn by both men and women. It is a voluminous wrap-around skirt, the ends of which are pulled up between the legs and tucked into the waist band at the back to form a kind of pantaloon. It is often compared to the Indian dhoti. Today the phanung is usually worn only by older women. Men sometimes are seen wearing it at formal court functions. Many Chinese women wear the "Chinese pants" which are wide-legged, wide-waisted, lightweight cloth pants which are pulled together and tied in a knot at the waist. With these pants a shirtlike blouse which hangs on the outside of the pants is worn.

The Chinese pants are popular items of men's clothing. Outside Bangkok many farmers and fishermen wear these pants made of a heavier cotton cloth dyed black, brown, or dark blue for work. In the city they are worn, too, by many workers in rough, outside laboring jobs. The lightweight rayon Chinese pants are worn by many Thai at all social levels. Some foreigners, too, when they come home from work, discard their tight suits, and relax in these comfortable pants which are much cooler. These lightweight pants are often used as pajamas by many men, and the pants come in all colors—red, green, black, brown, blue, yellow, violet, etc. Often these lighter pants have a small pattern of a lotus leaf or some similar Thai design in the material. At work or away from home, however, most men in Bangkok in nonlaboring jobs wear Western suits with or without the coat.

Women play an important role in Thai society, probably more important in Thailand than in most other countries of Asia. In most ways women are treated equal to men. Although there are no women cabinet members, there are women in high-ranking civil service posts and women have been elected to the National Assembly. There are women doctors, lawyers, bankers, store owners, vendors, hotel owners, publishers, and in almost every other field of economic endeavor. Thai women are especially important in the ownership of real estate. During my first period of residence in Thailand I had to negotiate about a half-dozen leases in Bangkok. Except for one piece of property owned by the government, all of the other property was owned by women. Why this should be, I have never had convincingly explained.

In one way women are discriminated against, at least from a Western viewpoint. Thai marriages need not be registered. If they are not registered and the couple later separates, the woman has no legal grounds for claiming any support for herself or her children from the ex-husband. Some rich Thai men are able to afford more than one wife, but they can only register one at a time. That means the unregistered wives have no enforceable claim on his property or his support, and he can abandon them, if he so desires. Some women are willing to accept such a situation for the security it can bring under the right circumstances, and they often have been fully supported throughout their lives by their husbands although they may be his second, third, or fourth wife. There have been some attempts by women leaders in recent years to make the woman a more equal partner in Thai marriages.

The Thai marriage ceremony is a simple one. The actual marriage ceremony itself is not religious, although Buddhist monks are now often called in at some time just before the wedding to recite appropriate Buddhist texts which will bring blessings to the couple. As in most important personal events, the day and time of a wedding are chosen by an astrologer who picks the auspicious time. On the day of the wedding the couple, sometimes dressed in white, but not necessarily so, will kneel together at a small *priedieu* each with hands clasped together over the edge of the stand above a decorated silver or bronze bowl. A single white cord is wrapped around the heads of the bride and groom joining them together. Wedding attendants, if any, stand behind the kneeling couple.

Wedding guests line up and one at a time approach the couple. The guest is given a conch shell containing lustral water. The guest pours a small amount of the water over the hands of the groom and the bride while giving them his blessings and best wishes. The guest then goes to another room where an elaborate meal and celebration will take place. As the guest leaves the room where the bridal couple is kneeling he usually receives (at least this is true in Bangkok today) a small gift from the wedding couple as a token memorial of the day. If there are a great many guests (at one wedding I attended there were several hundred), the water-pouring cermony can go on for hours. Later the couple may or may not register the marriage as they decide. Many persons at the lower economic levels in Bangkok do not go through even this simple wedding ceremony. Instead, they just start living together, and eventually everyone accepts them as married.

Sometimes when I visited the stevedore and his family his sons and a few friends would form a circle in the open area of the lane and begin to play *takraw*. Takraw is played with a rattan ball about the size of a grapefruit. Although woven tightly, the ball is hollow and there are openings around its surface between the woven strands. The object of the informal takraw played by these boys is to keep the ball in the air by use of the head, shoulders, upper arms, legs, and feet. The hands and forearms are not to be used, and no player is to strike the ball twice in succession. A good head bunt, a well-placed kick with the inside of the foot, or a well-directed back swing of the elbow so that the upper arm can hit the ball call for great skill.

There are other more formal games of takraw. In one, there are two teams spaced on opposite sides of a badminton net and the ball is batted back and forth across the net much as in volley ball except that the hands and forearms cannot be used. A second more formal game has a group of players in a circle with a three-opening net suspended above the center of the circle about twelve feet. The player gets points for placing the ball into the net through one of its openings. The game calls for great stamina and skill and for hardened heads, arms, legs, and ankles which can take the punishment of striking repeatedly the hard, rattan ball.

Another Thai sport of unusual interest is kite-flying. During the hot, windy months of March and April regular kite-flying matches are held on the Phra Mane Ground in Bangkok and elsewhere. There are two teams, one with a male kite called a *chula* and one with a female kite called a *pak pao*. The chula is a five-pointed star stretched in one direction so that it is about seven feet long and four feet wide. The pak pao is about half the size of the chula. The object of the contest is for one of the kites, through skillful maneuvering on the part of its team, to bring down the other. Sometimes the cords used to fly the kites are waxed with a hardening substance which will enable one cord to cut the other in a way to either bring the second kite down or free it to fly away. In any case, the winner is the team that can force the other kite to the ground without losing its own kite.

The Thai are insatiable gamblers. Not only is the national lottery three times a month well supported, but the main interest in most sporting events seems to be not in who wins and who loses, but in the wagers to be made on the side. Thai sporting events include all kinds of animal fighting, including cockfighting, fishfighting, cricket fighting and, in the South, bullfighting. Unlike Spanish bullfighting, Thai bullfighting is between two bulls rather than man and bull, and a kill is not necessary to win. One bull may win by chasing the other out of the ring. All of these fighting events are accompanied by heavy betting on the part of the spectators.

So far, the Thai have imported few major sports from the West. One that they have brought in is European-style football, or soccer. The annual football game between Chulalongkorn and Thammasat universities is a spectacle to outshine most college or New Year's Day football spectaculars in the United States. One year when I attended, the parade of elaborately decorated floats and smart marching units and the pregame festivities of bands and drill teams and other performing organizations lasted four hours before the football game, which ended in a tie and kept thousands of spectators in the National Stadium on the edge of their seats. After the game there were torchlight parades by students of both universities back to their campuses and a continuation of the festivities long into the night. Football is also played by many secondary schools, and several business firms and government departments organize teams as well. On several occasions Thailand has been able to send outstanding teams to international matches and has returned home victorious.

I suppose the one sport most foreigners associate with Thailand is Thai-style boxing. It should be noted, too, that Thailand has produced some excellent boxers at the lighter weights in the international style of the sport. When I was first in Thailand a Thai international-style boxer, Pone Kingpetch, was World Flyweight Champion and a national hero. But the more colorful, more exciting, and sometimes more bloody Thai-style boxing claims first place in the interest of any fan who has seen it.

In Thai-style boxing the fighters are not limited to using their hands; they may also kick, elbow, or knee their opponents. Of particular effectiveness for a spectacular knockout is a high kick to the opponent's jaw with the foot, but kicks are also delivered to the legs, stomach, back, throat, head, and anywhere else that will weaken the strength of the opponent. A Thai boxer may hit his opponent on any part of the body; there is no such thing as a rule against hitting below the belt. Almost every foreigner blanches the first time he sees the Thai boxer use the very effective tactic of locking his opponent's head between his gloves, pulling the head down, and then bringing his knees up in rapid succession to strike the opponent's face and head. It often appears as if nothing is barred, but a few things, such as judo, biting, or kicking the opponent when he is down, are fouls. After watching a few bouts it is easy to understand why Thai-style bouts are never more than five rounds long and often do not go the whole length.

There are other aspects of a Thai boxing match of interest to the foreigners who attend the nightly matches in either the Rajadamnoen or Lumpini stadiums in Bangkok. The program descriptions of the boxers, who are either in the red corner with red trunks or in the blue corner with blue trunks, are often amusing and tantalizing. In the main event of a match several years ago the man in the red corner was described in English as:

Highlight of Dechachai Camp, the most valuable product of limb bartering frivolity, Chumporn, Southern Thailand now patronized by the Royal Thai Air Force. Podh-thaung (his name) is one of the colourful tough kicking artists who prefc. able marched forward lead followed by punch and dangerous kick to land in the solar plexus or on chins, and gives the referee some jobs to do in singing One—, two—, —ten into opponents' ears whilst dreamed happily.

His opponent in the blue corner was characterized as:

Super star of Kaeo-suriya Camp, the best issue of cauliflower industry, Songkhla, Southern Thailand and now patronized by The Thai Railway Organization Camp. Sornsingh (his name) is a leading violent fighting machine with good combination of limbs which provided sensation for fans completely to their hearts' content from gong to the homestretch.

When the boxers appear they often kneel before entering the ring to pay homage to the guardian spirit of the ring. Many boxers wear a sacred cord around their heads; this cord is removed usually by the trainer before the bout begins. Many also wear similar bands around their upper arms. These are kept on during the fight and may contain a charm of some sort to protect the fighter.

Before the fight begins each boxer, ignoring his opponent, performs a ritual. They may pray by crouching down facing their place of birth and the four points of the compass. They also pay homage to their teachers and then exercise one or more different movements which demonstrate what they plan to do to their opponent, such as stomping him or burying him. They may also perform movements which are supposed to hex their opponent. Sometimes a boxer will walk slowly around the ring with one hand on the top rope. He does this to seal off the ring from any bad spirits or other possible interference including bad advice from his seconds.

During this preliminary ceremony and the match itself a small orchestra keeps up continuous music. The orchestra consists of a *ching,* or small cymbal, one or two drums beaten on both ends, and a *pi chawa,* which is a reed instrument sounding like a high-pitched oboe. The ching is used to beat time. During the first round the ching will play slowly, but it speeds up the beat with each new round and the rising excitement of the bout.

Much of the excitement takes place in the stands where from the time of the beginning of the preliminary ceremony to the end of the final round, if it is a close match, shouting bettors move around placing bets wherever they can. When the bout is over, the audience's roar quiets a little as losers pay off and money exchanges are made throughout the crowd. The pattern is repeated until the evening's boxing card of eight spell-binding bouts is completed and all bets are paid.

*Wat Saket, the Temple of the Golden Mount,
Bangkok.*

Wat Benchamabopitr, the Marble Temple, Bangkok.

Bangkok's Weekend Market at the Phra Mane Ground.

A Stand at Bangkok's Weekend Market.

A Bot, Wat Phra Singh, Chiengmai.

A Portable Restaurant in Bangkok.

A Vihara, Wat Phra Singh, Chiengmai.

A Bell and Drum Tower at a Wat in Nongkai.

A Monk Visiting Wat Phra Keo, the Temple of the Emerald Buddha, Bangkok.

Demons Guarding an Entrance at Wat Phra Keo, Bangkok.

Stone Lions Guarding a Doorway at Wat Po, Bangkok.

A Wat in Nakornsrithammarat.

Wat Doi Sutep near Chiengmai.

An Elaborately Decorated Facade at Wat Chieng Mun, Chiengmai.

Bas-relief Sculpture in Wat Ruins at Sukhothai.

Bas-relief Sculpture in Temple Ruins at Pimai.

The Busy Corner of Yawarat and Vorachak Roads in Bangkok.

A Chinese Outdoor Theatre at a Wat Po Fair in Bangkok.

A Chinese Temple in Saraburi.

Life along the Chao Phya River, Bangkok.

On the way to the Floating Market in Thonburi.

A Typical Modern Style House in Nontaburi near Bangkok for Wealthy Persons.

New Buildings of the Medical University in Bangkok.

A Quiet Beautiful Klong in Thonburi.

A Spirit House Factory in Bangkok.

The Lake in Khao Din Park in Bangkok.

A Mountain Village in Northern Thailand.

A Man-made Waterfall in Khao Din Park, Bangkok.

Floating Houses along the Nan River in Pitsanuloke.

A Samlor and Driver in Chiengmai.

A Woman Carries her Goods to Market Using a Shoulder Pole.

Ruins of an Old Wat at Thailand's First Capital at Sukhothai.

Ruins of Wat Sri Chum in Old Sukhothai.

The Elephant Corral near Ayudhya.

Ayudhya in 1969.

Old Ayudhya Destroyed in 1767.

A Palace of King Narai (1657–1688) in Lopburi where he Received the Embassy of Louis XIV.

The Ruins in Lopburi of the House of Constantine Phaulkon.

Ruins of Khmer Style Temple in Sukhothai.

Ruins of Khmer Style Temple in Lopburi.

Wat Ruins in the Old Capital of Ayudhya.

The Seven-headed Naga (snake) Forming the Balustrade of the Stairs to Wat Doi Sutep, Chiengmai.

A Guardian Demon at Wat Doi Sutep.

Decorating Lacquer Bowls in a Chiengmai Factory.

A Lahu Village House, Doi Chiengdao.

A Lahu Man and his Son, Doi Chiengdao,
Northern Thailand.

A Christian Church in a Lahu Village on Doi Chiengdao.

A Boy and his Buffalo.

The Morning Market in an Upcountry Town.

The Fishing Village of Hua Hin.

Central Tower of the Khmer Style Temple at Pimai in Northeastern Thailand.

An Overall View of the Temple at Pimai.

The Mekong River at Nongkai with Laos on the Far Side.

Women Construction Workers at Nongkai.

A Main Street of Hotels, Restaurants, Stores, and Night Clubs Catering to American Troops from the Airbase outside the City at Udorn.

A Thatch House, Phuket.

Unloading Fish in Songkhla.

A Shrubbery Zoo in Songkhla.

Wat Phra Mahathad in Nakornsrithammarat.

The Present Bridge on the River Kwai (Kwae) Kanchanaburi.

Fishermen scrubbing their drying racks.

6

Palaces and Coups

About one mile from the Phra Mane Ground at the other end of a handsome broad boulevard called Rajadamnoen Road is a huge paved plaza near the center of which is a magnificent equestrian statue of King Chulalongkorn facing in the direction of the Phra Mane Ground. At the end of the giant square behind the king's statue is an impressive building, the Ananta Samakon Hall, which King Chulalongkorn built as a palace throne hall. It is probably the most un-Thai-like architecture of any government building. Designed by Italian architects in a European style with a large dome and built of white marble, the building would seem more at home in Venice, although Bangkok, with its canals, is sometimes referred to as "the Venice of the East." This Marble Throne Hall, as it is also known, is now the home of Thailand's National Assembly.

East of the plaza is Khao Din Park, one of Bangkok's largest and most beautiful parks and home of the Bangkok zoo. Here amid artificial lakes and man-built waterfalls cooled by the shade of many trees one can walk along the paths that twist past the pens and cages of many animals including the king's white elephants. On the other side of the park from the plaza, across a street bordered with klongs on both sides, is the Chitralada Palace, the home of the present king of Thailand. Its attractive grounds, with several buildings to house the king and his staff and with space to develop demonstration agricultural projects, cover an area much larger than the compound of the older Grand Palace. Surrounded by an open fence and a klong moat instead of a high wall as is the Grand Palace, Chitralada Palace is open to the eye, but not to visitors except by special invitation. In this attractive setting the much-loved king and his beautiful queen live with their family when in Bangkok.

Rajadamnoen Road is probably the widest and one of the loveliest streets in Bangkok. It is divided into two sections. The first section, running east from

154

the Phra Mane Ground to a large canal, the Klong Banglampoo, is lined on both sides with rows of monotonous neat four- and five-story buildings of a dull faded red brick or yellow stucco. Originally built as government offices and hotels the buildings now house banks, private businesses, a newspaper plant, hotels, night clubs, and a movie theater as well as some government offices and government corporations.

Across the Klong Banglampoo under the watchful eye of Wat Saket, or the Temple of the Golden Mount, Rajadamnoen Road turns northeast and runs to the plaza before the National Assembly building. This second section is much more attractive than the first. It is wider and has broad grass-covered dividers between the lanes of traffic. The government buildings along this section are set back from the sidewalk in individual compounds rather than joined together in rows as they are in the first section. Trees line both sides of the avenue and are also planted along the road dividers, making this second section the most beautiful boulevard in Bangkok.

At one end of Rajadamnoen Road is the Phra Mane Ground and the Grand Palace, a reminder of the absolute monarchy that ruled the Thai for seven hundred years. At the other end of Rajadamnoen is the National Assembly building, symbol of Thailand's current experiment in government by constitution and with a constitutional monarchy.

Three days after the bloodless revolution of June 24, 1932, the "Promoters" of the coup, renaming themselves the People's Party, published what was apparently a hastily drawn provisional constitution and began working on a permanent constitution. The latter was finished and put into effect December 10, 1932, and that date is now a national holiday celebrated as Constitution Day. Since that first revolution and those first two constitutions Thai politics has consisted of a series of coups, and constitutions, a few elections, and several unsuccessful attempts to overthrow the government by force. The newest permanent constitution was announced in June of 1968. It is still too early to tell how long it will endure.

The first constitutions provided for a National Assembly of which one-half was elected and one-half appointed. The number to be appointed, in a unique feature of the constitution, was to be decreased over the years as the percentage of the literate Thai population and those with a primary education increased so that they could participate intelligently in the election process. This feature enormously increased the importance of an elementary education for all, and the government began to enforce the compulsory education law more strictly. The transition period to achieve any substantial decrease in the number of appointed members was expected to take at least a decade or longer. In the meantime, the People's Party could easily control the government between its share of the elected members and selecting the appointed members named formally by the king.

The coup group turned to an older representative of the traditional bureaucracy to serve as first prime minister. Chosen for that post was a conservative high court judge, Phraya Mano, and soon he and Nai Pridi Phanomyong, the brilliant young lawyer who was the recognized intellectual as well as the principal civilian leader of the Promoters, clashed.

Soon after the new government had taken over, Pridi proposed an economic plan for the country which became the center of controversy. Among other provisions the plan called for the nationalization of all farmland. Farmers would be government employees and would be paid salaries with special government checks which could be spent only in government stores. Such a plan, of course, was completely contradictory to the whole history of Thailand with its proud emphasis on the independent, self-sufficient farmer owning his own land, and the plan immediately provoked an uproar. Pridi was charged with being a Communist by some of his compatriots. A serious split in the ruling group developed between the military and civilians and the older and the younger coup leaders. Pridi had to resign and he left the country.

Pridi was not gone long, however, when the military group itself became divided. In June 1933, almost a year after the revolution, a new coup took place in which the younger military group threw out the more conservative older government led by the civilian Phraya Mano. The new prime minister was a general, Phraya Phahon. Although himself an older man and the senior military officer in the 1932 revolution, he was supported by the younger military faction among whose members was Colonel Luang Pibun Songgram. The new government recalled Pridi from abroad. Pridi was cleared of any Communist charges and became the minister of the interior. His earlier economic plan was not revived.

In October 1933, the government in Bangkok was confronted by a counterrevolution. Prince Boworadet, a former minister of defense under the absolute monarchy, had organized provincial troops in the Northeast and with other royalist supporters was marching on Bangkok. The central government sent troops to meet the prince's forces and a battle took place near Don Muang Airport. The prince's forces were defeated and there was no revolt to support him among the military and other groups in Bangkok, as he had expected. The prince fled and his rebellion was suppressed within a week. The military leader who most distinguished himself in leading Bangkok's forces against the prince was Luang Pibun Songgram, who was fast becoming the most important military leader in the government.

During the Boworadet revolt King Prajadhipok, who by coincidence was again, as in 1932, at Hua Hin, fled by ship to Songkhla in the South of Thailand. His exact motives for doing so are not known, but his action resulted in some suspicions, never proved, that he supported or at least sympathized with the attempted royalist takeover. The king, however, was not in the best of health. He was losing his sight and finally the government gave him permission to go abroad for medical treatment early in 1934. He was not happy with the way the ruling group was governing and an extended correspondence between the king and the government did not improve matters from his viewpoint. At last, on March 2, 1935, the disappointed king abdicated. He lived in exile in England until he died in 1941. The government in Thailand selected a ten-year-old nephew of King Prajadhipok to become king. The new king was named Ananda Mahidol and is designated as Rama VIII. Except for a short visit to Thailand in late 1938, the king continued to live in Switzerland, where he was attending school, until after World War II.

In 1938, Phraya Phahon retired as prime minister and Luang Pibun Songgram succeeded him. Nai Pridi Phanomyong became minister of finance. This highly talented lawyer had also held the post of minister of foreign affairs in addition to his earlier position of minister of the interior. Pibun was a strong nationalist and under his direction several restrictive measures were enacted by the government which had their main effect against the Chinese minority. The name of the country was changed in 1939 from Siam to Thailand with the implication (considered a threat by some of Thailand's neighbors) that Pibun had ambitions to build a "greater Thailand" which would unite the Thai peoples in Laos, Burma, and possibly China as well, into one Thai state under his leadership.

Thailand and the whole world was concerned in 1939 with the approaching war in Europe and Asia. The Japanese had already invaded China, with indications of soon moving elsewhere in Asia. Pibun seemed to admire the plans and ideas of the Germans, Italians, and Japanese and tried to model his Thai government on the governments of those countries, at least in part. When the Japanese finally moved into Thailand on December 7, 1941, it was not too difficult for Pibun to lead his government at first into acquiescence, then into assistance, and finally into alliance with the Japanese forces.

Other Thai had different ideas, however. When the Thai declared war on England and the United States the Thai ambassador to Washington, M. R. Seni Pramoj, refused to deliver the declaration to the United States government. He claimed the declaration was not an expression of the true will of the Thai people. In England his counterpart did deliver the declaration to the British government and this difference in Thai ambassadorial behavior was to have different effects on the behavior toward Thailand of these two allied nations in the postwar world. M. R. Seni Pramoj actively began to organize a Free Thai Movement, drawing mainly upon Thai students in the United States and England to be trained and sent back into Thailand to organize an underground resistance movement and to gather intelligence for the Allies.

Back in Thailand a situation, almost like a comic opera in its plotting, was developing. Nai Pridi Phanomyong, with his known strongly democratic ideas, was not an especial favorite of the Japanese allies of the Thai. Consequently, Pridi resigned from his ministerial post and Pibun appointed him to the regency which ruled in the name of the absent king, who was still a minor. At first Pridi was a member of the Council of the Regency and before the war was over he was serving as the sole regent of the kingdom. From this invulnerable and prestigious spot as regent Pridi became secret head of the Free Thai Movement inside the kingdom and protected the movement with all his official powers. By 1944, British and American agents responsible to Lord Mountbatten's Southeast Asian command in Ceylon were living secretly in Bangkok palaces under the regent's control and were even using a radio in central police headquarters to send messages to Ceylon. Pibun probably knew what Pridi was doing and so did the Japanese, who were infuriated but in no position to act against the regent.

By 1944, too, it was becoming apparent that the Japanese were losing the war. Having antagonized the Japanese by not stopping Pridi's undercover activities and yet unacceptable to the wartime Allies because of his pro-Japanese policy before the war and during its first years, Pibun resigned as prime minister at the end of July 1944. He was succeeded by a civilian from the early days of the Promoters, Nai Khuang Aphaiwong, who served until the Japanese surrendered in August 1945. At that time an interim prime minister was appointed who served less than a month until the Thai could bring M. R. Seni Pramoj back from Washington to serve as postwar prime minister until the peace treaties were signed. The Thai figured, and rightly so, that because of Seni's wartime position as head of the Free Thai Movement abroad, he was not tainted with any collaboration with the Japanese and would be able to deal with the Allies better than a Thai leader who had remained in the country under the Japanese occupation.

A few months later, after successfully concluding treaties with the major Allies, Seni resigned and Khuang Aphaiwong became prime minister again, but only for a few months. Then Pridi took control of the government as prime minister. This was the only period when this major figure of the 1932 revolution served as prime minister and his term was not to last long.

In May 1946 Pridi introduced the first new constitution since 1932. It replaced the one-house National Assembly with a bicameral elected body. The new constitution was only a month old when Pridi was faced with a crisis that contributed to his downfall. On June 9, 1946, under mysterious and never completely explained circumstances the young King Ananda Mahidol, who had returned to Thailand after the war, was killed in his bed. He was succeeded by his younger brother, the present King Bhumibol Adulyadej (Rama IX). Rumors about the king's death by a gunshot wound developed quickly and the government was never able to dispel them completely or to explain the circumstances of the king's death satisfactorily for many people. Among the rumors were some that reported Pridi's implication in the regicide. Although these rumors were never proved, Pridi resigned in August 1946.

For a little more than a year Thailand's prime minister was an admiral, whose government in that postwar period was haunted with reports of scandal and corruption. On November 8, 1947, a new military coup by supporters of former Prime Minister Pibun Songgram threw out the admiral's government. Pibun had been arrested after the war as a collaborator, but then shortly released on the grounds that he could not be tried for something that was not illegal at the time he did it. He had been steadily rebuilding his political strength since his release, but in 1947 he was still not ready to antagonize the former Allies who had fought Japan. A new provisional constitution was put into effect and for the third time Khuang Aphaiwong, with Pibun's support, became prime minister. The new constitution retained the bicameral assembly, but made the upper house appointive rather than elective. This constitution combined elements of the 1932 constitution and the Pridi constitution of 1946.

Elections were held for the lower house in January 1948, and Khuang's party elected the largest number of representatives. He stayed on as prime minister. By April, however, Pibun was secure enough to move. Khuang was told to resign. When faced with the decision to resign or to stay and try to fight it out with the support of his parliamentary group, Khuang checked with the military and found he had no military support. When he learned that fact, Khuang did not even bother to ask for the support of his party members in the Assembly, but resigned immediately. This action illustrates the strength in the government of the military and the weakness of the elected parliament. Pibun again became prime minister. Among the leaders of this new coup group in late 1947 and early 1948 were two generals who were to become the most important political powers in the next decade. One was General Phao Siyanond who in time headed all the police forces; the other was General Sarit Thanarat who rose to be commander in chief of the army.

Pridi fled the country after the 1947 coup and eventually reached Communist China where, it is believed, he has resided ever since. He has not been heard from in the last few years except for an occasional statement reported in the Peking press. The most recent of these came in December 1968 when Peking reported in the news that Pridi had sent a message to Chinese leaders congratulating them on the success of their hydrogen bomb tests. That was the first time his name had appeared in the Chinese press since 1964.

During Pridi's first years out of Thailand he still had supporters who hoped to return him to power. In February 1949 some of his supporters in the Thai navy and marines attempted a military revolt, but they were suppressed by General Phao's police and General Sarit's army forces.

In June 1951, the navy again revolted in an episode which once more had certain comic-opera aspects to it. Pibun was attending a ceremony on a vessel in the Chao Phya River at which the vessel was being transferred from the United States to Thailand. In full view of the entire diplomatic corps Pibun was kidnapped by the navy and placed on a naval vessel. This time the air force joined the police and the army to suppress the revolt. An air force plane bombed the navy ship on which Pibun was held. In the ensuing confusion the prime minister escaped by jumping overboard and swimming to shore. It seems almost needless to write that since that date after two unsuccessful revolts, the navy has been kept in a subordinate military position in Thailand.

In March 1949, after the attempted coup in February, Pibun put a new permanent constitution into effect. This one lasted until late 1951 when a military group with both Phao and Sarit in prominent roles restored the 1932 constitution of December that year in place of Pibun's latest constitution. With some revisions in 1952 the restored constitution stayed in effect until 1957.

During much of the second Pibun government period in Thailand, the prime minister was not as free to act as he had been in the 1930's. Directly under him were Phao and Sarit, two powerful rivals who could not be ignored, and much of Pibun's energies went into maintaining a balance between these two, each supported by his own armed forces. It should be noted that the Thai police are essentially almost as well equipped as the army, for the police have their own ships, airplanes, and tanks, and are the only real rival of the army.

In 1955, Pibun returned from a world tour with some surprisingly liberal ideas. He began to allow public speeches by persons opposed to the government and even permitted the organization of political parties, one of which he organized to support his government. The active head of this government party was General Phao. General Sarit stayed quietly in the background. In February 1957, the elected half of the National Assembly was chosen. Pibun's party won amidst many charges of voting frauds and other irregularities, and students, especially from Thammasat University, which had been founded on the initiative of Pridi in the 1930's, took to the streets in protest. The protests were put down, but General Sarit, who had not been smeared by the allegedly corrupt election because he had taken so small a part in it, let it be known indirectly that he supported the students in some of their protests.

On September 16, 1957, General Sarit and his army followers staged a coup forcing Pibun and Phao to flee the country. Nai Pote Sarasin, a civilian who had served as secretary general of SEATO, was called in to be prime minister for a ninety-day period during which new elections were to be held. They were held on December 15, 1957, and not surprisingly, the party supported by General Sarit won. Sarit's deputy in the army, General Thanom Kittakachorn, became prime minister. General Sarit was seriously ill and went abroad for treatment. During the next few months the government of General Thanom was faced with many problems with which it could not cope successfully. In October 1958, General Sarit, once again healthy, returned to Bangkok and proclaimed a new revolutionary government in power with himself as prime minister. General Thanom became deputy prime minister and minister of defense in the new government.

In January 1959, the constitution was set aside and replaced by an interim constitution which authorized the government to take almost any action it felt necessary for the security and welfare of the country. Under the interim constitution there was an assembly which was completely appointed. Once, when checking the membership of the assembly, I found that about 80 percent of the appointees were military or police officers. This assembly had the duty of approving the legislation proclaimed by the government, and at the same time was to act as a constituent assembly to draft a new permanent constitution. It took several years to complete this second task. A new permanent constitution was announced by the king in June 1968, and the first national elections under the new constitution were held in February 1969. In the meantime, General Sarit died (in 1963), and once again General Thanom became prime minister as well as minister of defense. The succession was accomplished smoothly and under the new constitution of 1968 now in operation Marshal Thanom continues to serve in his two posts. He shares his power, however, with another important military leader, General Praphas Charusathien, who is deputy prime minister and minister of the interior. In his latter position General Praphas has control of all the police forces.

Despite the frequent changes of constitutions and governments since the revolution of 1932 the actual number of persons in leadership positions is quite small and most of them are either Promoters of the 1932 revolution or leaders of the Pibun coup in 1947 or of the Sarit coup in 1958. The same names appear over and over in one assignment or another. In the 1930's and 1940's the most important names were Pridi Phanomyong, Pibun Songgram and Khuang Aphaiwong. After the war, until 1957, one could add the names of Generals Phao and Sarit and M. R. Seni Pramoj. Since 1957, Generals Thanom and Praphas would be added and possibly the name of Pote Sarasin. There were many others, of course, but these are the most prominent over a period of years. At the beginning of the 1970's, of these leaders Pridi is in exile apparently in Communist China; Marshals Pibun and Sarit, General Phao, and Nai Khuang are dead; Marshal Thanom, General Praphas, and Nati Pote Sarasin are all in the cabinet; and M. R. Seni Pramoj is leader of the largest opposition party elected to the National Assembly in 1969. With the exception of Pridi, those living leaders long in power still are in power.

For almost four decades military power to support the political leadership has been of major importance. In Thailand this means power in the army first of all, and the police and air force second. The navy and marines have been of much less significance in most of the last twenty years. No government has existed for any length of time without army support.

The total politically concerned population in Thailand is a small precentage of the entire population. The coups, countercoups, revolts, and even elections have generally involved a small number of persons. Perhaps the elections under the new constitution will change this pattern from the past. At the top of the concerned group is a handful of men, probably no more than twenty or twenty-five top military leaders, a few civilian cabinet leaders, and a few individuals associated closely with the king. Beneath them is a larger group amounting to several hundred persons, including other senior military officers, some members of royalty, senior civilian government officials, and a few powerful businessmen, including some ethnic Chinese business leaders tied by interlocking boards of directors to some of the members of the Thai elite. The largest group of politically concerned is made up of the other educated people in the nation who are often civil or military leaders at lower grades, academicians and students, businessmen, and professionals. This largest concerned group, whose representatives may be found in all parts of the nation, is mainly concentrated in Bangkok-Thonburi and a few other cities.

Outside of these politically concerned groups is the great mass of Thai farmers and other rural and urban workers. By tradition they tend to look to leaders with prestige who tell them what to do and what to believe. This huge group, accepting the Buddhist belief that a man achieves honor and power because of his karma, is a great conservative group and in the past has tended to support whatever political group is in authority regardless of how that political group gained that authority. In the election of 1969 this unconcerned mass generally supported the government while, in contrast, the largest politically concerned group tended to oppose the incumbent government. All the Bangkok assembly seats, for instance, went to opponents of the party supporting the existing national government. It is too early to tell if this heralds a change in any traditional divisions of the Thai political population or if the old patterns will continue under the new constitution.

Finally, throughout the history of Thailand since 1932, effective political pressure groups are unknown. Political parties, when they were permitted, tended to be cliques around a leader rather than independent groups with ideological stands and action platforms separate from personalities. Independent interest groups such as professional organizations, labor unions, youth groups, women's groups, and so on, have had little importance in Thailand's political history. The membership of many professional and civic groups, when they do exist, is often composed mainly of government officials. Labor unions have been prohibited for more than a decade and before that were ineffective as major political forces. Buddhist monks in Thailand, unlike Burma or Ceylon or Vietnam, have had almost no political role. Some individual monks who have dabbled in politics have been defrocked and returned to layman status. The limited role of the monk is expected to continue under the new constitution in which he is denied even the right to vote.

Almost ten years passed between the appointment of the Constituent Assembly at the beginning of 1959 and the promulgation of the new constitution in the middle of 1968. The assembly moved slowly by studying earlier constitutions of Thailand and those of other countries before deciding what to include in the new document. The result is a combination of elements drawn from several sources—the American constitution, British parliamentary practice, and the earlier constitutions of Thailand.

The 1968 constitution is divided into eleven chapters plus transitory provisions. The first two chapters state that Thailand is a kingdom with a democratic form of government. The king is head of state, but must act in conformity with the provisions of the constitution. The role of the king, his privy council, and a regency, if necessary, are all discussed, and provisions for succession are included.

Chapter Three states the rights and liberties of the Thai people and covers a broad range, including religious liberty, presumption of innocence, equality under the law, privacy, the right to assemble peacefully, and several others. It should be noted, however, that some of these rights are qualified so that it is difficult to determine just from a reading how they might be applied or possibly abused at some future time. For example, full liberties of speech, writing, printing, and publication are granted, but restrictions can be placed on them by law for the purpose of "safeguarding the liberties of other persons, avoiding a state of emergency, maintaining public order or good morals, or protecting young persons from moral degeneration." What precisely is meant by these qualifications, especially the last ambiguous one, is not defined.

Chapter Four sets forth the duties of the Thai people. These duties include defending the country, giving military service, abiding by the law, paying taxes, and others.

Chapter Five is especially interesting in that it sets forth what are called "directive principles of state policies" which by the word of the constitution itself are intended as guiding principles for legislation and administration. Among the directive principles are the promotion of friendly relations with other nations, the promotion and advancement of education, the encouragement of research in arts and sciences, the encouragement of private economic initiative, the promotion and encouragement of social work for the happiness and welfare of the people, the promotion of public health, the promotion of local government, and several others.

According to Chapter Six, the legislative power rests with a bicameral National Assembly consisting of an elected House of Representatives and an appointed Senate which is to have three-fourths the number of members elected to the House. The present National Assembly has 219 members in the House chosen on the basis of one for 150,000 people except that each province has a minimum of one, and 164 appointed members in the Senate. The chapter spells out in detail the powers of each house, the qualifications for membership, the qualifications for voting in elections, the procedures for passing bills, for settling differences between the houses, etc. It might be noted that voting in an election is authorized for Thai nationals who are at least twenty years old on January 1 of the election year. But there are exceptions. A Thai national whose father is an alien or a naturalized citizen must meet certain additional qualifications to be stipulated in an election law. On the surface this appears to be discriminating against many ethnic Chinese citizens in Thailand, but it would be necessary to see what extra requirements are in the election laws and how they are administered before drawing any final conclusions.

It might also be noted that the officers of both houses are appointed by the king (in effect by the government in power) and are not elected by their own bodies. This gives the government one more control of the assembly in addition to that gained through the appointment of members of the Senate.

The executive power, as stated in Chapter Seven, is in a Council of Ministers of fifteen to thirty ministers presided over by a president. All council members are appointed by the king. As in the United States, ministers are not concurrently members of the assembly. At the same time, however, as in England, the ministers can be summoned before the assembly for questioning. Under certain conditions the assembly can pass a vote of no confidence in the government in which case the Council of Ministers resigns.

The last chapters cover the judicial system, a constitutional tribunal which has specific functions delegated to it under the constitution, amendments, and what are called "final provisions." One of these last is of special importance for it permits legislation by command of the king through the Council of Ministers during a state of war or of special emergencies "when the normal exercise of the legislative power through the National Assembly may be impeded or unsuitable for the situation." What this provision, especially the words "unsuitable for the situation," will mean in future practice cannot now be determined.

One final observation about the constitution can be made at this early stage in its life. It is probably as democratic as any of the previous Thai constitutions and perhaps even more so. Within its framework a genuine working democratic system can be developed, but also within its terms there are enough hedging qualifications that an unscrupulous government in power will be able constitutionally to do almost anything it wishes and still maintain itself as the legitimate government in power. Undoubtedly the new constitution is a big step forward from the short interim constitution in effect during most of the 1960's, but whether or not the new constitution will help achieve real democracy in Thailand, only future experience will be able to demonstrate.

In Thailand, as in many other countries, regardless of what happens to constitutions and politicians, the government continues to function with moderate success because of the ongoing work of the administrative bureaucracy. Thailand is divided into seventy-one *changwad* (provinces); all of them except the one in which Bangkok is located bear the same name as their principal city. In the case of Bangkok, the province is named Phra Nakorn. The provinces, in turn, are divided into more than four hundred *amphur* (districts), the districts into more than three thousand *tambon* (communes), and the tambons into almost fifty thousand *muban* (villages). The governors of the changwad and the chief officers of the amphur are appointed direct from Bangkok by the Ministry of the Interior. The villagers choose their own headmen, and all the headmen in a tambon choose their own *kamnan* (headman of a commune). The choices for kamnan must be approved by the district officer.

There are also a few municipalities whose lord mayors are appointed by the Ministry of the Interior. The department within the ministry responsible for local government, confusingly, has the same name as the ministry; it is called the Department of the Interior. Since Thai government administrators at the upper levels sometimes hold more than one office, Bangkok had the unusual and potentially humorous situation for several years in the 1960's of the posts of director general of the Department of the Interior and the lord mayor of Bangkok being held by the same person. The lord mayor was theoretically subordinate to the governor of the province, but if he did not like what the governor ordered he could always switch to his other office as director general of the Department of the Interior, in which position he was the governor's superior, and could countermand the order.

Several of the other national ministries and departments, such as education, public health, agriculture, finance, and the police, appoint their own officials at the changwad and amphur levels. These officials are responsible to their national offices in Bangkok rather than to the changwad governor or district officer. Yet, these two chief officials regularly bring together the representatives of other ministries in their jurisdiction to provide the governor or district officer with at least an informal advisory cabinet. In this way the governor or district officer is kept informed of what each ministry is doing in his territory and some coordination can be attempted.

The Thai bureaucracy and administration is a highly centralized organization and operation. This centralization is intensified by the fact that all finances must come from the national government in Bangkok. Local villages may build a school or a new road as a community development project, but this is done with local resources other than tax funds unless the central government is a partner in the project. Expenditures from taxes are controlled by the central government for all levels of Thai public administration.

Speculation is often heard about whether the king of Thailand does or does not have any real political power or has only ceremonial functions. The present king, Bhumibol Adulyadej, Rama IX, is certainly loved, respected, and held in awe by all levels of Thai society. During the second half of 1960, the king and queen made a world-wide tour lasting about six months. I was in Bangkok the day they returned to their capital city early in 1961. The crowd that lined the streets of Bangkok to welcome their majesties was without a doubt the largest crowd I have ever seen anywhere for any occasion— including New Year's Eve in Times Square. The cynic will say that an authoritarian government can organize any size and type of demonstration, and the Thai government certainly did what it could on that occasion to insure a large turnout. The day was declared a holiday. Special trains and buses were used to bring in people from the upcountry provinces. Still, the people came willingly and many came without government urging or assistance. I think everyone in that crowd, Thai and foreigner, could feel the electric excitement and genuine affection that flowed from those thousands and thousands of Thai people to their king and queen. The same sense of good feeling toward their majesties can be seen and felt, on a smaller scale, at every gathering where they appear.

For many Thai citizens it makes little difference who actually rules the country as long as the king is still safe on the throne. This was recognized quickly at the time of the 1932 revolution when, after sending an insulting ultimatum to the king, the leaders of the revolution later apologized. Since that time each change of government has always gone through the formality at least of gaining the king's approval for the change. To that extent, as the representative head of the nation with wide support among his people, the king can certainly have some political influence on his government.

Under the new constitution the king is given many responsibilities which, of course, he exercises mainly as an instrument of the government in power. But an intelligent and well-informed king can use his formal responsibilities at least to impart his views to his ministers and to that extent again can have some influence. This role of the king was openly recognized, even before the new constitution, by the late Prime Minister Sarit at the time of the Khao Phra Viharn decision in early 1962.

Khao Phra Viharn is a magnificent temple ruin in the architectural style of the Khmers at Angkor. It is located in an area which was claimed by both Thailand and Cambodia. After long years of dreary arguments and threats, the two countries finally submitted their dispute to the International Court of Justice at The Hague, and the court awarded the land and the temple to Cambodia, the smaller and less well-armed of the two. The award was followed by a mighty uproar in Bangkok. Demonstrations against Cambodia were organized with government blessing (the first demonstrations allowed by the government since the student demonstrations of 1957 protesting the Pibun elections of that year). Some senior government and military officials began talking of war or using the military forces to prevent Cambodia from taking the site of the temple. Then the prime minister suddenly announced that Thailand would abide by the court's decision and respect its international obligations. The tumult quieted. While there were undoubtedly several factors involved, the prime minister in explaining his decision gave credit to the cautious and sensible counsel he had received from the king.

King Bhumibol Adulyadej was born in Cambridge, Massachusetts, on December 5, 1927, while his father, Prince Mahidol of Songkhla, a son of King Chulalongkorn, was studying medicine in Boston. The new prince was a younger son and no one had reason to expect that he might be king some day. He studied in Thailand and later in Switzerland with his brother, who became King Ananda Mahidol on the abdication of King Prajadhipok in 1935. The younger brother studied science, but after the tragic death of his older brother, the new king switched his studies to law and political science. In 1950, King Bhumibol Adulyadej returned to Thailand for the double ceremony of his marriage in April and his coronation on May fifth.

Queen Sirikit, often described accurately as one of the world's most beautiful women, is the daughter of a Thai prince who served in several senior diplomatic posts in Europe where she as a student met the king. They have four children. Their oldest child, Princess Ubol Ratana, is studying in the United States, and the crown prince, Prince Vajiralongkorn, studied in England.

After his coronation the king went back to Switzerland to complete his studies. He returned to Thailand in 1951 and has stayed there ever since except for several official trips which he has made to other countries. He has traveled widely in Thailand and has come to know his country and his people well. In addition to his duties as a constititonal monarch outlined in the new constitution, which include the important duty of putting his signature to laws (withholding it can require a reconsideration of the law) and to the appointment of major officials, he is also the head of state for relationships with foreign countries and for the domestic duties associated with state ceremonies. As defender of the faith the king appoints the religious leaders, although for political purposes he gets the advice of his government first. The king's reputation in the eyes of most Thai was greatly increased in 1956, when he became a monk for two weeks at Wat Bovoranives, the temple of his great grandfather, King Mongkut.

On June 9, 1971, the king will be celebrating twenty-five years (his silver anniversary) as king. That anniversary will also represent twenty-one years since his coronation and twenty years since he took up permanent residence in Thailand, giving his full time and attention to his duties as the Thai king. This makes him the country's only leader with such a long continuous time in office. He has used this period well, as all evidence indicates, to learn much about his country, his people, their needs and desires. I would assume that a king as intelligent, informed, experienced, and loved, as is the present king of Thailand, could not be a nonentity on the political scene, but within the limits of the constitution and the framework of his own wisdom and desires would exercise some real political influence and, perhaps on occasion, even some political power within the policy and decision-making processes of the government.

There is a traffic circle at the intersection of Rajadamnoen Road and a cross street. In the center of the circle is a monument. It has four independent pillars which look a little like concrete half-wings standing on end. In the middle of the circle is a small building with what appears to be a large urn on its roof. This whole complex is the Monument of Democracy built after the revolution of 1932 to commemorate the achievement of democracy in Thailand. Perhaps it was a little premature and it would be better to consider this monument as one to the future rather than to the past. Thailand has not yet achieved democracy, but perhaps it will under the newest constitution or perhaps under a still newer one after that.

Part Two

Beyond Bangkok

7

Sukhothai

By observing the people of Bangkok, their customs, the places in which they live, work, and worship, much can be learned about the Thailand of the past and present. Bangkok and Thonburi together have about 10 percent of the country's total population. Bangkok is the capital of Thailand in many ways. It is the seat of government, the base of trade and commerce, the headquarters of business and finance, the locus of the Buddhist hierarchy, and the center of education and the arts. Still, it is a cliché to say of Bangkok that the city is not the whole of Thailand just as it is a cliché to say New York is not the United States.

To learn more about Thailand, its people, its history, and its culture, it is necessary to go beyond Bangkok, to travel to the smaller cities and towns and in the rural areas which collectively, regardless of the direction traveled, are referred to as upcountry. There is no better place to begin than Sukhothai, a town and a province in the Northern region of Thailand. Sukhothai is generally considered to be the site of the first major independent Thai kingdom on the Southeast Asian peninsula in what is today Thailand and, therefore, the father of the present-day kingdom of Thailand.

Sukhothai, about three hundred miles north of Bangkok, is almost two-thirds of the way between Bangkok and Chiengmai, the largest northern city and the second largest city in Thailand. The countryside between Bangkok and Sukhothai is one of low hills and flatlands of the Central Plain over which a train can move at rapid speed. The shorter distance between Chiengmai and Sukhothai is through the mountains of the north over which a train must crawl at what is sometimes an exasperatingly slow speed.

Sukhothai, located on the Yom River, one of the four major rivers that join to make up the Chao Phya, is not itself located on the railroad line between Bangkok and Chiengmai. About thirty-six miles slightly to the southeast of

171

Sukhothai another old city and a provincial capital, Pitsanuloke, is located on the railroad line and it is often used as the gateway to Sukhothai. A newly paved road links the two cities. Pitsanuloke is situated on the banks of the Nan River, which joins the Yom a short distance above the point where they meet the Ping River coming down from Chiengmai and where they form the Chao Phya. One of the interesting features of Pitsanuloke is the houses on the Nan River. On both banks houses built on floating rafts are anchored to the shores in long lines. Connected to the banks with gangplanks, these houses, and also some stores and other business places, can rise and fall with the level of the river. Unlike the boats in which Thai live along many rivers and klongs, these are regular houses built on rafts and cannot be sailed around. Similar raft dwellings were common in Bangkok many decades ago.

My visits to Sukhothai have always begun with train trips to Pitsanuloke. On my most recent visit I went to Pitsanuloke from Chiengmai and the slow train ride was a fascinating experience itself as we rode through the sparsely populated and in some areas sparsely forested mountains of the north. As the train twisted and turned its way along the serpentine path out of the mountains we could see once in a while a rugged mountain village clinging to the hillside near the railroad tracks. Part of the journey was at night and I was startled to see a spectacular and slightly frightening fire display along the right of way. A few times during the daylight hours I had seen glimpses of smoke wisps rising from areas of the hills where there were no visible signs of human habitation. At night the wisps of smoke turned into numerous small forest and brush fires throughout the hills from beside the tracks back through the hills as far as one could see.

The tiny forest fires, usually covering areas of only a few feet to a few score yards in diameter, added a beautiful and eerie backdrop to the train trip. But this was the dry season in Thailand and I feared the possibility of a general forest fire. I expressed my fear to a provincial education officer with whom I had been chatting earlier on the trip, but he seemed undisturbed and said the fires were burning all the time. In response to my inquiry on their cause (I thought they might have been started deliberately to clear land), he told me most of them were the result of natural causes and a few were attributable to the carelessness of man. This blazing background stayed with us almost until we reached Pitsanuloke.

The train reached Pitsanuloke late in the evening, about ten thirty. I had no hotel reservations, but had been given the name of the "number one" hotel. I took a samlor from the station and arrived at the hotel only to find it was full except for one room, which I immediately agreed to take, sight unseen. While waiting for a boy to escort me to the room I looked around the hotel and saw that it was a typical upcountry hostelry. The ground floor was a great open area the full width of the building in the front half. In the rear only the

center of the floor had an open area. On the left-hand side was a small office
and a storeroom area with walls of wire fencing and filled with cases of various
brands of soft drinks. On the right side were two or three other small rooms
with regular solid walls. The center of the rear part of the ground floor was the
bottom of an open well space that extended to the roof of the four-story building.

Like most of the newer buildings in town the hotel was stucco over brick or
concrete blocks and the floors were bare concrete. The exterior was painted a
pastel green which was streaked in many places from rain.

Along both the left and right walls of the large front open area of the
ground floor were a few wooden chairs and couches with thin cushions on
them. The furniture was arranged in a rigid military row. This was the "lobby"
of the hotel. But like most small upcountry hotels in which I have stayed the
lobby doubled as a garage at night. One car, two motorcycles, and five small
trucks had been driven into the lobby and filled all the open area between the
street and the back wall of the hotel. If you sat in one of the lobby chairs, you
stared at a truck about two feet in front of you.

The room boy arrived at last and I was escorted to my room. It was a small
bare room with a low, hard wooden bed, without springs, as usual, and covered
only by a thin mattress. The room was located on the inside well. With only
a small ceiling fan turning weakly and with no outside windows I knew I was
in for a hot night. More disturbing, however, was the fact that as soon as the
room lights were turned on I saw that the room had already been occupied
once that evening. Tired as I was after the long trip I might have overlooked
that minor fact except that the earlier occupant had eaten watermelon and
left watermelon seeds, rind, red flesh, and soggy stains all over the floor and on
the bed itself. The cockroaches were out in force under the command of a
couple of the largest roaches I have ever seen, and they all seemed to be having
a great time. After strongly voicing my dissatisfaction at this state of affairs to
the room boy and then to the hotel manager I finally persuaded the latter to
have the former clean up the mess and change the one sheet on the bed before
I could fall into that backbreaker for the hot, fitful sleep I expected to have. I
should point out that this experience is probably not typical of Thai hotels,
although similar ones can be encountered from time to time.

Some upcountry hotels have unusual features. In one hotel at which I
stayed small advertisements had been pasted on the walls where the visitor
was most apt to see them. Next to the mirror one could read about a cola
drink. Above the door handle was a notice for tires, and beside the toilet paper
was pasted a sign for sewing machines. In many upcountry provincial capitals
first-class hotels, which are as modern and comfortable as many of the hotels
in Bangkok, have been built in recent years.

While the room was being cleaned I decided to find something to eat. At that hour of the night all restaurants seemed to be closed. As I wandered down the main street toward a circle with a beautiful fountain, I passed one store from which music could be heard and in front of which several persons were seated on folding chairs set up in the road. A wake for a Chinese merchant was underway. Except for an occasional samlor the rest of the street was quiet. I did not want to disturb the wake so I headed for the local movie house hoping that the evening's film would not yet be over so that neighboring restaurants might still be open. I was lucky and found the cinema, as I expected, with restaurants on both sides of it empty but open. I chose one and had an all-purpose meal of rice and beef and vegetables with a good hot sauce to perk it up. After the meal and a cold drink I walked back past the fountain. Many upcountry towns in Thailand today are decorated with a central fountain. This one had lights playing upon it which added to its quiet beauty. Six or eight men and women sat around its edges, not speaking, just watching the water playfully rising and falling. I, too, watched for a few minutes, then drifted back to the hotel, threaded my way among the trucks, and climbed the stairs to my hot cell above.

The next day I hired a taxi to drive me west to Sukhothai. The city today is not precisely on the same site as the capital of the ancient kingdom of Sukhothai. The old capital lies five or six miles farther west of the present city. I noticed as we drove through new Sukhothai that the city had apparently had a major fire relatively recently. Because buildings are built in rows close together in all cities in Thailand and because most towns have inadequate fire-fighting equipment, once a fire starts in an upcountry town it frequently burns out a large area before it can be extinguished. Whenever the fire had occurred that had burned out a business section of Sukhothai, it had been long enough before so that some rebuilding had begun. Temporary shanties had been built behind many of the stucco façades that had been left standing after the fire, and business had started again. From the rear these one-story shanties with two- and three-story stucco façades reminded me of old Western ghost towns and their false-front buildings.

West of the new city are the ruins of the old capital of the Sukhothai kingdom. Like most old cities in Southeast Asia only the temples and some of the palaces were constructed of brick and stucco while the rest of the buildings were of wood. The wooden buildings have long ago disappeared and the pillars, foundations, and parts of walls jutting up from the flat plain in front of the not too distant hills farther west are the remains of Sukhothai wats. Old statues of Buddha gaze serenely down among the ruins of what must have once been a large city with many wats built by expert craftsmen with bas-relief sculptures of great beauty carved on the walls. One of the ruined buildings that still can be seen (Wat Sri Chum) has four high windowless, almost ten-foot thick brick walls and a narrow open, tapering door going from the ground almost to the top of the walls. Inside the thick double wall on one side of the square building a stairway is built to the top of the wall. Inside the roofless building a large seated Buddha calmly watches those who come to pay tribute or to gaze. Numerous other wat and chedi ruins can be found throughout this area.

Who the first men were to live in the area that is now Thailand is not definitely known, and the early history of the Thai peoples themselves is obscure. What I shall relate here is the traditional history of the area based on what little is known. New archeological studies now underway in Thailand may in time show who the earliest pre-Thai dwellers in the area were, and these discoveries may demonstrate that men began living in this area much earlier than had been assumed.

Early Thai history is made more difficult to discover by several factors. For one thing, the earliest-known Thai people did not have a written language of their own. What has been learned about them has been gleaned from the writings of neighboring peoples such as the Chinese. The Thai people suffered a staggering loss when the Burmese captured and sacked the capital of Ayudhya, destroying all records and archives on which they could lay their hands. Since that year of 1767 Thai historians and historians of Thailand have tried to reconstruct the early history of this proud people from bits and pieces brought together over the years from many sources. There are, however, gaps in Thai history still unfilled except by legend and which may never be completely and accurately filled.

The earliest-known references to the people known as Thai occur in early Chinese chronicles. As early as the seventh century the Thai are mentioned in wars among China, Tibet, Annam, and the Thai kingdom of Nanchao which existed in the southern part of what is now China. In the south Chinese province of Yunnan there are still a few hundred thousand Thai-speaking persons, and the Communist Chinese have used this group for political and propaganda purposes against Thailand.

By the end of the ninth century the independent Thai kingdom of Nanchao had become a vassal state to the Chinese emperor. Although remaining independent, Nanchao was subjected to continuing political and territorial pressure as its overlords, the Chinese, forced their way southward. As these pressures increased, groups of Thai began to migrate still farther south ahead of the advancing Chinese. This was not a rapid migration, but one that took place over several centuries.

As they moved southward the Thai followed the most accessible routes along the river valleys of all the major rivers of Southeast Asia. They proceeded down the Irrawaddy, the Salween, the Mekong, and the Chao Phya system. Various groups of the Thai people organized small city-kingdoms in the areas to which they moved, and their descendants are found today in several areas of Southeast Asia. In Burma the Thai people became known as the Shans, and along the Mekong valley the Thai became the Lao people. Both of these groups are closely related in language and customs to the largest group of Thai who moved down the center of the peninsula into the valley of the Chao Phya and its main tributaries. Among some of the oldest of the early Thai-Lao city-states still in existence are Chieng Rai and Chieng Sen in northern Thailand.

As the Thai moved into Southeast Asia they found other settled kingdoms already there. Among those the Thai encountered were the Burmese and Khmer (Cambodian) empires each of which at one time or another controlled most of present-day Thailand. Sukhothai, eight hundred years ago, was a Khmer city and a subcapital in the northwest of the great Khmer empire which had its major capital at Angkor Thom. Remnants of Khmer architecture can still be seen among the Sukhothai ruins. Farther south in the area around Nakorn Pathom, the Thai met the Mon people, who had moved into the area from southern Burma.

In 1238, two Thai chieftains defeated the Khmer general in command of Sukhothai and set up an independent Thai kingdom which is generally considered the forerunner of the present kingdom of Thailand. The first king of this new state was Sri Intaratitya, often more popularly referred to as Phra Ruang, one of the two chieftains about whom little is known and surrounding whom many legends have developed and been passed off as history.

One event during this early reign had a major impact on Thai history; this was an event that occurred far to the north of Sukhothai. The Mongols were pressing their conquest of China, and in 1253, under the leadership of Kublai Khan, the Mongols defeated the northern Thai kingdom of Nanchao and ended its existence as an independent state. After the subjugation of Nanchao the slow trickle of southward-moving Thai became a swift-moving river as larger groups of Thai migrated to the new Thai kingdom of Sukhothai and to other areas in Southeast Asia where earlier Thai settlers had established their own small states.

The new Sukhothai kingdom did not last long as an independent state. It continued only for about a century and a half, although much of its power and influence were gone even sooner. As an important Thai state most of its significance had disappeared by the middle of the fourteenth century.

Despite the relatively short hegemony of Sukhothai among the Thai states, the kingdom produced one of the most important kings in Thai history, King Ramkamheng the Great. His accomplishments were many and legend has added more to his glory. His forty-year reign from 1275 to 1315 saw a great expansion of the territory under Sukhothai control. He crossed the mountains to the west and extended the Sukhothai kingdom to the Bay of Bengal, taking control of part of modern-day Burma, and he marched his forces southward almost to the present-day border with Malaysia. He was the first Thai ruler to expand the kingdom to areas which were to become major integral parts of the present Thai kingdom.

In this early period, however, distance from the central kingdom at Sukhothai determined to a considerable extent the amount of control that was actually exercised. Some of the outlying areas had vassal status and were only loosely controlled. A few of them even continued to pay tribute to the Khmer king as well as to the Thai king. In the north, Chiengmai and some other city-states remained independent Thai-Lao kingdoms not subject to orders from Sukhothai.

King Ramkamheng is known for other achievements in addition to his military ones. He adopted and adapted the Khmer alphabet in 1283 for use by the Thai and thereby gave the Thai their first written language. Centuries later a stone pillar was found on which this great king had written a description of his country and his life. This pillar with its inscription is the earliest-known example of Thai writing and can be seen in the National Museum in Bangkok. It is believed to have been written in 1292.

The king also began a custom which continued, at least symbolically, into recent times. He had a bell set up outside his palace in Sukhothai. It could be rung by any person who had suffered a wrong or injury from someone else. When the bell was rung, the king answered and personally tended to the matter at hand and gave judgment. The custom faded gradually over later centuries, and an attempt to revive it in the nineteenth century failed either because of apathy on the part of the people or because they were too much in awe of royalty by that time to summon the king to attend personally to their problems.

With the death of King Ramkamheng in 1315, the kingdom of Sukhothai began to disintegrate. His successors were weak kings unable to hold together the expanded kingdom bequeathed to them by Ramkamheng the Great.

In the middle of the fourteenth century a prince of Utong, an area to the south and west of the Khmer city of Lovo (the present Thai city of Lopburi) near Supanburi, began to extend his control over some weaker parts of the Sukhothai kingdom. In a short time the prince of Utong took over Lopburi and other former Khmer areas which had been under the rule of Sukhothai. When an epidemic attacked his capital, the prince built a new capital for himself in 1350 farther to the south on the Chao Phya River. He named it Ayudhya after the mythical kingdom of Ayodhya in the Hindu epic, the *Ramayana*. He took for himself the title of Rama Tibodi I, the name by which he is known to history as the king of Ayudhya. He was the founder of a new Thai kingdom at Ayudhya which was to last for more than four centuries, until the Burmese captured and destroyed the capital city in 1767.

Within a few decades after establishing his new capital at Ayudhya, Rama Tibodi I forced Sukhothai itself, much weakened by then, to become his vassal state and eventually part of the more powerful Thai kingdom at Ayudhya. Thus ended the independence of the first Thai kingdom predecessor to the present kingdom. The remnants of its strength and glory can be seen by the visitor today only in the impressive ruins of the magnificent wats in old Sukhothai and in Ramkamheng's pillar in the National Museum.

8

Ayudhya

Although Sukhothai remained independent for some years after the prince of Utong established his new capital at Ayudhya, the focus of the development of the Thai kingdom shifted from Sukhothai to Ayudhya after 1350. From that year until the fall of Ayudhya to the Burmese 417 years later the kings of Ayudhya dominated a Thailand which expanded or contracted in size depending on the strengths and weaknesses of its immediate neighbors as well as on that of the central area of Ayudhya itself.

This relatively recent period of Thai history is far from being completely and accurately known due to the thorough destruction, as noted earlier, by the Burmese in 1767 of the Thai records and archives found in the captured capital of the Thai. Some of what is known was reconstructed early in the reigns of King Taksin and King Rama I while there were still persons alive who had lived and worked in Ayudhya. More was unearthed by later scholars working among Thai sources as well as sources in Burma and other neighboring areas in Asia.

The Ayudhya period in Thai history also saw the arrival and residence of the first Westerners in Thailand. Many of these Western visitors kept extensive diaries or wrote their memoirs which have added to the available information on the Ayudhya of the sixteenth and seventeenth centuries.

The Ayudhya period in Thai history was the third era and the second longest of four known general periods. It was the longest period of Thai history in the area that is now Thailand. The longest of the four periods, however, was the first, or Nanchao, era which extended roughly from A.D. 650 to the Mongol conquest in 1253. The second and shortest era was the Sukhothai from 1238 to 1350 or a few waning years thereafter. The third period is the Ayudhya, and the fourth is the Bangkok-Thonburi period from 1767 to the present.

More than thirty kings of several dynasties ruled during the period of Ayudhyan supremacy. As king of Ayudhya, the prince of Utong is known as Rama Tibodi I. In time, he extended his rule over most of the area under the control of Sukhothai and reached south all the way to Malacca deep in what today is Malaysia. Much of the Ayudhya period is devoted to struggles among the major kings of Southeast Asia for territorial control. The rivals included the kings of Ayudhya, Burma, and Cambodia with occasional strong intervention from rulers of the Lao states of Luang Prabang, Vientiane, and the descendants of the Chiengsen dynasty in Chiengmai, all to the north and northeast of Ayudhya. Sometimes Annam, farther to the east, and some of the southern states such as Nakornsrithammarat and Songkhla were strong enough to act independently to affect developments in the center of the Southeast Asian peninsula. The principal rivals through most of the period, however, were Ayudhya, Burma, and Cambodia. As often happens in history the center power geographically of the three, Ayudhya, found itself facing attacks on both sides. In an attempt to take advantage of Ayudhya's involvement on its western front, it was not unusual for Cambodia to attack Ayudhya in the east when the latter was engaged in war with Burma. The back and forth shifting of territorial control was to continue into the nineteenth century until Burma became a British colony and Cambodia lost its sovereignty to France.

Rama Tibodi I was known for more than his territorial expansion and consolidation. He is known today to the Thai as a great lawgiver, for within the first decade of his rule several major laws were published for his kingdom. Among these new laws were those on evidence, on offenses against the government, on abduction, and on relationships between husbands and wives, all given to the kingdom in the 1350's in considerable detail. For example, the law on evidence prohibited many persons from appearing in judgments to give evidence. Included among those prohibited were:

Infidels, debtors of the parties, slaves of the parties, diseased persons, children under seven, old persons over seventy, backbiters, covetous persons, professional dancers, beggars, homeless persons, the deaf, blind, prostitutes, pregnant women, hermaphrodites, impotent persons, sorcerers, witches, lunatics, quack doctors, fishermen, bootmakers, gamblers, thieves, criminals, and executioners.

In the first century of Ayudhya's prominence the Thai frequently engaged in skirmishes and wars with the Cambodian or Khmer empire which had its capital in the magnificent city of Angkor Thom with its enormous and beautiful temples and other structures, the most noted of which is Angkor Wat built by the Khmer King Suryavarman II in the first half of the twelfth century when the Khmers had one of the most powerful kingdoms in Southeast Asia. At the time this huge temple of Angkor Wat, covering with its surrounding lands and moats an area of approximately one square mile, was built, the Thai were still migrating in small numbers from southern China to the Sukhothai area, and an independent Sukhothai and the first Thai kingdom were still a century in the future.

By the end of the fourteenth century when Ayudhya and the Khmer empire were engaged in almost continuous wars, the Khmer empire was declining in strength and effectiveness. In 1393, the Thai successfully raided Angkor Thom and brought back to Ayudhya an estimated ninety thousand Cambodian prisoners, including government officials, dancers, and artisans of many crafts who, as slaves, made important contributions to the development of Ayudhya.

The Thai also brought back from Angkor new concepts of law and new ceremonies drawn from Brahmanical practices long observed in the Khmer empire. Among these practices were those that elevated the king to semi-divine status. In time, the Thai absorbed this concept of the god-king into their own system of kingship.

In 1430, the Thai under King Boromoraja II (1424–1448) were again pounding on the giant four-headed gates of Angkor Thom, capturing and sacking the city in 1431. The following year the Khmer decided to abandon Angkor Thom and to move their capital to a safer location farther away from the attacking Thai. Within a few years a new capital was built at Phnom Penh, the modern capital city of Cambodia.

The next major king of Ayudhya was King Trailok, who had a forty-year reign from 1448 to 1488. During the last part of his reign he moved the capital from Ayudhya to Pitsanuloke, but on his death his son, Boromoraja III, returned the capital to Ayudhya.

King Trailok made several innovations in his kingdom which were to set the pattern for Thai government administration throughout the rest of the Ayudhya period and into the Bangkok period right down into the reigns of King Chulalongkorn and his successors who reformed the Thai monarchy and government along Western European lines.

The land of the kingdom, which theoretically was all owned by the king, was divided among all free men of the kingdom according to rules set by the king based upon the individual's position in the kingdom and his value to the kingdom as understood and interpreted by the king. Each man received from twenty-five to ten thousand *rai* (ten to four thousand acres). He was expected to live off the income from this plot of land so that the system reflected not only his position and worth to the king, but determined his economic level in society. This system of grading all men and placing them in a definite position in relation to all others was called the *Sakdi Na*. A man's position in the Sakdi Na determined almost everything he did—his job, his responsibilities, his authority, his income, his rewards, even his fines and his punishments, if convicted of a crime. For the same crime, a man higher in rank with more resources would be expected to receive greater punishment than one at a lower level in the Sakdi Na system. This system continued until recent modern reforms were instituted in the nineteenth century.

Both slavery and the corvée system existed in ancient Thailand. All subjects were required to give a part of their time to military service and to other projects for the king. Slaves and aliens were exempt from this requirement. The amount of time in this corvée system varied at different periods of history, but was probably most often set at three months a year, although it was known to go higher.

The slaves in early Thai history were usually war captives such as the thousands of prisoners brought back from Cambodia. By the sixteenth century debt slavery was also allowed and a large percentage, sometimes as high as one-third, of the subjects in Ayudhya were slaves.

Slavery was a relatively mild institution in early Thailand, at least when compared to that which existed in the West, and volunteers to slavery were not infrequent. A man heavily in debt could volunteer to be a slave to a patron who would assume the debt in return for the slave's services. A slave was not subject to the corvée and slavery was sometimes used as means to avoid that kind of forced service. A slave could not be sold from one patron to another without the slave's consent, and his family, unlike the practice for slaves in the United States, was kept together. The institution of slavery existed in some vestigial forms until it was completely abolished by King Chulalongkorn in 1905.

King Trailok reorganized the government of his kingdom. Prior to his time the ministers were territorial ministers with both civil and military functions over a defined territory. King Trailok separated the civil and military administrations and set up five civil ministries. They were a Department of Interior, whose minister served as the prime minister, a Department of Local Government concerned with the governing of Ayudhya which had become a great city and city-state, and departments of the Treasury, Agriculture, and Royal Household. The last concerned itself with palace business and with justice. The Treasury Department was headed by an official with the title of Phra Klang who in time also handled matters of commerce and trade. This function, in turn, led him to concern himself with foreign visitors both from Asia and Europe, and in this way he took on the duties of a minister of foreign affairs in addition to his treasury duties.

Although it may have been known earlier, it was King Trailok who made the position of second king or uparaja, a formal institution in Ayudhya with the installation of his son as uparaja a few years before the king died. Probably the king took this action with the presumption that the uparaja would succeed him. While this may have been the initial presumption, it was not to be a binding one in the future.

King Trailok is also known for instituting the new palace law which governed the relationship of tributary states to Ayudhya and also determined the rights and duties of queens, princes, and other members of the royal household. Some of the punishments in the palace law were quite severe by present standards. For example, for shaking the king's boat the punishment was death; for whispering at a royal audience, death; for a palace official to allow stray animals in the palace, death, and the sentry on guard was to have his eyes put out; for introducing love poems into the palace, death; and for kicking the palace door, loss of a foot.

After a short reign by Trailok's son, another long reign began by a king who took the title of Rama Tibodi II (1491–1529). The second Rama Tibodi's reign is especially notable for the arrival of the first envoy to Ayudhya from a Western European nation.

At the beginning of the sixteenth century the viceroy of Portuguese India was Alfonso de Albuquerque. During the first decade of that century he raided and seized control of the Malay state of Malacca and there came in contact with the Thai, whose territory had reached that far south during the time of the first Ayudhyan king. In 1511, Albuquerque sent to Ayudhya an envoy, Duarte Fernandez, the first European known to call officially on the Thai king. For a long time the Portuguese were the only Europeans to have any official relations with the Thai. By the end of that century, however, the Thai had signed a treaty with the Spanish from Manila, and in subsequent years at the beginning of the next century, traders and mercenaries of the Dutch, French, and English joined the Portuguese and Spanish in Ayudhya. The Japanese, too, expanded their interests in the Thai kingdom at that time.

During most of these years wars continued to be fought among the princes of Southeast Asia over territorial issues, succession to vacant thrones, and other matters. Although the Cambodians had been roundly defeated in the fifteenth century, their defeat did not prevent them from later reorganizing their strength and attacking the Thai whenever they had the opportunity and the Thai were occupied with problems elsewhere. Conflicts leading to battles occurred periodically between the rulers of Ayudhya and those of the Lao kingdom of Chiengmai which often found its independence threatened either by Ayudhya or by Burma.

Although wars between Burma and Ayudhya had gone on from time to time, starting with the middle of the sixteenth century Burma became the most serious and persistent enemy the Thai had to face. Both sides were capable of throwing huge armies into the field; sometimes these armies involved more than a hundred thousand men on each side. Both sides won at one time or another, and both sides were decisively defeated at other times. Still the wars continued.

Sometimes the two countries fought over unusual demands. One of the best-known wars between the two was the war over white elephants in 1563–64. White elephants are held to be special animals in Buddhist countries for they allegedly represent one of the reincarnations of a future Buddha. All white, or albino elephants are the property of the king and if one is found, it is turned over to the king amid great festivities and the finder is honored and greatly rewarded. Finding a white elephant during a reign is considered to be great good luck for that particular king and his subjects.

In 1563, the king of Ayudhya, King Chakrapat at the time, had seven white elephants and the king of Burma demanded that two of them be turned over to him, for he had none. King Chakrapat refused and the war was on. The demand for the white elephants was probably only an excuse to renew hostilities, for the itching king of Burma was eager to avenge earlier defeats he had suffered at the hands of the Thai. In one of these earlier battles one of King Chakrapat's queens donned fighting clothes and rode into battle with her husband. She was astride an elephant and succeeded in placing herself between the king and one of his attackers in such a way that she took the heavy blow and sacrificed her life for the king, her husband. This warrior queen is one of the most revered heroines in Thai history. In the war of the white elephants in 1563, the Thai lost and the king of Burma took back to Burma four of Chakrapat's white elephants as prizes in the war.

In 1569, Burma attacked again and this time captured Ayudhya itself. This was the first time, but not the last, that the Thai were to surrender their capital city to the Burmese. After seizing the city, the Burmese destroyed all of Ayudhya's defenses, and for the next fifteen years the Thai capital, while remaining independent, was little more than an appendage of Burma. The conquerors introduced new laws based originally on an Indian legal system into Thailand which changed some of the legal bases of the government and which, in time, were largely absorbed into Thai law.

To guarantee peace in Ayudhya the Burmese put a vassal king on the throne and took a group of hostages back with them to Burma. Among these hostages was Prince Naresuan, a fourteen-year-old son of the vassal king, a son who was destined to play a decisive role in the Thai-Burma rivalry in the years ahead. Naresuan spent several years in the Burmese capital during which he learned all that he could about his captors, their military forces, and the Burmese princes who were likely to succeed to the Burmese throne. In time, Naresuan returned to Ayudhya, where his father appointed him to the post of second king.

During this period of weakness in Ayudhya, the Cambodians followed their usual pattern of attacking the Thai in an attempt to win back lost territory and authority. Prince Naresuan was sent against the Cambodians in a series of engagements and successfully defeated them. The time came in 1584 when Naresuan felt he was strong enough to act against the Burmese masters of the Thai and he declared Ayudhya once again independent of Burma. The Burmese immediately reacted by dispatching a series of armies against the forces of Naresuan (known to the Thai as the Black Prince) and his able younger brother (known as the White Prince) over the next three years, but the Thai were able to defeat the Burmese armies. The Thai kingdom was completely free from Burmese control by 1587.

Three years later Naresuan succeeded his father as king of Ayudhya and the Burmese attacked again with an army reported to have more than two hundred thousand men. Again the Burmese were defeated, but they did not give up easily. In 1592 came another attack on Thailand by the Burmese with a still larger army. Once more this huge Burmese force was routed. During this particular phase of these continuous wars, King Naresuan engaged the Burmese crown prince, whom Naresuan had known while a hostage many years before, in single combat on elephant back. The crown prince was killed. This famous battle of the king and the crown prince has frequently been depicted in Thai art and a statue of the king on his elephant stands in Supanburi Province northwest of Bangkok near the spot where the battle is supposed to have been fought.

By the end of 1593, King Naresuan had taken back from the Burmese the provinces of Tavoy and Tenasserim on the west coast of the Malay Peninsula. Today, these provinces are once more Burmese; they have often changed back and forth between the two countries for several centuries of their history. The following year (1594) King Naresuan turned his attention to Cambodia, which had been restless during the recent Thai-Burmese conflicts. Once more Naresuan invaded and defeated the Cambodians. It is easy to understand why King Naresuan is regarded as one of Thailand's most illustrious heroes. He died in 1605 and was succeeded by his brother, the White Prince, who became King Ekatotsarot.

Toward the end of the sixteenth century a treaty had been entered into between Ayudhya and the Spanish at Manila. In the first decade of the 1600's Ayudhya increased its contacts with the Portuguese, Spanish, and Japanese and signed an agreement with the Dutch. The Japanese had one especially unusual role in Ayudhya. A group of approximately six hundred Japanese mercenaries under the leadership of a man named Yamada was hired as a royal bodyguard. Yamada and his men soon became increasingly powerful in the palace and began playing a role in the process of selecting successors to the throne. Since Thailand had no automatic succession there were usually several potential candidates. In 1632, Yamada and his group interfered once too often and backed a candidate who lost. The new king seized and killed many of the Japanese troops and the rest were forcibly expelled from the kingdom. This incident seemed to have no adverse effects on the relations, mainly trading, between Thailand and Japan.

Throughout all these years and many before and after the Chinese, too, had been in Thailand. But the Chinese followed old habits of concerning themselves primarily with trade and shipping and did not interfere politically in the country's affairs as did these Japanese and later some European countries. Consequently, the Chinese were permitted to continue to trade and conduct business in Thailand when nationals of many other countries were not openly welcomed.

Through much of the first half of the seventeenth century Thailand was confronted with wars, one right after another, with Burma, Cambodia, Luang Prabang, Chiengmai, and some of the other smaller states around the fringes of the Ayudhyan domain. Some of the Thai vassal states farthest from Ayudhya also were difficult to control. Particularly in the South, Ayudhya faced revolts in such vassal states as Pattani and Nakornsrithammarat, old cities which themselves were major trading ports and once had been completely independent states. The revolts were put down and they remained Thai vassals. Through much of Thai history vassal states followed the custom of sending periodically to Ayudhya small gold and silver trees as a symbol of their allegiance to the suzerain state. Many of these trees, which are about two and a half feet tall, can be seen in several Thai museums and old palaces today.

In the second half of the seventeenth century a king named Narai came to the throne of Ayudhya by forceful seizure in 1657 and ruled until 1688. A few years after he began to rule, French Catholic missionaries arrived. Coming in 1662 they were not the first Catholic missionaries, for the Portuguese had sent missionaries as early as 1606. The Portuguese had had little success and did not energetically press their mission. The French Jesuits and the other French orders were something else altogether. More vigorous and more zealous and with the strong support of Louis XIV and the pope, the French missionaries were eager and determined to convert the Thai and especially King Narai. The missionaries worked on the assumption that the conversion of an absolute monarch would bring the mass conversion of his subjects. Thus, quietly, began one of the most bizarre and fascinating periods of Thai history and the history of the relationships between Thailand and the Western European nations.

Through much of the seventeenth century the Dutch traders going to Ayudhya had grown stronger and stronger until they had replaced the Portuguese as the most important European trading partner of the Thai. Although the Spanish and British also had trade agreements with the Thai, they did not become as important as the Dutch.

The British, in fact, who had started trading only a few years after the Dutch in the early part of the century, had withdrawn their representatives after only a few years and did not return to more active trading for several decades until after the middle of the century. The British, mainly interested in trade and profits rather than in conquest, were concentrating on trade with India where the East India Company held a monopoly.

With their increasing strength the Dutch decided to exert more power in Ayudhya and in 1664 they signed a treaty with King Narai which gave the Dutch the first extraterritorial privileges ever granted by the Thai. The treaty permitted the Dutch to take their citizens out of Thai court jurisdiction and submit them only to the jurisdiction of Dutch courts.

King Narai was becoming disillusioned and fearful of the growing power of the Dutch and began looking for offsetting power among other European nations interested in trading with the Thai. By this time the British had re-opened their trading stations in Ayudhya and King Narai began to give them more attention. The arrival of the French missionaries had introduced another group to Ayudhya and King Narai took a tolerant attitude toward them and what they were trying to do. He provided the missionaries with land and even helped them to build a church. This apparent encouragement by the king led the French to dream of the king's conversion as a possibility in the near future. Apparently, they could not understand the king's actions for what they were—his desire to find a European power to counterbalance the Dutch and the general tolerance which Buddhism has for all other religious beliefs. Tolerance of this kind was unknown to Christian and other Western Asian religions at that time which believed they had the only way to truth and salvation. Certainly Europe had suffered tremendously from religious intolerance and the confusion of the missionaries when confronted by Buddhism was understandable. This narrow outlook of the missionaries led them to misjudge the situation in Ayudhya at the time. The religious picture was further complicated by the presence of Persian ambassadors who hoped to convert King Narai and his subjects to the Muslim religion. The French missionaries heard a rumor that the king had said if he were to change his religion from Buddhism it would not be to Islam. Because of their own hopes and wishful thinking the missionaries interpreted this as a favorable sign that the king might be converted to Christianity.

While the British East India Company had a monopoly in India, it was often troubled by independent British traders referred to as interlopers. As long as the interlopers confined their endeavors to the Indian intercoastal trade the East India Company took little action, but the company tried seriously to prevent interlopers from engaging in Asian-European trade.

Among these interlopers in the local trade was a former employee of the British East India Company, George White. He traded along the Coromandel Coast of India and farther north. In 1675, George White transferred his base of operations from India to Ayudhya and within a short time, his brother, Samuel, also an able sea captain, joined him at the Thai capital.

The Malay Peninsular provinces under Ayudhya's control were especially important in Asian-European trade at that time. The various European, Arab, and Persian companies brought their goods to the west shores of the Peninsula where they were shipped across the narrow Peninsula overland to the Gulf of Thailand and up to Ayudhya by land or water. There they were exchanged for Asian goods brought that far by Chinese and Japanese merchants and traders. The route across the Peninsula was much shorter, faster, and safer than the long journey around the Peninsula through the pirate-infested waters of the Straits of Malacca and the other narrow strips of water around the tip. The trip from Madras to Ayudhya around the tip took about six months while the cross-peninsular route took only one to one and a half months.

The principal port of the Peninsula's west coast was Mergui in Tenasserim, the province that had been contested by both Ayudhya and Burma. From Mergui goods could be transshipped upriver a considerable distance before the overland trip began. King Narai engaged in this trade himself and had several vessels sailing from Mergui to India. Soon after Samuel White joined his brother in Ayudhya, King Narai hired Samuel as one of his ship's captains. Samuel did such a satisfactory job that within a short time he became the king's officer in charge of the port of Mergui and thus in a position to play a major role in the transpeninsular trade and enrich himself at the same time. Samuel White turned out to be an adventurer who, by cheating King Narai whenever he could, imperiled the position of his brother in Ayudhya and caused considerable trouble to the British East India Company at the same time.

Of more importance to Thai history in general, however, was the arrival on the scene in Ayudhya in 1678, of a young Greek adventurer, Constantine Phaulkon. Born in Greece with a family name of Gerakis (or Jerakis) meaning falcon, he had gone as a youth to England, where he became a sailor, changed his name a couple of times, and eventually rose to be a mate on a British East India Company ship. While in the company's employ he met George White and after a few years in company positions in various parts of Asia, Phaulkon arrived in Ayudhya as a company employee and renewed his acquaintance with White, who was an interloper or "free merchant" in Ayudhya.

With White's help and encouragement, Phaulkon left the company's service soon after arriving in Ayudhya and went to work as a clerk for the Phra Klang, the Thai minister of the treasury who was also responsible for foreign trade supervision. No doubt George White could see many business advantages to having a friend in the government's foreign trade section and his brother, Samuel, in charge of the principal trading port on the west coast of the Peninsula. Within two years the able Phaulkon had gained the respect and the strong support of the Phra Klang and the king and was named superintendent of foreign trade in the king's service. The British East India Company was unhappy with the rise of its former employees whom it regarded as increasing the trade competition on the peninsula trade route unfavorably for the British company.

Phaulkon was well aware of the king's growing fears of the power of the Dutch. At first Phaulkon thought his old employers might be able to offset the Dutch, but the British company was not interested in plans of its former employee and did not want to become involved in Thai politics in any way. Phaulkon and, therefore, the king turned to the French, and the French, in turn, immediately saw in this potential new Greek ally an instrument for speeding the conversion of King Narai. Phaulkon himself had been born a Catholic, been converted to Protestantism in England, and now had converted back to Catholicism under the guidance of the French missionaries. Phaulkon also had a more personal reason for becoming a Catholic again. He wanted to marry, and did, a Catholic girl who was half Japanese and half Portuguese.

With the support of King Narai and the Phra Klang, Phaulkon rose in power until he became the most powerful lord in King Narai's service. Phaulkon in less than five years had risen from clerk to a position comparable to that of prime minister in a country that was not his own. He was being courted by Thai and foreigner alike.

To improve his relations with France, King Narai sent an embassy to France in 1680. The Thai embassy was lost at sea, but the news did not reach the king for many, many months. In 1684, a second embassy was sent at Phaulkon's urging. The Thai ambassadors officially saw the French foreign minister and privately saw Louis XIV. With their exotic clothes and manners they made a great impression on the French court. In response, Louis XIV sent a French mission back to Ayudhya under the leadership of the Chevalier de Chaumont.

The interests of both sides in the negotiations were clear. King Narai and Phaulkon wanted an alliance against the Dutch. The French wanted to improve trade relations and to convert the Thai king as their price for an alliance. The French hoped to use Phaulkon to persuade the king to convert, and

Phaulkon, well aware of the Buddhist king's true feeling on the matter of conversion, resisted French pressure and would not bring the matter before the king. At the same time Phaulkon let the French believe he was acting on their behalf. Unfortunately, the Chevalier de Chaumont was a convert from the Protestant Huguenots and a religious zealot who would not budge on the alliance unless he first got a conversion. In the end a treaty was signed providing favorable treatment for the French missionaries and for the French East India Company, but without either an alliance or conversion. The French mission returned home.

Two years later in 1687, a second French mission arrived, but in the intervening two years signs of a weakening of Phaulkon's position were growing, although apparently neither Phaulkon nor the king interpreted them as such. Many Thai officials and nobles resented the power and influence over the king held by the young Greek, still under forty, who had come to be the principal adviser to King Narai. The king had built a new summer palace at Lopburi and Phaulkon had built a splendid mansion nearby equal to many of the greatest palaces in Europe in the splendor of its gilt-decorated interior.

Among the officials opposing Phaulkon was Luang Sorasak, who was especially incensed at the way in which the Greek flouted Thai traditions and by Phaulkon's inducement of some Buddhist monks to leave the monkhood to enter government service under Phaulkon's direction. This was viewed as an attempt to undermine Buddhism and added to the Thai suspicions that Phaulkon was working with the French to convert the king. At one point Luang Sorasak in his anger physically attacked Phaulkon. The Thai official fled, but later surrendered to the king. Luang Sorasak was punished only mildly because of his long and close friendship with the king and because of the importance of his family.

The Muslims in Ayudhya, too, were distressed by Phaulkon's role. They wanted the king converted to Islam, if to anything, and felt that Phaulkon was a serious obstacle. Among the foreign groups residing at Ayudhya at that time was a group of Muslim Macassars. They had fled from Macassar in the Celebes before the Dutch took control of the East Indies and had been given refuge in Ayudhya. They organized a plot to overthrow the king and replace him with a younger brother provided the brother became a Muslim. Just before the revolt was to start in 1686, one of the Macassars weakened and revealed the plot. Phaulkon took swift and bloody action to suppress the rebellion. Leading some of the king's forces himself, Phaulkon came close to being killed and took revenge by torturing the rebels who were not killed, and thereby increased the number of his enemies.

Thus, when the new French mission came in 1687, the situation had changed, at least beneath the surface. The French had sent six hundred soldiers along with the mission but a few more than a hundred had died along the way. They were led by a general, M. Des Farges, who planned to take both Bangkok, then a small village and fort site, and Mergui, the important port, by force, if the Thai did not grant him control of the towns voluntarily. Eventually, his forces were landed at Bangkok and occupied a fort on one bank of the Chao Phya River while the Thai remained in the fort on the opposite bank. A few French troops were sent to Mergui, also.

The French still had hopes of converting the king and of achieving both military and trading domination of the Thai. To win Phaulkon's support they brought him insignia of honors from Louis XIV and the pope. Phaulkon was made a knight of the Order of Saint Michel and a count of France. In less than ten years the Greek sailor on the payroll of the British East India Company had become first minister of an Asian kingdom and a count of France, who carried on correspondence with Europe's most powerful political and religious leaders. It is easy to understand why this young man might have thought he could accomplish anything to which he set his mind.

Despite their honors the French encountered great difficulties with Phaulkon. He wanted an alliance first, and only then would he bring the matter of conversion to the king's attention. At the same time, he discouraged the French from thinking they would ever succeed in converting Narai. The mission departed in 1688 having accomplished almost nothing. There was still no alliance and no conversion, but the French did have a treaty in which the Thai ceded all islands within ten miles of Mergui. If the French had occupied these islands in strength, they could have exercised effective control over whose ships used that major port.

When the French mission departed for home, the French troops under M. Des Farges stayed behind with their main body still stationed in Bangkok. Frequently drunk, they bullied and antagonized the people of the villages around Bangkok and made many enemies.

During the early months of 1688, King Narai was seriously ill at his palace in Lopburi. Thai officials began quietly to think about a successor. These Thai leaders had been upset by the attempts of the French to convert the king and to spread the Catholic religion. They were growing to hate the foreigner who held the powerful position of a minister of state, and they strongly opposed the presence of foreign troops stationed on Thai soil.

One of the major leaders of the Thai opposition to the Greek and his control of the government was an old enemy of Phaulkon's, Phra Petracha, who, against Phaulkon's interests, supported one of Narai's brothers as successor to the ailing king. Phaulkon was supporting a different candidate. To strengthen his hand Phaulkon sent a message to Des Farges in Bangkok to bring his French forces to Lopburi. Des Farges brought his men upriver as far as Ayudhya, where he spent a night and met two Frenchmen who advised him to turn back. For personal reasons these two French advisers to Des Farges disliked Phaulkon. One adviser was a not-too-honest respresentative of the French East India Company who feared the Greek because Phaulkon knew of his irregularities in handling company funds. The other was a French abbé who resented Jesuit influence on Phaulkon. Des Farges listened to their advice and turned back to his fortress in Bangkok. Again Phaulkon sent for him, but it was too late.

On May 18, 1688, Phra Petracha and his followers seized the king's palace in Lopburi and Phra Petracha began acting as regent in place of the ailing king. Without his foreign troops and the support of the king Phaulkon stood with his family alone in his mansion near the palace. He had time to escape, but to his credit, he remained loyal to the king and refused to flee. He was taken prisoner by Phra Petracha much to the satisfaction both of the Thai nobles and the Buddhist leaders. Phra Petracha also seized the king's two brothers and had them executed in the customary velvet sacks with the sandal-wood club beatings.

With the king and Phaulkon in his power and the king's brothers dead, it became obvious that Phra Petracha planned to make himself king. On June 5, 1688, Phaulkon, fallen even quicker than he had risen, was taken to a forest outside Lopburi and there executed, it is believed, by beheading and then hacked to pieces. He was not of royal blood despite his high rank so that it did not make any difference if his blood was spilled.

On July 11, 1688, the long-ill King Narai died and Phra Petracha proclaimed himself king. To legitimize his claim he promptly married the two surviving princesses of King Narai's family. Petracha named his son uparaja. That son was Luang Sorasak, the young man who had assaulted Phaulkon some years before.

The French troops tried to fight their way out of their Bangkok fort, but were held under seige. By November of that year the Thai permitted the French troops still under Des Farges' command to leave the country under the indignity of rented ships because none had been sent from France to take them home.

Phaulkon's Japanese-Portuguese widow was held captive for a while, but eventually was freed and employed by the new king. In time, she became superintendent of the royal kitchen. Phaulkon's infant son grew up and entered government service in Ayudhya. A grandson also served the government and was among those prisoners taken to Burma in 1767 when Ayudhya was destroyed. Later the grandson returned to Thailand, and there may be descendants of the Greek adventurer still living unknown in the country.

The immediate aftermath of this episode in Thai history was the first religious persecution seen in Thailand. Several French missionaries in the country were imprisoned, released, reimprisoned, and released again. But this action was probably more political than religious, because missionaries from other nations were not arrested. Within a year all the French missionaries were free again and religious freedom had been completely restored.

Of much longer range effect was the antiforeign suspicion that bloomed in Ayudhya after these events. Thai contacts with Europe, much like those of Japan, became severely limited, and full restoration of trade and diplomatic relations between Thailand and the West did not recur until the Chakri kings of the nineteenth century welcomed British, American, and other envoys.

Today a visit to Lopburi helps one recall the events of this strange period in Thai history. The ruins of King Narai's palace are still there. One can see the shell of the reception room where he received the envoys from France. A short distance away a marker points to the foundation stones of the room in which it is believed the king died. A newer pavilion built within the palace walls by King Mongkut is now used as a museum holding many Buddha images, votive tablets, and other items which the visitor will find of great beauty and interest. Not far away outside the walls of the palace, near the center of modern Lopburi, stand the crumbling remains of the magnificent mansion built by the Greek minister of state who had dominated Thai political life for almost a decade.

Lopburi has other ruins well worth a visit. These ruins date back long before the period when Lopburi was a summer capital for King Narai. Among the ruins two are especially well known. Near the railroad station stand three towers in the Khmer style of architecture reminding the viewer of the ancient kingdom of which this city was once a part. A short distance from these towers are the remains of an old chedi in a small park now inhabited by large numbers of playful, chattering monkeys and at times a few goats. The monkeys climb over everything, sometimes riding on the backs of the goats, and sometimes reaching into a man's pocket or a woman's handbag to grab what can be stolen.

The end of European interference in Thai life was not the end of Thai international relations, however. The Thai still were confronted by frequent wars with their neighbors over the usual problems of successions, territorial rights, and other related matters.

For a long period Burma was relatively quiet as far as the Thai were concerned. A series of clashes among the princes and rulers of Burmese provinces kept the country too weak to consider external aggression. By the middle of the eighteenth century new rulers had arisen to unify and strengthen Thailand's old enemy, and in 1759, the Burmese armies invaded Ayudhya's territory from the south, coming up the Malay Peninsula. At first the Burmese had several victories and reached Ayudhya to which they laid seige. The Burmese king, however, had been seriously injured and when he died his forces withdrew without taking the Thai capital.

A few years later, in 1763, the Burmese again struck at Ayudhyan vassal states and territory. The Burmese captured Chiengmai and followed that victory with a successful campaign against Luang Prabang at a time when Thailand had a relatively weak king. They followed their northern victories with another invasion of the southern peninsula area, and there they were stopped by an exceptionally able half-Chinese general commanding the Thai forces. His name was General Taksin, who was to become an outstanding Thai hero and a future king of the Thai.

Three years later, in 1766, the Burmese again invaded Thailand and reached the capital at Ayudhya, where they once more laid seige. Ayudhya, because of its islandlike character surrounded on all sides by rivers and klongs, was a difficult city to capture. The Burmese demanded unconditional surrender of the city, but the city refused and held out for more than a year. Finally, in April 1767, the city fell to the Burmese and the Burmese laid it waste. They plundered, burned, and destroyed the entire city and everything in it. Not even the Buddhist temples of Burma's own religion were immune to the destruction. Prisoners were taken by the thousands and many others were tortured and killed. The only purpose the Burmese seemed to have was to destroy Ayudhya, their old enemy which had so often defeated them, and to eliminate the Thai as a power in Southeast Asia.

Ayudhya was destroyed. A city which had at one time been larger than contemporary London was left in complete ruins. It was never to be restored to its earlier size and glory. Succeeding kings built their capitals in Thonburi and Bangkok. Ayudhya today is a small city, a provincial capital along the Chao Phya River. At one edge of it lie the ruins of the temples and the old palace, memorials to the important Thai kingdom that had its capital there for more than four hundred years.

Despite the destruction of the capital of Ayudhya, that kingdom left major imprints on Thai history. It was during that period that Thailand began to centralize and modernize its government administration with the shift from territorial ministers to functional ministers responsible directly to the king. In Ayudhya Thailand received its first delegations from European countries and extended its relations with China, Japan, India, Persia, and the Arab states of Western Asia. With the capture of Ayudhya by the Burmese in the sixteenth century, and even earlier and more importantly with the capture of Angkor Thom by the Thai, new concepts of law and legal practices were introduced to Thailand. The idea of the king-god which had been of major importance in the Khmer empire became a part of the Thai political and religious structure although modified in some ways to fit the Thai scene. The impact of this idea is still felt today even though the absolute monarchy no longer exists. Many of the royal ceremonies which add to the majesty of the Thai king are based on Brahmanic practices brought into Thailand from the Khmer empire and

other outside sources. Thus, much that occurred in Ayudhya shaped and continues to some extent to shape modern Thailand.

A trip down the Chao Phya River from Ayudhya to Bangkok can be one
of the most pleasant experiences a visitor to Thailand can have. The country
is flat in this area and one can see rice fields for great distances in all directions
either green with newly growing rice or golden with rice waiting to be har-
vested and threshed. Water buffalo with young boys crazily clinging to their
backs or lazily sleeping on the grazing animals can be seen everywhere. Perhaps a line of women shoulder to shoulder will be seen extended across a
klong near the river. Each woman grasps a woven basket held bottom up. As
the line of women moves slowly up the canal suddenly the baskets will be
thrust into the klong water to entrap a fish to be cooked and eaten with rice
that evening. Not far south of Ayudhya the river traveler comes to the island
of Bang-Pa-In, where King Chulalongkorn had a summer palace built on the
site of a much older palace. The summer palace is unusual in that each of its
several buildings is built in a different architectural style—European, Chinese,
Thai—and in the middle of a smooth pond stands an exquisite Thai-style
pavilion with many-colored, multiple roofs, and a graceful spire reflected in
the water which surrounds it. On a nearby island the king even had built a
Buddhist wat in the shape of a Christian church with a belfry and all.

Arriving by boat in Bangkok at dusk one has the city on his left and the
quiet lush tropical forest growth of Thonburi on his right. The river bustles
with heavy traffic from boats of all sizes, and the city sparkles with lights of
many colors. With Ayudhya forty miles upstream in ruins, the Burmese
thought the power of the Thai had been destroyed along with its capital, and
the conquerors returned to Burma. But General Taksin and his small band of
followers had other ideas. Within months they had resurrected the Thai kingdom and established a new capital at Thonburi. In one decade the political
power of the Thai was restored and under the series of kings who made Bangkok their capital and one of the great cities of Asia, the kingdom of Thailand
resumed its position as one of the major nations of Southeast Asia.

9

Chiengmai

Chiengmai seems to be everyone's favorite city in Thailand. No one asks a foreign visitor if he has seen Pitsanuloke or Srisaket or Yala, but everyone asks the visitor if he has been or is going to Chiengmai. Usually the questioner smiles broadly and a kind of misty longing appears in his eyes, especially if he is a Thai, even though he himself may never have seen Chiengmai. The name itself conjures up a kind of magical aura which makes the visitor ask what can be so special in Chiengmai. The answer he receives is a simple one which manages to embrace visions of Chiengmai's cool, invigorating climate, its beautiful girls, its slower pace of life, its Songkhran festival celebration, its elephants at work in the teak forests, its numerous craftsmen's industries, and its general sense of well-being and happy living. The visitor, if he has any time at all, soon feels it is absolutely necessary for him to visit this Northern city that calls forth so much praise.

Chiengmai, Thailand's second city, is located at the end of the Northern railroad line approximately five hundred miles north of Bangkok. In the most recent census, Chiengmai City had a little more than sixty-five thousand population in a large province of about three-quarters of a million people. Actually the population was larger, but the hill tribe people, of which there are many in Chiengmai Province, were not counted. At the present time the population of Chiengmai City is probably closer to a hundred thousand, which still leaves it substantially smaller than Thailand's one giant metropolis of Bangkok-Thonburi.

Located on the upper reaches of the Ping River, Chiengmai is situated in a beautiful valley surrounded by mountains. Because of its elevation, the city is generally cooler than the capital and at times is cool enough for sweaters and jackets and even fires in the fireplaces that decorate some of the mountain homes. On a clear day a visitor can see across the whole valley from the mountain, Doi Sutep, in whose shadow the city lies. The mountain is a place of special pilgrimage for Thai Buddhists because of its famous temple, and more recently all Thai have been attracted to the mountain because the king has built a holiday palace high up on the mountain above the temple.

Founded in its present location in 1296 by King Mengrai, Chiengmai is one of the oldest Northern kingdoms in Thailand. King Mengrai was a contemporary of King Ramkamheng of Sukhothai to the south. In fact, King Mengrai died in 1317, two years after the first great king of Sukhothai and of modern Thailand. Mengrai, the founder of Chiengmai, came from the family that ruled Chiengsen, an earlier kingdom still farther north, but a kingdom whose importance was soon overshadowed by the new state with its capital at Chiengmai. This state remained independent for almost five hundred years although during many long periods of those centuries it was vassal to one or another of its neighbors, including Ayudhya, Burma, and Luang Prabang.

King Mengrai's state was known in its early days as Lanna Thai and encompassed the area today included in the Thai provinces of Chiengmai, Lampang, Lampoon, and Chieng Rai, and the Burmese Shan state of Kengtung just north of the present Thai-Burma border of the provinces of Chiengmai and Chieng Rai. King Mengrai's successors for generations had wars with their neighbors over territory and over succession to the throne. Often potential candidates for the throne called upon neighboring Thai, Burmese, or Lao princes to support their candidacies and frequent battles were fought before one candidate succeeded in controlling the state. Whenever the Burmese attacked Ayudhya in the centuries of Burmese-Ayudhyan rivalry, they usually attacked Chiengmai as well and used the latter as a base in their wars with the Thai kingdom farther south. Thus, Chiengmai was captured by Burma and became a Burmese vassal in 1556 and again in 1762; both years were just shortly before Burma seized Ayudhya itself. In 1775, the forces of King Taksin took Chiengmai back from the Burmese and made it a part of the new Thai kingdom at Thonburi. Although subject to later pressure from the Burmese, Chiengmai has been a part of Thailand throughout the Chakri period. At first Chiengmai was in a kind of vassal status and continued to have its own princes to rule over it. In 1874, King Chulalongkorn sent a resident Thai commissioner to Chiengmai and the province became an integral part of the Thai kingdom, although it continued to have hereditary chiefs. The last of the rulers died in 1938, and under the constitutional monarchy in effect since then, no one has been named to succeed him. When King Taksin took Chiengmai his forces were assisted by those of the prince of Lampang under the leadership of one of the prince's sons. King Taksin made that son prince of Chiengmai and hereditary ruler. It was one of his descendants who held that title until thirty years ago.

Most visitors to Thailand think of Bangkok as a city of temples, which it is, but Chiengmai fits that description even more accurately. Bangkok, with its three or four hundred temples, is approximately twenty times the size of Chiengmai, yet the smaller city has almost half as many temples as Bangkok. In one area of the old city of Chiengmai, a little more than one square mile, there are forty Buddhist temples either still in use or whose ruins can be clearly seen.

Chiengmai is two cities in one. Some distance west of the Ping River is located the old capital city which was once surrounded by a thick wall and a moat. The moat is still there and in a few spots just inside the moat, sections of the old city wall can be seen. All around the old city, between its moat and the river, as well as across the river on the east bank, is located the newer city of Chiengmai with its rows of stores, its modern hotels and movie theaters and, of course, its modern fountain. The railroad terminus is east of the river and visitors, until recently, stayed at the old-fashioned Railway Hotel, which consisted of a wooden one-story building and several bungalows. The one-story building, where I stayed on my first visit to Chiengmai, had a few rooms on each side of an open veranda the center of which served as the dining room and lounge. Within the last five years the old hotel has been replaced by a beautiful, modern, six-story hotel on the same site, and two or three other new hotels have been built to accommodate the thousands of tourists and other visitors to this city.

Taxis and samlors are readily available to get around the city, but the old city of Chiengmai is small enough that one can easily walk to many of its main points of interest. As in most old Thai cities the principal sights are the ancient Buddhist temples, some of which in Chiengmai go back several hundred years in history and in construction.

The best known of Chiengmai's temples is Wat Phra Singh named for the Buddha image which it houses. This fine old temple located within the old city and dating back six hundred years or more has several buildings distributed around its large compound which is covered carefully with the fine, clean sand found in most temple compounds. The main Buddha image, the Phra Singh, is even older. The image was made in Ceylon and came from there in about the year 1300 although it is believed to have been made there several centuries earlier. Thailand has often turned to Ceylon on matters related to Theravada Buddhism and an image coming from that country is highly revered. There are two other Phra Singh images in Thailand. One is at the National Museum in Bangkok and one is at Wat Mahadhat in Nakornsrithammarat in the South of Thailand. Each possessor claims the original and asserts the others are copies. The image during its long life has moved from city to city and legend says that at one time it was on a ship that sank and the image miraculously floated to shore. Whatever the circumstances of its long history, the doubts about which of the three claimants has the original image have not yet been resolved to everyone's satisfaction.

Wat Phra Singh is important to the Sangha in two other special ways. It is the administrative headquarters for the Fifth Buddhist Region, and the wat has a school of higher Buddhist studies which attracts many young monks and novices.

Many of the trees in the compound of Wat Phra Singh have little signs tacked to them with short sayings painted on them in Thai and English. Several of the proverbs sound similar to those in the West, from which they may actually have been copied, while others are uniquely Thai and Buddhist. Among those I jotted down while strolling one time through the quiet temple grounds were the following:

"Barking dogs seldom bite."

"Fatigue is the best pillow."

"He that walketh with wise men shall be wise."

"Hope is the poor man's bread."

"To be conscious that you are ignorant is great step to knowledge."

"Courtesy costs nothing."

"By oneself is one purified, by oneself is one defiled."

The oldest temple in Chiengmai is Wat Chieng Mun built when the old city was founded by King Mengrai in 1296. It has been restored many times since it was first constructed. The gleaming white main building with its three-tiered roof has a broad portico across the front. The decorated front of this portico is intricately carved and painted in gold. The arches around the door and windows from the portico into the building are made of small bits of colored glass—blue, gold, green, maroon, and white. In the sunlight the bits of colored glass sparkle like mirrors reflecting many colored lights. Behind the vihara is a tall chedi on a base of carved elephants almost of life size.

A third temple of some note in the old city is Wat Chedi Luang. A visitor to this temple can see the ruins of an old chedi which at one time was almost three hundred feet high, one of the tallest chedi in Thailand. This temple is particularly notable because it housed the Emerald Buddha during a period of time some centuries ago before its removal to the more eastern Lao states and still later to Bangkok where it is now housed in its own temple in the Grand Palace.

The visitor can spend days visiting the temples of Chiengmai, but the one temple that everyone tries to see is Wat Phra Tatu, more frequently referred to by the name of the mountain on which it is located as Wat Doi Sutep. At one time the visitor could reach this lovely temple, standing at about the thirty-five-hundred-foot level on the mountain, only by walking. An automobile road was built about thirty or thirty-five years ago; it twists back and forth in sharp turns as it climbs up the mountain which overlooks the valley of the Ping River. From several points along the way one can stop and get magnificent views of Chiengmai and the valley in which it is located.

Legend has it that this wat on Doi Sutep was built in the fourteenth century when the king in Chiengmai at that time had received a relic of the Buddha. The king and his advisers could not decide where to build the temple to house the relic, so the king decided to let the relic make its own decision by using an elephant. One of the king's white elephants was chosen for the task and the relic was placed on its back. The king decided that wherever the elephant finally rested would be the spot where his new wat would be built. The elephant started at the west gate of the old city of Chiengmai, the gate closest to the mountains and Doi Sutep particularly. It started climbing Doi Sutep and finally stopped at the present site of the temple. The elephant refused to move any farther until the relic was removed from its back. The king built his new temple where the elephant had halted. Today there is a small statue of an elephant near the entrance to the temple to commemorate the beast that chose the site. For some unknown reason this statue is painted a loud, flat brown color, unlike any real elephant in appearance.

From the parking area to the temple itself is a stairway of more than three hundred steps. The balustrade on either side for the whole length of the stairs is the undulating body of the sacred seven-headed naga (snake) brightly decorated with bits of colored glass and colored stones. The heads of the snake are at the base of the stairs and the tail is at the top. The temple at the top with its carved and decorated doors and windows, its Buddha images, lacquer work, and gold chedi surrounded by umbrellas, small shrines, pillars, and other objects also carved and decorated in gold, is well worth the long climb. On cloudy days at the temple one can easily be cut off from the valley below.

Modern Chiengmai is known for more than its temples. It is also a city of good educational institutions. For approximately a century now Christian missionaries, both Protestants and Catholics, have been in Chiengmai, where they have built hospitals and excellent secondary schools for both boys and girls. The Thai government, too, has been active in education in Chiengmai beyond the ordinary schools found in most provinces. On the road to Doi Sutep one passes the new buildings of the Chiengmai Medical University, the only medical school in Thailand outside the Bangkok area. In June 1964 the University of Chiengmai, with faculties in science, social science, and the humanities, was opened, and this, too, was a first. Until that time all universities in Thailand were located in Bangkok. With the opening of the Chiengmai University the Thai government broke its traditions. It has since followed this new path by opening other universities in the Northeast and Southern regions as well. The campus of the University of Chiengmai has been well designed, and when it is completed it will be one of the most attractive campuses in all of Asia. On the same road one passes an older small zoo and a quiet, shady arboretum which is a delightful spot to pause and relax on the way to or from the wat on the mountain.

Chiengmai is also the center of many Thai handicraft industries. Within the city or nearby one can find houses clustered together in small groups where cotton and silk are woven, silver bowls and plates have complex designs pounded into them, bronze Buddhas and other temple decorations are cast, and lacquer boxes and bowls are carefully decorated with gold leaf. In still other clusters there are doll factories and woodcarving shops, pottery shops and paper umbrella factories. As the demand for these products increases, much of this work may be done by machine, but for the moment most of these industries are still small family enterprises in the back yards or in the open spaces under the houses on stilts.

Most of these village shops can be visited and the work seen at first hand. Several of the shops are located in the area just outside the southern moat of the old city. Here may be found the silver shops. Workers squatting on the dirt floors of the open shedlike areas behind the retail stores show the raw material from which the silver bowls are made. They use old rupee coins from British India and Burma. The coins are melted down over tiny, hot charcoal fires which are fed with air from a small bellows the workman pumps with his foot. The coins are made into round slugs or globs of silver. These globs are heated and pounded and heated and pounded thin and shaped by this process into bowls of various sizes. The silver is kept soft and pliable by heating and reheating over the charcoal fires. Once the bowls are shaped, they are filled with black tar or pitch and another worker pounds the intricate design into the silver with a hammer and small chisel-like tools which he can use to make the lines and the round dots of the design. When his work is finished the tar can be melted and run off, and the bowl polished.

At another workshop I visited, this time inside the old city, small bronze Buddhas and temple lions were being cast. The models were made of beeswax. They were then encased in a mixture of clay and straw to make the mold. The mold was heated and the wax ran out to be replaced by the molten metal poured in. After it had cooled and hardened the mold was removed, the rough edges of the image that had been cast were filed away, and the statue polished vigorously until it shone almost like gold. The whole process was handled by two or three men in one family working in the open back-yard area covered with a simple thatch roof to provide shade and coolness on the hot days and protection from the rain on wet days.

Near the silver shops are the lacquerware factories. Thai lacquerware is a very old craft going back several centuries. But the process has changed little and the use of the word factory is somewhat misleading. A factory is usually no more than a shed with perhaps a few rooms in which different parts of the total process are carried on by hand usually by women, although men may sometimes be found working in the factories, too. Chiengmai lacquer factories are justifiably proud of their work, for down through the centuries these factories have produced some of the most beautiful lacquer pieces in the country.

At one time lacquer work was used to decorate Thai palaces and temples. Such lacquer was made in panels for walls and for window shutters or as boxes used for the storage of manuscripts, wearing apparel, and other items. Bookcases were commonly made of lacquered wood. Many lacquer bookcases can be seen yet in temples throughout the country and in the National Museum in Bangkok, which has some fine examples on display. In Bangkok, too, at the Suan Pakkad Palace, open to the public on certain days only, is a whole library room with rare and beautiful walls of lacquer panels. The lacquer panels used in these bookcases and wall decorations usually show scenes of both real and mythical animals amidst heavy tropical foliage, or scenes from the *Ramakien*, similar to scenes in many Thai temples in their painted murals, depicted in gold leaf on a black lacquer background.

Today, most of the lacquerware made consists of smaller items—bowls, plates, vases, cigarette boxes, music boxes, and similar decorative pieces which are sold largely to the tourist trade. Their gold-leaf decorations still emphasize traditional Thai scenes and the heavy jungle foliage, typical of Thailand, is usually found in some part of the decoration.

Two kinds of lacquerware are currently manufactured. In one, the box or vase is cut from a piece of wood to which the black lacquer is applied in several layers and made smooth. In the second, bamboo strips are tightly woven into bowls and other objects to which the lacquer in many layers is then applied. Sometimes as many as fifteen or more layers of lacquer are needed on this woven bamboo to give it a smooth surface. The design in both cases is applied after the lacquer and is carefully put on the item with a small paintbrush. A slightly gummy paint, whitish-yellow in color, is put on the parts which are to remain black. Then the whole piece is covered with a thin layer of lacquer. On top of this thin layer of lacquer sheets of gold leaf are affixed to the whole area of the design and the bowl or other item is allowed to set for about twenty hours. At the end of that time, the piece is washed and the gold leaf attached to the gummy paint comes off with the paint leaving those areas black, and the other areas to which the leaf still adheres are gold. The hand painting of the design to leave certain areas black takes great skill and long training especially for the delicate foliage designs used in much of the lacquer work of the Thai.

Lacquer, of course, is a resin product of the Thai forests. But when one speaks of forest products in Thailand in general and in Chiengmai in particular, the one wood that comes to everyone's mind is teak. Along the highways and railroad of Northern Thailand mile after mile of logs waiting for transportation to the sawmills are stacked in a haphazard way on both sides of the road or tracks. Along the rivers of Thailand from the far north down to Bangkok itself can be seen the giant-size rafts of teakwood and sometimes bamboo and other woods which float down to sawmills in the capital city. On the boat trip, familiar to many tourists, to the floating market in Thonburi, the boats pass several small boatyards where the boats and barges to carry rice and other products on Thai rivers are being constructed of teakwood. Of great use inside the country, teakwood was also a major export, although its value as an export has slipped in recent years and been superseded by new agricultural products.

Teak trees do not grow in great forest clusters. Instead, they tend to grow singly or in small groups and, depending on the area of Northern Thailand, there may be only twenty-five to around 350 mature teak trees per square mile of forest. The trees grow in the lower levels of the mountains, and a tree takes about 150 years to reach the minimum legal size at which it can be cut in Thailand. The long growth period means that trees cannot be quickly replaced, and the Thai government has begun in recent years to exercise more strict controls over the cutting of teak trees. Still, illegal cutting is not unusual and there are frequent reported thefts of teak logs between the time they are cut and delivered to the sawmills.

All the teak forests are now legally under the control of the Thai government, but this is a development of the last couple of decades. Many years ago Lao princes across the northern area of Thailand cut teak regularly. They used the wood as decoration for their palaces and for Buddhist temples. In the 1880's the British, continuing their expansion of territorial control in Burma, conquered upper Burma with its teak forests, and teak became an important export from Burma to Europe. In time, teak lumbering companies expanded their operations to Thai forests, too, under concessions from the Thai king. At one time more than one hundred concessions in the Thai teak forests were held by Thai, Chinese, Burmese, and Europeans. The difficulty of access to the teak forests required heavy capital investment for equipment to get the cut trees out of the forests and to provide living quarters for the workers in the remote forest areas. These capital requirements forced many of the smaller companies to drop out of competition until finally the Thai teak concessions were held by eight large companies of British, Danish, French, and Chinese ownership. In 1955, all concessions were ended and the Thai government took control of the teak forests and teak lumbering.

The process of cutting teak is well set. A government agent selects the trees to be cut from those which have reached the legal minimum size. The trees are then girdled. A cut is made around the tree about two feet above ground. After it is girdled the tree stands for another two years until it dies by drying out. Only when it is dry is this extremely hard wood light enough to float. The dead trees are cut during the rainy season so that when they fall they will be cushioned on the soft earth and the dry hard wood will not splinter. Once felled they are cut into logs fifteen to thirty feet in length and hauled by elephants to the nearest waterway. Elephants cannot stand heat well and often suffer illness from sunstroke. Because of this the lumbering companies used to give the elephants the whole hot season off. In their place during the dry season, ox carts were used for the hauling. At one time thousands of elephants and their trainers were a major part of the heavy investment made by the foreign companies. Other means of transporting the heavy logs to waterways have been tried, but the elephant and the oxcart have been found still the best.

The logs are floated down the waterways during the high water season from June to October. At first the logs move singly until they get past any rapids in the streams and rivers. They are then formed into huge rafts. At especially difficult spots along the streams where the logs might jam elephants and men are stationed to keep the logs moving. Eventually the rafts move down the major rivers into the Chao Phya River itself. Shortly before that point they are checked and graded by government inspectors. Some logs may be sold along the way while others move farther downstream where the rafts wait in storage along the riverbank until they are taken to sawmills in Bangkok and other cities along the river. This difficult passage down the waterways from the time the tree is cut until it finally reaches its destination at a sawmill in Bangkok takes a long time; usually several years pass in the process of transportation. Some sawmills have been built in recent years in areas closer to the Northern forests and logs are now moved these shorter distances by train and truck as well as by water. Drivers in the North often encounter the great trucks hauling a load of two or three logs, and sometimes it needs only one of the huge teak logs to make a load for a truck.

Thai forests are rich in many products useful to the Thai people. Besides teak and resins they grow bamboo, rattan, other hardwoods, and many varieties of palm trees which can be used for food, fuel, and building materials of many kinds.

Driving north from Chiengmai with a Thai friend on one recent jeep trip we passed through a rich and varied agricultural area. Besides the rice which is grown almost everywhere in Thailand, we passed fields of soybeans, maize, and tobacco, and orchards of oranges and *lamyai,* that small fruit growing in bunches a little like grapes, but having a hard brown skin covering the sweet-tasting flesh inside.

A little more than thirty-eight miles north of Chiengmai on the road to Fang we turned off and stopped while a gateman came to open the gate that barred access to the side road on which we had turned. As we waited for the gate to be opened I could see banana trees on both sides of the road and beyond them, clinging precariously to the hillsides, were tea bushes. We were entering the experimental station area on Doi Chiengdao of the Hill Tribes Division of the Department of Public Welfare. On the property of the station a tea plantation is thriving.

The side road on which we entered the station was thickly covered with red dust and soon we were, too. I was glad that we were in a four-wheel-drive vehicle because no ordinary automobile or light truck could have made it along what I am generously calling a road. The jeep started up the mountain, doubling back on itself at each sharp horseshoe turn, sliding at times in the soft dusty surface of the road. From time to time a tree or a boulder which had fallen partly blocked our path and the jeep had to drive along the drop edge of the road where sometimes the road itself slipped away down the hillside under our wheels. After grinding our way five miles up the road we reached the station headquarters at an elevation between 4,500 and 4,600 feet. Here thirty to thirty-five persons, in what must be one of the loneliest and most remote government stations in the country, bring several specialties to their tasks for the Hill Tribes Division. Among these young government workers are specialists in agriculture, medicine, education, social welfare, and security, who try to keep track of nearby hill tribes and their needs. The station staff attempts to meet some of the tribes' basic wants as well as it can while at the same time encouraging experimentation with new methods and new ideas for the tribes themselves to meet their needs.

Down in the valley on the campus of the new University of Chiengmai is located the Hill Tribes Research Center of the Department of Public Welfare. At this center a small group of Thai and foreign scholars is trying to learn as much as it can with limited resources about the hill tribe peoples scattered throughout the mountains all across Northern Thailand and down its mountainous western border with Burma. The center has established a small museum in two parts at its base on the university grounds. In its main building is a collection of hill tribe costumes, jewelry, tools, and other artifacts, and in a large parklike area behind the main building are model houses, typical of the dwelling places of each of the six major hill tribes.

The Department of Public Welfare is not the only Thai government agency concerned with the hill tribes. A major agency working in this area is the Border Patrol Police, an organization with security and intelligence responsibilities in all Thai border areas and in some other remote districts of the mountains. In carrying out its responsibilities the Border Patrol Police has inaugurated a kind of community-development program among some of the hill tribe villages and has started schools for tribal children and training programs for young hill tribe leaders.

In addition to these two agencies, the provincial police, the Ministry of Education, the Ministry of Defense, the Ministry of Health, and the Department of Forestry all have special responsibilities of some kind toward these hill tribe peoples. Indeed, one of the problems of the Thai government in dealing with the hill tribes is its own administrative hodge-podge. Too many agencies are working independently on the same general problems with too little cooperation or even coordination. The result is that the limited resources available do not achieve all that they might if the programs were better organized across all the government agencies involved and if central, coordinated direction were given to the programs.

Who are these hill tribe peoples and why is so much attention being given to them? The hill tribes are non-Thai-speaking peoples who live generally in small villages in the mountains usually above an elevation of two thousand feet. (It should be quickly added that some individuals in these tribes have come into contact with the Thai and do learn to speak the Thai language in addition to their own hill tribe language.) The total number of persons in the hill tribes is unknown because they have not been counted in any census. Furthermore, most tribes move their villages every few years so that it is difficult to keep track of them. Many of the groups do not limit themselves to moving inside Thailand. In fact, the country of Thailand may be a concept of which they have little or no knowledge at all and national borders have no special meaning. Because many of the tribes are related to similar groups across the borders in Burma, Laos, and Yunnan Province in China and some to tribal groups as far away as Vietnam, it is not unusual to find tribal villages moving from one country to another. Despite the enormous difficulties in keeping track of the tribes, persons who have studied the hill tribes estimate that the total in Thailand is probably as high as three hundred thousand. Collectively, therefore, they are an important minority group.

If the different languages and dialects spoken are used to classify the hill tribes, there are probably twenty or more distinct tribal groups. Six of these are believed, however, to account for well over 80 percent of the total. These are the Karen, Meo, Yao, Lahu, Lisu, and Akha. The first two are much larger than the other four. Each group is distinctive not only in language, but in costume, the elevation at which it chooses to live, its religious beliefs (although most are animists), and in many other cultural features.

The main concerns about the hill tribes by the Thai government, as well as such international organizations as the United Nations and SEATO, are two. First, experience, especially in Laos and Vietnam, has shown that hill tribes can become an important part, either negative or positive, of any security plan or problem. In Laos there are Meo tribal soldiers on both sides of the political conflict. In recent years there have been government and newspaper reports in Thailand that Communist infiltrators from Laos have begun to work among Meo and other hill tribes in Thailand. Some Meo tribesmen in Pitsanuloke Province near Laos are said to have become part of Communist terrorist groups operating in that area. The extent to which hill tribes are or will become security problems in Thailand is not yet definitely known, but some attempt is being made to find out and to counter, not always successfully so far, any disaffection which may appear.

Secondly, while most of the hill tribe villages are small and much more primitive than the Thai villages, and most hill tribes cultivate crops needed primarily for their own subsistence, there is one cash crop of the hill tribes that causes much concern to the Thai and to international organizations. The hill tribes are opium growers and much of what they grow finds its way into the illegal international trade.

At more than one time in history the use of opium was legal in Thailand, as it was in much of Asia. Early Chakri kings tried to forbid its use and issued edicts banning it. But they were not completely successful due partly to the active promotion of its use by some Chinese and some European merchants. The Thai government again prohibited its use in 1959, and this time closed the Bangkok opium dens and took other steps to enforce the ban. Unfortunately, one of the results of making opium illegal has been to introduce refined and more dangerous forms of opium, such as heroin, into the illegal narcotic trade in Thailand.

The hill tribes practice slash-and-burn agriculture to grow the opium poppy. A small field, inaccessible to the Thai authorities, will be burned over and planted with poppies. After a few seasons and a few harvests the ground is often exhausted and the village moves to some other site where new fields are cleared by burning. Several Thai government agencies are seeking to find satisfactory cash crops to substitute for the opium. This is the reason for the agriculture experts at the experimental station on Doi Chiengdao. They are trying to demonstrate how tea and coffee can be profitable substitutes for opium. So far, none of the government agencies has had much success. Only a few of the hill tribe villages are making satisfactory progress toward new cash incomes by growing these and other agriculture crops.

The hill tribe peoples in Thailand today are relative newcomers to the country. Some have been there fifty or sixty years while others, it is believed, have come only in the last decade or so from troubled areas of Laos and Burma. Some of the hill tribes, such as the Meo, are part of a much larger society. The total number of Meo who live in several countries may reach as high as 5 million, and they have been a distinct nation known in Chinese history perhaps as far back as four thousand years. All the hill tribes are proud of their histories and cultures. While there has been some assimilation with the Thai by the tribes that generally live at lower elevations and come into contact with the Thai and whose men, in some instances, have worked for Thai mining and lumbering companies, most of the hill tribes tend to withdraw from too close contacts with the Thai people of the valleys. This separation is becoming increasingly difficult to maintain as pressure on the valley rice-growing lands increases and the Thai farmers are moving more and more often into higher elevations.

Not all the hill tribes can be traced back to the same origins. Some are believed to have come originally from Chinese areas. Others seem more closely related to the Mons and Khmers, and a few might be related to other Southern peoples such as those found in the Malay states and Indonesia. Tribal skin colors range from light to dark and other physical features also vary. Most of the hill tribes are animist and the belief in spirits determines the location of their villages and many other aspects of their daily lives. A few of the tribes have mixed Buddhism with their animism and a few have sprinkled in Christianity, also.

Although each tribe cannot be described here, two might be mentioned because of their special characteristics. One of these is the group called Haw. These are Chinese from Yunnan. Unlike the main body of Chinese in Thailand who live in the towns and cities and who generally came to Thailand originally by ship, these mountain Chinese came overland and continue to live in rural settlements. They are not true hill tribes in the sense that the Meo or Lahu are, however. Many of the Haw tribesmen lived on settled farms in Yunnan before they left China and now in Thailand engage in more advanced agriculture than the other hill tribes. The Haw are also active as traders in the mountains. Many of the Haw are newcomers who crossed the Chinese border into Laos and Thailand only after the Communists took control of mainland China in 1949. Some of these refugees are Chinese Muslims who fled before the religious persecution of the Chinese Communists.

At the time these Haw Chinese farmers fled Yunnan other Chinese were also fleeing from the Communists into Thailand and other Southeast Asian countries. Among these other Chinese were remnants of Nationalist Chinese armies. Some of these soldiers settled in the hills of Thailand and Burma and conducted raids on the Chinese mainland territory. When this warlike activity became more difficult they turned to the smuggling of opium. The Burmese felt these former troops were endangering their border areas and opening these areas to potential retaliatory raids by the Communist Chinese seeking to capture or suppress these former Nationalist troops. The Burmese brought the situation to the attention of the United Nations in the mid-

1950's. In time, it became an open secret that these troops were continuing to get supplies from the Nationalist forces in Taiwan and allegedly from American intelligence sources, too. Some of these Nationalist Chinese troops began interfering in Burmese internal affairs and fleeing to sanctuaries across the Thai border, which led to some antagonism between the two neighbors. Finally, at Burmese insistence and with United States help, thousands of these troops were repatriated to Taiwan, although it is known that small remnant groups of these troops are still in the northern hills of Thailand, Burma, and Laos.

A second, but smaller group of Chinese that fled Yunnan about the same time as the recent Haw arrivals, were bands of Chinese bandits driven out by the Communists. Little is known about these small groups but, like the Nationalist troops, these bandits sometimes pose as Haw and are confused with them. The legitimate Haw tribesmen are farmers and traders who have settled in the Northern mountains. Although many of them are strongly anti-Communist because of their own experiences in Communist China, their racial and cultural similarities to the Yunnanese Chinese Communists across the border open their ranks to infiltration without too much difficulty. In this way they may become a security problem for the Thai.

A second specific hill tribe group that might be mentioned is the mysterious people who call themselves Yumbri (or perhaps Mrabri, according to some recent investigations), but who are often better known by the romantic name of the Phi Tong Luang which means the "spirits of the yellow leaves." They are mysterious because it is still not known for certain that a genuinely distinct tribal group really exists or if they are an offshoot or an outcast group from some other tribal group or groups. Their romantic name has been given to them because of their living habits. They are foragers and hunters and are among the world's most primitive peoples. Their main concern is survival. They have no permanent villages. Instead, they travel in small groups, often with less than ten members, and build lean-tos in which they live until the leaves turn yellow, which may be within a few days after they are built. Thus the Phi Tong Luang are constantly roving and when their lean-tos of yellow leaves are found in the forests they have fled and only their spirits are around.

What little is known about these people comes mainly from other hill tribes and a few Westerners and Thai who have reported seeing small groups of the Phi Tong Luang. No Westerner was reported to have seen any member of the group before 1936, and since then only about a dozen Westerners have encountered either Yumbri or Mrabri people. The Phi Tong Luang have really trusted only the Meo, who have assisted them at times. Occasionally the "spirits" have been seen by the Lahu as well. A few Thai have also reported encountering the Yumbri or Mrabri but, like the meetings with Westerners, these encounters have been very infrequent and for short periods of time. The numbers of Phi Tong Luang must be very small, probably no more than one or two hundred. As they continue to retreat deeper and deeper into the mountain jungles, prey to the tigers and other vicious jungle animals, they may disappear altogether before anything is really learned about them. Perhaps one day the yellow leaves of the lean-tos and the spirits of the yellow leaves will all be gone from the mountains of Northern Thailand.

On a recent trip to Doi Chiengdao I visited a Lahu village. The village had simple thatch and wood houses at several levels on the mountainside and was similar in many ways to extremely poor Thai villages. This reflected the fact that these Lahu had come into contact with the Thai and were adopting some of the Thai village features. The houses, for example, were separated by bamboo fences in a manner similar to the Thai rather than to most mountain villages. The Lahu village had twenty-nine households, including two which were Lisu families who had recently joined the village. The total number of persons in the village was about 180. This village was on the land under the jurisdiction of the experimental station and, working with the staff of the station, the villagers were growing a small coffee crop at the edge of the villages. The Lahu village had twenty-nine households, including two which as the middle man.

A group of Lahu men and boys and girls gathered around the jeep, which seemed to fascinate them much more than the foreigner who had arrived in it. One man wearing the wide Chinese-style pants wrapped around him as many Thai wear them, and with his baby son slung on his back, spoke Thai to my companion and told him, in response to my question, that it was all right for me to take pictures. I immediately took one of a house, or what I thought was a house. I chose it because it had no fence around it, was a little separate from the others in an open area and, therefore, could be clearly photographed. A few minutes later—this was late Sunday afternoon—a steady stream of villagers, mainly women, but including some older men and several young men, came down the hill from the houses farther up the mountainside and entered the building which I had just photographed. I asked what the building was and was surprised to learn that it was a Christian church. This was one of the few hill tribe villages in this area which had been converted by missionaries many years earlier. No missionaries remained in the village, but Lahu leaders themselves now carried on the service each Sunday. The Lahu man explained this to my companion and then stopped a young man on his way to church and took from him a book which he showed to me. It was a New Testament. Although the Lahu have no written language of their own, they were using a missionary script with Romanized letters on a phonetic base. The book was as much a matter of interest to my Thai Buddhist companion as it was to me. A few minutes later we left the village and began the hazardous twisting descent down the mountain back to Chiengmai.

10

Nongkai

Rice farming, despite the promotion of agricultural diversification and industrial development, is still the base for the Thai economy. More than 10 million tons of rice are produced each year. Of the total production approximately nine-tenths is consumed locally and one-tenth is exported. One should not picture every Thai rice farmer producing a portion of his crop for export. Many Thai rice farmers are subsistence farmers in the sense of producing only enough rice for their own needs while relying upon secondary crops to provide what little cash income they receive each year. Most surplus rice for export is grown in the rich valley of the Chao Phya River of Central Thailand with much smaller amounts coming from the other regions of the country.

A trip by road or train from Bangkok to Nongkai, a small provincial capital on the Mekong River border with Laos and the terminus of the north branch of the Northeastern railroad line (a second branch terminates in the east at Ubol), takes the traveler through the richest and the poorest agricultural regions of Thailand, the Central Plain and the Northeastern Plateau respectively.

The average cash income of Thai farmers is quite low, but this does not adequately measure their real income for most Thai farmers are self-sufficient producers and worry little, if at all, about food (except in severe drought years), clothing, shelter, and other basic needs. Recently, of course, in many rural areas of Thailand, contacts with the cities, with foreign troops and other farangs, and with an increasing number of government teachers and officials have increased the demand for goods which cannot be produced on the farm. In such instances the farmers have come to desire larger cash incomes, and as these new desires spread wider in the country, there can be expected changes in the rural economy.

212

For the most part the present rural life and economy are closely tied, as they have been for generations, to the seasonal rice cycle. (Most of this discussion is applicable to all of Thailand except the Southern peninsula area which has different seasons.) Officially, the rice-growing season begins in May or early June with the coming of the rains after the long dry season. The actual date on which a farmer begins his first plowing may still be set by astrologers consulted to select an auspicious time which will insure a good crop.

The small rice field surrounded by low dikes to hold the water on the field is familiar to every visitor to Thailand and to many other countries in Asia. Usually one of these fields is selected by the farmer for a seedbed, and the farmer's rice seed preserved from the previous year's harvest is set out in this special field. While the rice plants are beginning to grow, the farmer's task is to prepare his remaining fields by plowing, weeding, repairing dikes, and in other ways seeing that his fields are ready for transplanting from his seedbed.

When the rice in the seedbed is about a foot and a half tall—or about a month to six weeks after the seeds have been planted—the rice plant is carefully removed from the seedbed, the excess dirt knocked off skillfully and delicately so as not to injure the plant, and the plants tied together with bamboo strips into small bundles. The bundles are heavy and they are transported by farm men carrying several bundles on a pole across the shoulder to the fields where the plants are again carefully, but with great speed and dexterity, transplanted in the water-covered field. (In some areas and in some fields the method of planting by broadcasting rice seed, eliminating the need for transplanting, is used.)

After the transplanting the farmer has a more relaxed period of his year until harvest time in November or December. There are many varieties of rice and each has a different growing cycle. The farmer may deliberately use different varieties in different fields so that his planting and harvesting schedules will be staggered. This relaxed period on the farm comes at the same time as Buddhist Lent and permits young men from the farms to enter the monastic order for Lent and still be available when they leave the monkhood three months later for service in rice harvesting and threshing. Threshing usually takes place in December and January. Often it is done by yoking oxen or buffalo together and tying them to a central pole in the threshing floor. As the animals walk in circles about the pole the grain is threshed beneath their hoofs.

Work in the rice fields calls for the participation of the farmer's entire family. Usually men, women, and children old enough to do the work all join together in the main field tasks. At the times of transplanting and harvesting many rural schools have vacations to permit the children to work with their parents in the fields. While most of the family is out, the older folk will stay at home to tend the children too young to be working or to take care of any marketing or other work which must be done around the home.

Thai farmhouses typically consist of a large room which usually has an open veranda, and a few small rooms which are used for bedrooms. At one time the farmer built his house of teak, but where teak nowadays is often too expensive, farmhouses may be built of bamboo, woven palm mats, thatch, or a combination of several materials. The houses are ordinarily built on stilts high enough so that a man can stand under the house. The lower open level has many uses. One of the main reasons for building a house on stilts is to prevent it from being flooded when the rice fields are inundated. But building houses in this manner also permits the lower ground level under the floor to be used to shelter chickens, pigs, buffalo, oxen, ducks, and other farm animals. Thai houses in the country as well as in the city are kept clean, and it is easy to sweep the dirt through cracks in the floor to the ground below. Even food scraps can be disposed of this way to be eaten by the chickens and other animals. Building the houses on stilts also reduces the menace of snakes getting into the living quarters.

Farmhouses are usually sparsely furnished. The clean floors provide both sitting and eating space. There may be a table and a few chairs as found in Bangkok houses. Often, however, the furnishings are limited to a low table, a stove, some pots and pans, including a large jar which is used to store water for bathing and drinking, some storage chests and baskets, and mats or mattresses for sleeping. Again, these furnishing arrangements are changing and farmhouses near the cities and towns are being furnished more like their urban neighbors.

Thai farm families are usually small rather than the large extended families found in many other countries. The family ordinarily consists of the husband, wife, and unmarried children, and perhaps one married son or daughter who in time will take care of the aging parents and probably inherit the household compound. Other children will set up separate homes when they get married.

The typical farm day begins at dawn when the wife rises, starts a fire, and cooks rice to give to the monks. The presentation of rice or fruit or flowers to the monks is made about six o'clock. Then she begins to prepare the food for the family. At the same time the husband and the children are rising, bathing, and getting ready for the day's activities. The first family meal comes about seven or seven thirty. Although the family unit is relatively small, it is a strong unit and a farm family ordinarily works and eats together as a unit. There is little difference in the food served at each meal. It usually consists of rice and vegetables and fish served with hot sauces, fish sauce, or in curries. Sometimes, especially at breakfast, the rice is made into a tasty, thick soup, and on special days the curries may be made of meat or poultry in addition to or instead of fish.

Outside many farmhouses built along a klong can be seen a long pole weighted down at the end on the klong bank. A few feet from the weighted end the pole rests on a short pillar stuck in the ground; the pillar acts as a fulcrum. At the other end of the long pole extended over the water are two shorter crossed poles fastened to the tip of the long pole. The four ends of the cross poles form the corners of a square. To these cross poles is tied a fish net which can be dipped into the klong by raising the weighted end on shore and lowering the net end. Most Thai farm families catch their own fish and this is one of several common methods.

After breakfast each member of the family begins his day's work. If it is one of those times when the whole family is not needed to work in the fields, only the man may go to the fields while the woman cleans the house or goes to the market and the children go to school. Not every Thai village has a market. Many villages are too small and the villager must go to a nearby provincial capital or other market town. The morning market is one of the busiest and most exciting times of the day and provides a chance, while shopping, to see one's friends and neighbors and exchange gossip.

I once stayed in a country hotel overlooking a market and was awakened at four thirty in the morning when the first vendors, the butchers, arrived and began chopping and cleaving their meat on the heavy blocks. By five thirty the earliest customers were beginning to appear and by eight the market was crowded with customers seeking the day's food supplies. Beside the butchers with their muddy red and fatty meat were the rice merchants with several different grades of rice stacked in great open bags for all to see. Nearby were the sellers of spices and cooking sauces with many varieties of peppers. A little boy played with his toy soldiers in a big bag of green peppers. Fish in many forms and varieties were for sale. There were dried fish and fish pastes and fresh fish. The last were sold from concrete stalls at floor level. The concrete floor was covered with a couple inches of water in which the live fish lay surrounding their seller who stood or squatted barefoot in the middle of the pool. All around her (for most vendors are women) were big fish, little fish, prawns, eels, squid, and sea creatures I could not identify, all waiting to be mixed in someone's curry.

Large sections of the market were used to display the fruits and vegetables which are a part of the Thai diet. Most of the food part of the market was in an area of covered stalls, counters, and fish pools crowded together under the great roof of a large shed. Even so, this covered area was insufficient space and the market spilled over into the street around it where one could find clothes, shoes, jewelry, trinkets, stationery, cosmetics, and drugs for sale in numerous stalls shaded by flimsy cloth awnings. Nearby could also be found many of the more permanent stores usually including a row of Indian cloth merchants.

Returning from the market the farm woman may prepare a midday meal after which the family will probably rest during the intense heat of early afternoon. Sometimes there is no midday meal because the family prefers to replace it with a series of snacks eaten by each individual whenever he feels hungry. The final meal is eaten early in the evening after the work of the day is done, the animals fed, and everyone has bathed again. In the period following the meal the family may sit around and chat among themselves or visit with neighbors. They usually go to bed soon after dark especially in the areas without electricity.

There are many variations of this typical day. Visits may be made to the temple on some days. Wat fairs enliven many a rural evening. Radios or visiting theater groups can alter the usual patterns or the return of a traveler (and young Thai men delight in traveling around the country before settling down to marriage and a family) with many tales to relate may add a special fillip to a routine visit with a neighbor. In recent years, motion picture theaters have been opened in many larger towns and rural folk from all the villages within walking or bicycling distance find their way to these entertainments from time to time.

Rural Thai villages are usually found physically organized in one of two ways. They may be spread out in a long line or two along one or both sides of a river or klong or highway or they may be clustered together compactly surrounded by the fields owned and farmed by the villagers. A farmer's fields are not necessarily contiguous to his house compound or to each other, so that he may own fields in several different locations at some distance from his house. These fields may be far enough apart and have sufficiently different soil and water conditions that he will plant different varieties of rice in them to get the best possible harvest. Only in a few sections of Thailand, mainly in the Central Plain near Bangkok, do you find the isolated farmhouse surrounded by its own fields.

Within each village certain work is done cooperatively. The particular groupings, however, may differ from task to task. Within the rice-growing cycle transplanting and harvesting are done by groups larger than a family and on a reciprocal basis. There are tasks assigned to the village as a whole which are also shared among all the villagers. The whole village is responsible for the upkeep of the wats, schools, roads, and the important irrigation system, where there is one, except for those major highways, canals, and higher schools which are maintained by the central or provincial government.

At the head of each village is a headman selected by the villagers. Women take an active, equal, and independent part in village life and make important contributions to village decision-making. The headman often shares his village leadership with resident monks at the village wat, if there is one, and with the village schoolteacher. The teacher and the monks are usually the best-educated persons, in the sense of formal education, in the village. Although the headman is often one of the wealthier farmers in the village, wealth *per se* has little to do with the individual prestige on which any person's social position is based. Once outside the major cities with their official hierarchies and away from such established institutions as royalty or military leadership, there is almost no sense of class as the basis for individual prestige. Prestige is based on the individual's merit which, in turn, is based on such factors as age, sex, whether or not a man has been a monk, and any special talents (for example, in farming or healing or astrology) that a man may demonstrate. An older poor man who has been a monk will usually be held in higher respect than one of similar age, who has never served in the Sangha and whose main claim to leadership is based on wealth. With many factors contributing to the estimation of one's worth, the social structure of leadership in the village is a fairly flexible one.

While rice continues to be the most important farm crop, many others are grown for use and sale. Maize, kenaf and jute, and cassava (tapioca) are all important exports along with rice and rubber, but other crops such as peanuts, sesamum, soybeans, coffee, sugar cane, tobacco, cotton, peppers, and a little tea are grown for domestic use. One of the most useful of all tree crops is the coconut palm. The nut is used for food, milk drink, oil, fuel, cattle feed, vinegar, and fermented drinks, and the leaves and branches are used for containers, thatch, and fiber for building. Thai fruits, as anyone who has eaten them will report, are among the sweetest and tastiest in the world. They include bananas of many varieties served in many forms, papaya, pineapple, mango, lamyai, pomelo and other citrus fruits, mangosteen, watermelon, custard apple, durian, and many others.

The most valuable animal for the farmer is the buffalo which can be found all over the rice country tended by young boys in the farmer's family who sit or sleep astride the animal's back. The great strength of the buffalo makes it an ideal animal for working in the heavy mud of the water-covered rice fields. Oxen, too, are important, but more as animals for transportation, pulling carts along the dry roads. Oxen do not have the strength of the buffalo to do the heavy work in the mud.

The work animal of the forests is the elephant. But upcountry rural Thailand has many animals which are less friendly toward the farmer. Among them are the tiger, leopard, black panther, Himalayan black bear, and wild pigs. Many kinds of monkeys and gibbons are also found. At one time Southern Thailand was the home of both one- and two-horned rhinoceroses, but they are believed to be close to extinction. They have been killed for their horns which, when powdered, are used for aphrodisiacs and in Chinese medicines.

Most visitors to Thailand soon become familiar with the tiny rubbery-looking lizard that is found in all houses and buildings. This little fellow, who is a great help to humans because he consumes great quantities of mosquitoes and other insects, is one of more than three-score varieties of lizards known to live in the country. One ugly-looking lizard about a foot and a half long is called a *gecko* after the sound he makes. This lizard lives in the rafters of many houses and is rarely seen, but is usually heard every evening. He is supposed to bring good luck to the house in which he lives. I was told that if a gecko says his name seven times in a row without interruption that will bring especially good luck to the householder. I had a gecko living in my house and though I heard him almost every night, he never said gecko more than six times without interruption. Yet, every time I heard him I found myself stopping whatever I was doing and automatically counting—hoping he would go to seven.

Other reptiles common to Thailand include the deadly king cobra, the regular and equally deadly ordinary cobra, several kinds of vipers, and several varieties of poisonous sea snakes. After every heavy rain in Bangkok when I lived there, I would see one or two six-foot-long snakes stretched out on the lane between my apartment house and the main street. Thailand also has the huge pythons which stretch out to twenty or thirty feet, but I never saw any except in the zoo. In some of the rivers of Thailand crocodiles can also be found.

Many varieties of fresh and salt-water fish are found in Thai waters. Among the more unusual ones is a climbing perch which is able to move about on dry land, and another variety of perch which is able to adjust to the drying ponds of the hot season by burying itself in the mud in a kind of hibernation. Some Thai fish in fresh waters grow to unusually large sizes. Carp have been known to grow up to six feet, and the largest fresh-water fish in the world, called in Thai *pla buk*, grows to ten feet long and is found mainly in the Mekong River and some of its tributaries.

Of the many birds found in Thailand I will mention only one which is prized for its contribution to gourmet meals. The bird is a kind of swift which builds its nest on cliffs mainly on islands in the Bay of Bandon section of the Gulf of Thailand. The nests are made with bird saliva containing a kind of gelatinlike material to hold the nests together. These nests are gathered from the high, steep cliffs at considerable danger to the gatherers.

Once cleaned they are made into birds' nest soup, which is a delicacy on the menus of Chinese restaurants in Bangkok and other Asian cities.

Almost midway between Bangkok and Nongkai beyond the city of Khorat, but still within that province, is the town of Pimai which merits a visit by any traveler by car to Northeastern Thailand. In Pimai are the ruins of a large temple which is slowly being restored by the Thai government. The temple is one of the largest Khmer-style temples so far found to have been built in Thailand. Apparently erected a few years or at most a few decades before the great temple at Angkor Wat in Cambodia, the similarity in architecture is remarkable and obvious. It is part of that chain of Khmer ruins scattered across Thailand which can be seen in Sukhothai, Lopburi, and other provinces as well as in Pimai and which date back eight hundred to a thousand years. Pimai is almost two hundred miles from Bangkok, but the whole distance is now served by a paved road and is well worth the trip for any visitor who is interested in a fascinating major example of the work and art of a former civilization which produced some of the greatest stone artists the world has ever known.

The river port of Nongkai at the north end of the railway line is the port of exit for travelers going from Thailand to Vientiane, the capital of Laos, on the other side of the Mekong River and upstream about fifteen miles. Nongkai is a sleepy little town built along three roads parallel to the river. (The road right on the riverbank has been washed away in places leaving only two roads that run the full length of the town.) It is a long, narrow town with few trucks or automobiles on the streets. The main means of transportation is the bicycle in one form or another. Besides the ordinary two-wheel bicycles, there are samlors, three-wheel push-type delivery wagons, three-wheel pull-type wagons, motorcycles, and motorscooters, all of which dodge in and around each other and apparently rarely collide.

The Mekong River at Nongkai is almost a kilometer wide. In the dry season the town sits high up above the river because the level of the river rises and falls about forty feet depending on the time of the year bringing the rainy or dry season. One evening a Thai friend took me for refreshment to a restaurant built on a large, handsome barge anchored to the river's shore beneath the town. The barge, I was told, had been used for ceremonies when the kings of Thailand and Laos met in the middle of the Mekong to inaugurate a new flow of electricity from Thailand to Laos. Darkness came soon after we were seated at a table at the river edge of the dimly lighted barge. Above us were the lights of Nongkai and across the river were fewer lights from a Lao town and from vehicles on the road to Vientiane. Only one other table was occupied and the evening blackness seemed thick with silence. We heard a slow, gruff chugging approaching and out of the blackness emerged a large white river boat only about fifteen feet away. When it passed we could read the words "United Nations" painted on the stern.

One of the largest and most dramatic of all the development projects sponsored by the United Nations and supported by many governments, international organizations, and private agencies is the multifaceted project for developing the Mekong River Basin. In 1957, the UN Economic Commission for Asia and the Far East (ECAFE), which has its headquarters in Bangkok, established a Committee for the Coordination of Investigations of the Lower Mekong Basin. The area within the committee's interest is that part of the Mekong basin below the point where the river turns away from the Burmese-Lao border to flow through Laos, along the Thai-Lao border, and through Cambodia and South Vietnam. Thailand, Laos, Cambodia, and South Vietnam are the four state members of the committee, and the most remarkable aspect of the project is that the four have continued to cooperate in the committee despite their political differences over the years and despite the unsettled conditions and fighting in much of the region.

The committee's first task was to investigate the potential for development of the river basin. For several years studies of many kinds were undertaken of the river and of the lands bordering it. Some of these studies still are in progress and new ones are regularly being started as needed. As a result of the preliminary studies it was found that the river could be used economically for irrigation, for navigation, for flood control, for power, and probably for other purposes, too, if it were properly developed. It was also found that the most effective, efficient, and economic way to develop the river and its basin would be through cooperative efforts on a regional basis. A piecemeal project approach or a one-country approach would not be able to achieve the same results at any cost as would a coordinated, well-planned project or series of projects for the whole region.

The coordinated approach was accepted by the committee members, and from the first general studies the committee turned its attention to more detailed studies of specific areas and specific projects. As these studies are being completed, the committee has moved its efforts into the construction stage. The first dams and electric plants have been built and more are under construction. There is still much to be done over many years ahead, for this was planned as a long-range project, but when finished it will harness the resources of one of the world's great rivers for the benefit of several nations.

The success of the Mekong development projects will contribute enormously to the development and well-being of Thailand's poorest region, the Northeast. While the area has soil less rich than Central Thailand, it mainly lacks enough water at the right time to make it a rich rice-producing area or to permit it to grow other agricultural crops profitably. Rice growing requires about seventy inches of rain a year, and the Northeast averages less than forty inches. The Central Plain does not get seventy inches either, but it does receive more than the Northeast, and the plains make up the difference needed through an extensive system of irrigation canals which have been built over many decades. With the completion of the Mekong system water for irrigation and new power will be available for the Northeast region. Even the small dam projects already completed have brought new irrigation to some acres and new power available to some areas.

The matter of developing the Northeast takes on added importance in light of the security factor which has become increasingly sensitive in the last fifteen years since the Geneva Conference of 1954 granted independence to the former French states of Indo-China. Since then there have been continuing efforts by Communist forces supported from Laos, North Vietnam, and China to stir up discontent among the Thai villagers of the Northeast, who are often remote and sometimes isolated from the mainstream of Thai society represented by Central Thailand and symbolized by metropolitan Bangkok. In circumstances of this kind, the villagers' loyalty is usually first of all to their local community. If their loyalty extends beyond the village, it is to the region in which their village is located, and only in some vague distant manner is there apt to be loyalty to the Thai nation as a whole.

Recognizing this situation and the fact that the overwhelming majority of Northeasterners are Thai-Lao ethnically and a minority are Thai-Khmer, the Communists have tried to destroy any inchoate loyalties the Northeasterners have to Thailand and to redirect them to Laos. They have had little success so far in directing these loyalties to Laos in general or more specifically to the Communist cause represented by the Pathet Lao. Although supplied with propaganda as well as weapons and equipment from across the Mekong and using terrorist tactics in some villages similar to those in Vietnam in the early stages of that conflict, the Communists have won few dedicated supporters. At the beginning of the 1970's, the number was estimated by different sources at fifteen hundred to two thousand in a population in the Northeast of about 10 million.

One of the specific problems Thailand inherited from the French Indo-Chinese war is a group of Vietnamese refugees living in the Northeast. Most of these refugees fled from the French during the period of 1947–54, and many are from North Vietnam. In 1961, the Thai and the North Vietnamese reached an agreement in Rangoon, Burma, negotiated under the auspices of the International Red Cross, for the repatriation of these refugees at the rate of approximately a thousand a month. They were to travel in Polish ships from Thailand to Hanoi. At that time the number of refugees was estimated at around forty to fifty thousand. About thirty thousand had been returned by 1964, when the repatriation was discontinued after the United States began attacking ships in the Gulf of Tonkin off North Vietnam. The Thai meanwhile had found out there were many more refugees than originally estimated. In 1969, there were still estimated to be forty-five thousand in Thailand.

Among that number were reported to be some who had been repatriated and found their way back overland from North Vietnam across Laos to Thailand. The chances are very great that these returnees are Communist agents sent to keep the refugees in line and under observation. Although many of the refugees have fared well economically both as farmers and as merchants, they have made almost no effort to become a part of regular Thai society despite the fact that some have lived in Thailand for twenty years or longer. They remain separate and most of them steadily insist they intend to return to North Vietnam. The *New York Times* reported in March 1969 that out of eight thousand Vietnamese refugees in the province of Nongkai, only two have adopted Thai nationality. Watched carefully by agents of North Vietnam, the refugee group constitutes a potentially dangerous security risk. Perhaps when a Vietnamese peace treaty is negotiated or maybe even before then some action can be started again to resume the repatriation of the remaining refugees from the Northeast of Thailand to North Vietnam. Two factors that may slow this process can be noted, however. Despite what they say, many of the refugees probably do not really want to return to North Vietnam. They are living well in Thailand and do not want to give up their advantages, including financial ones, to go back to a Communist nation. At the same time they do not want to accept the obligations of full Thai citizenship, and so they face a dilemma. The second factor is the very real possibility that North Vietnam, if it is planning further aggression in Southeast Asia and specifically against Thailand, would find it useful to have a potential "fifth column" group inside Thailand. The Communists may not be in any hurry, therefore, to repatriate these refugees as long as their agents can keep them under control.

Among the Thai-Lao leaders of the Northeast there are probably some who foresee an upheaval which would not be Communist dominated. Instead it would be an uprising of the poor of the Northeast who would attempt to join with their brethren in Laos to form a greater Lao state which would be independent of Thai or Vietnamese control. Some Westerners have talked of this possibility in the sense that they speak of an irredentist movement among the Thai-Malay in the South. The two situations are in no way similar. In the South, a Thai-Malay minority proposes to join a larger Malay group in a well-organized nation although Malaysia is faced with major ethnic problems of its own. In the Northeast, the Thai-Lao are a much greater number than the Lao-Lao. For the Thai-Lao to join an independent Laos does not appear to be a real political alternative as does the possibility of Thai-Malays joining an independent Malaysia. For the Thai-Lao to switch loyalty, weak as it may seem to some, from the king of Thailand to the king of Laos, who for many Lao is really only king of Luang Prabang, one of several historical Lao states and one which for centuries before French intervention was frequently subordinate and tributary to the king of Thailand, does not seem to be highly probable.

The Thai government seems finally to have recognized the problems it faces in a poor region with weak loyalties in remote areas and subject to propaganda and pressures and promises from both internal dissidents (and such do exist quite independent of the Communists) and external trouble-makers. We have noted the development steps to build dams and irrigate the Northeast as part of the Mekong development projects. Other steps have been taken, too, to develop the area economically. Perhaps one of the most important is the building of improved main roads and more access roads to extend communications between Central Thailand and the Northeast as well as to provide transportation routes for any products the farmers might now or in the future have to sell.

Ten years ago even the main roads were rough laterite roads often compared to the old-fashioned washboard ridges. Driving over them the traveler had two choices—drive slowly and try to ease over the ridges or drive as fast as possible and still hold on to the steering wheel in hopes of missing a few ridges and flying over the rest. Bridges were rough planks and logs laid over streams and klongs. Today the main highways to all regions are paved, all-weather roads. Most of the access roads and many of the main roads branching off from the main highways, however, are still rough and teeth-shattering. Many sections of the country are isolated, especially during the rainy season, which means that while much has been done, much more needs to be done.

Western writers talking about the Northeast often leave the impression, probably unintentionally, that the Northeast is cut off from Central Thailand by high, almost impenetrable mountains. Such an impression is far from the truth. The mountains separating the Northeast from the Central Plain are not the Himalayas or even the Rockies. Much of the Northeast Plateau is only a few hundred feet above Central Thailand and the mountains are more like hills. In Northern Thailand and parts of the Northeast there are higher mountains, but few that reach as high as eight thousand feet. Even low mountains, of course, can be a barrier to people who must rely on their feet and animals for transportation on primitive roads and whose only modern link with the rest of the country is a single-track railroad. New rail lines have not been built, but the new roads that have been built throughout the Northeast and the buses, trucks, and automobiles that use them have helped tremendously to reduce the mountain barrier between the Northeast and the rest of Thailand. The last decade has seen the two regions of the country, previously separated by the mountains, become more closely linked together.

The Thai government in recent years has also taken steps to improve the general security of the Northeast both against Communist infiltration and against bandits, cattle rustlers (or rather buffalo rustlers), and other criminal nuisances. Much more in this field can and should be done as soon as possible. The government has taken other steps, too, to tie the Northeast more closely to the rest of the country through education both at the lower levels and through the establishment of a university at Khon Kaen. Government development teams have gone into villages, which had never before seen any government officials except tax collectors, and supplied information and assistance for agriculture, medical services, and community development programs. Only a small percentage of the villages in the Northeast has been reached so far. Some of the programs have failed due to incompetence and insensitivity on the part of the Thai officials directing and participating in them. Other programs have had no effect on the villagers because of the failure on the part of Thai officials to correct the pervasive petty corruption that exists at many levels of government and which makes many villagers suspicious of all government activities. Despite these obstacles, programs have been started and some have succeeded which indicate the government's awareness of the needs of the poor farmers of the Northeast and other regions of the country and the government's interest in doing something worthwhile to meet those needs.

The problems of poverty, corruption, and discontent among the Northeasterners are real enough. These problems are separate from any Communist problem, although the Communists have taken advantage of the circumstances and quickly exploited any weakness on the part of the national Thai government and any perfidy on the part of government officials. The Thai government, however, is fully aware of these problems and fully aware, too, that its steps taken so far are inadequate to the solution of the problems. Much more must be done.

11

Udorn

About thirty miles south of Nongkai is the larger and livelier provincial captial city of Udorn. On a recent visit to the Northeast region a Thai friend and his family drove me the short distance from Nongkai to Udorn after his day's work was finished. We made the journey at dusk and in the short trip between cities we were stopped three times at roadblocks manned by Thai soldiers and police, a reminder of the security precautions taken by the Thai in this remote and sparsely populated area near the Laos border. The police were searching for fugitive criminals from Bangkok and other areas of the country who disappear into the mountain and jungle areas of the Northeast, and the soldiers were keeping an eye open for strangers who might be Communist agents infiltrated across the Mekong River from Laos. After my friend informed the officers at each roadblock who I was and what I was doing in that part of the country, we were allowed to proceed.

We arrived in Udorn after dark and drove along the main streets, which were brightly lighted by flashing, colorful neon signs. Most of the largest signs were in English rather than in Thai. They pointed to the entrances of bars and night clubs with such names as New York, Crown, Anchor Light, Blue Heaven, and Silhouette. Interspersed among the clubs were several new, modern hotels and motels with convenient hourly rates and massage parlors with obliging female attendants. On one corner stood a new bowling alley. The city appeared to be a miniature reproduction of Bangkok and quite unlike most provincial capitals I had visited in Thailand. The reason was quickly apparent. Along the streets many young American men in casual civilian clothes strolled in pairs and small groups. They were American Air Force men on passes from the joint Thai-American air base, the largest in Thailand, at the edge of the city.

In 1969, an estimated total of 49,000 American troops were stationed in

Thailand. Of this number 36,000 were assigned to the six air bases the Americans share with the Thai at Ta Khli in Northern Thailand, at Khorat, Udorn, Ubol, and Nakhon Phanom in the Northeast region, and Utapao in the Southeast near Sataheep on the Gulf of Thailand. To support these troops there were an additional 11,000 troops under the United States Military Advisory Group stationed at various locations in the country. In addition, there were approximately 2,000 other American military personnel assigned to a wide range of special activities such as training the Thai in counterinsurgency measures.

The great majority of these American troops are in Thailand for one purpose, as the Thai government spokesmen have repeatedly stated. The troops, with the possible exception of the 2,000 on special assignments and some of the support troops, are there to aid the American efforts in Vietnam and are in Thailand only for the duration of the Vietnamese war. With few exceptions these American troops are not in Thailand as part of an American commitment to Thailand's defense against either external or internal enemies. The Thai contend that they are able to handle their enemies themselves, at least at this stage of history.

Besides the American troops in Thailand, there are, of course, several thousand American civilians living and working in the country. Included among the civilians are the U.S. Embassy personnel, representatives of the U.S. Agency for International Development and the U.S. Information Agency, volunteers of the U.S. Peace Corps, American employees of United States business firms, missionaries, and representatives or employees of other international and American charitable and educational organizations, and their families, as well as the few independent Americans found wandering around all countries in Asia. The total number of Americans resident in Thailand is probably close to 60,000.

The presence of such a large number of recently arrived Americans creates an impact which at times is unfavorable to U.S.-Thai relations. Compare the thousands today with the almost insignificant number of Americans in Thailand in the years immediately after World War II and one can understand to some extent the force of the impact. In his book *Brief Authority*, the late Honorable Edwin F. Stanton, first United States minister and later ambassador to Thailand after World War II, reports that in planning the annual Fourth of July reception at the American embassy in 1946, he and his wife expected seventy Americans. By 1960, when I first went to Thailand, the number of Americans in the country was probably around two to three thousand with less than a thousand of those military personnel. The Americans were the largest body of resident foreigners (excluding the Chinese) and even then we heard comments from time to time that there were too many

Americans around. Yet, nine years later their number has increased about fifteen to eighteen times.

The United States was a latecomer among Western nations in establishing relations with Thailand. The Portuguese, Dutch, British, and French all had trade and some political contacts with the Thai long before the United States became an independent nation. Early in the nineteenth century American trading ships began calling at Bangkok with cotton, hardware, and arms and taking back sugar, timber, and drugs. By the end of the 1820's American Protestant missionaries had also made their appearance in Bangkok.

An American envoy, Edmund Roberts, arrived in Bangkok in 1833, and the first Thai-American treaty was signed that year. It was a general treaty of friendship and commerce and neither side gained much by it.

With the defeat of China in the opium wars, the opening of Japan to Western traders, and the assumption of the Thai throne by King Mongkut, who was familiar with Western languages and learning, Thailand began to welcome and encourage contacts with the West as part of a deliberate new policy. The partial withdrawal from the West which had begun with the revolution of 1688 was coming to an end. The first major result of this new policy was the Bowring treaty of 1855 signed between Thailand and England represented by Sir John Bowring. The following year, the United States sent a representative to negotiate a new Thai-U.S. treaty on terms as favorable as those given to the British.

The representative of the United States was Townsend Harris, a New York City merchant who had lived in Asia for several years and was considered—and considered himself—to be an expert on Asian peoples and society in general. Although he had never been in Thailand, Mr. Harris was asked by the State Department to stop in Bangkok to negotiate a new treaty with the Thai before proceeding to his appointment as the first United States consul to Japan.

When Harris arrived in Thailand on April 13, 1856, he was enthusiastic about the country and the people he met. He expected the treaty to be negotiated quickly and to be on his way to Japan, which was the country of his main interest in Asia. He had been trying to get there for years. Soon after his arrival in Bangkok Harris met the Reverend Dr. D. B. Bradley, an American missionary friend of King Mongkut, and the Reverend Mr. Stephen Mattoon, another American missionary who acted as Harris's interpreter. He also found that the second king, or uparaja, at that time had a son named Prince George Washington, and Harris could have easily misinterpreted this unexpected discovery as well as some of the impressions he gained from the missionaries as signs boding well for a quick and satisfactory ending to his mission.

Harris was soon disappointed and grumbling. In his journal at one point he wrote, "It is an old saying here that those who come here for business should bring one ship loaded with patience, another loaded with presents, and a third ship for carrying away the cargo." As one reads the journal it becomes increasingly evident that Harris's first ship had a short load. At the same time, however, the journal gives an interesting description of Harris's experiences in the Bangkok of more than a century ago, his official procession by royal barge up the river, his audience with the king, his negotiations with officials including both the major and second kings, his living quarters, and his food. Some of the descriptions would fit as well today as they did a hundred years ago.

The basic annoyance that Harris felt was what he considered to be long unnecessary delays on the part of the Thai officials with whom he was negotiating. Part of the delay was due to the general Thai characteristic of not rushing into anything, especially an important agreement. Part was due to some hesitation on the part of the Thai who were not sure that they should give the same treaty terms to the representative of a republic as they gave to a monarchy.

Probably the main reason for the delay, however, was the presence in Bangkok of H. S. Parkes, the secretary to Sir John Bowring. Parkes had arrived in Bangkok some time before Harris and had brought with him the ratified copy of the treaty signed the year before. Parkes had also brought with him many questions raised by British officials in London about the interpretation of the treaty. It was rumored that the British diplomat had greatly angered King Mongkut by writing him too many letters asking for the king's understanding of particular treaty terms. The king was not about to negotiate with Harris while Parkes was there, and only when the latter had departed did the Thai-U.S. treaty negotiations move faster.

By the middle of May Harris was suffering ill health and this condition, combined with the delays which he could not understand, made him turn against Thailand. The entry in his journal for May 24, 1856, has this harsh statement: ". . . I hope this is the end of my trouble with this false, base and cowardly people. To lie is here the rule from the Kings downward. Truth is never used when they can avoid it." Despite his years in Asia Harris did not really understand Asian people and he made some very harsh judgments about the Thai people and their rulers. Yet, many Westerners who have followed him have encountered similar experiences and with frustration and impatience have sometimes made similar judgments.

Because he was annoyed and ill Harris ended his mission to Thailand by insulting the king. He was in a hurry to leave and get on with his journey to Japan. To speed the negotiations he set the end of May for completion of the treaty. It was signed May 29, 1856, just under his deadline. Then without waiting for the king's presents to the President of the United States, Harris hurried away, telling the king to give his gifts to the new American consul, the Reverend Mr. Mattoon, appointed by Harris. This precipitate action by Harris violated diplomatic courtesy, but Harris seemed to be unmindful of his insult to the king and sped away as quickly as his ship could depart.

In the end, the treaty which Harris signed did secure for the United States the same terms as the Bowring treaty secured for England. The main provisions allowed the United States to establish a consulate at Bangkok and to exercise extraterritorial jurisdiction over American citizens, and limited the Thai to placing an import tax of no more than 3 percent on American goods. This treaty was to govern Thai-American relations until 1920.

In the first decade of the present century Professor Edward H. Strobel of Harvard Law School went to Thailand at Thai request with the title of general adviser, but with responsibilities chiefly as a foreign policy adviser to the Ministry of Foreign Affairs. King Chulalongkorn had several foreign advisers including an Englishman on finance and a Frenchman on justice. After the first few Americans had served in Thailand as general advisers both their title and duties were changed to limit their role explicitly to foreign affairs. In that post until 1940, the American advisers gave substantial assistance to the Thai in revising Thai treaties with Western nations to eliminate completely the extraterritorial and other special privileges held by citizens of the Western nations.

The first of the revised treaties was the new American treaty in 1920. The Thai had participated in World War I on the side of the Allies which gave the Thai a position at the Paris Peace Conference. There the Thai delegates suggested to President Woodrow Wilson the possibility of revising the 1856 treaty negotiated by Townsend Harris. The President agreed and a new treaty was signed in 1920 which gave Thailand complete jurisdiction over American residents in Thailand and thus ended American extraterritorial rights. The United States also agreed to permit Thailand to levy any size duty on American imports provided other nations agreed to the same arrangement. By the middle of the 1930's all the Thai-Western treaties granting special privileges to the Western nations were revised following the pattern of the 1920 American treaty, and Thailand was freed from the restrictions imposed on it by the earlier nineteenth-century treaties.

Thailand was allied with Japan in World War II after Japan invaded the Southeast Asian peninsula. After a few weeks Thailand declared war on the United States, England, and other members of the wartime United Nations. The Thai ambassador to the United States, M. R. Seni Pramoj refused to deliver the declaration to the United States government. Instead, he sought and received United States support for a Free Thai Movement in exile. Because of his action the United States treated Thailand as enemy-occupied territory whereas the British considered Thailand an enemy. This difference in viewpoint was to affect the understanding between the United States and its wartime allies over the treatment to be accorded postwar Thailand. The United States used its influence with England and France to moderate their demands in their postwar peace treaties with Thailand.

Because of the long history of capable American advisers who gave outstanding service to the Thai Ministry of Foreign Affairs, because of the initiative taken by the United States in revising the unfair nineteenth-century treaties, and because of the post-World War II role of the United States in moderating the Thai peace treaties, the two countries entered the postwar period stronger friends than ever. This new friendship flowered at the time when the traditional great Asian power on the mainland, China, was undergoing internal upheavals which were to put a new aggressive Communist government in control.

Thailand traditionally had accorded recognition to nominal Chinese suzerainty over all of Southeast Asia and had from time to time sent tribute to the Chinese emperor since the days of the Sukhothai kingdom. Thai kings throughout history down to the beginning of the Chakri dynasty sought the approval of the Chinese emperor for their assumption of the throne, but rarely had the emperor directly interfered or intervened in Thai internal political affairs or in the relationships between Thailand and its Southeast Asian neighbors. After the nineteenth century Western interventions in China that demonstrated the weaknesses of the Middle Kingdom, Thailand discontinued its nominal tribute sent at irregular intervals to China. Now, in the middle of the twentieth century a new aggressive China was threatening extension of its control to all the lands over which the Chinese emperor once claimed suzerainty. The Chinese invasion and conquest of Buddhist Tibet in the early 1950's was a warning taken seriously by many other Asian nations faced by threats from Communist China. Thailand decided to align itself with those Western nations opposed to Communist China and hoped for protection from continuing Communist Chinese threats, if they were turned into positive action. First among those Western nations was the United States which, at that time for the other reasons mentioned, stood unusually high on the ladder among Thailand's friends.

In 1950, the North Koreans, with the support of Communist China, launched an attack against South Korea. The United Nations with the United States in the vanguard went to the assistance of South Korea. Prime Minister Pibun Songgram in Thailand supported the action of the United Nations by sending a contingent of Thai fighting forces to join the UN troops in Korea, and this Thai contingent compiled an enviable record for bravery in the Korean War.

At the same time, Pibun sought to strengthen his ties with the United States by signing several new agreements. In July 1950 the two countries signed an Educational Exchange agreement setting up a Fulbright scholarship program for Thailand. This agreement was followed in September by an Economic and Technical Cooperation agreement and in October by a Military Assistance agreement. With the signatures to these new agreements one has an excellent illustration of how quickly changes in international events can change international alignments. In late 1941, Thailand under Pibun's leadership allied with Japan and then declared war against the United States. Less than ten years later Thailand, again under Pibun's leadership, was closely tied in friendship to the United States and the latter's policy in Asia.

This cooperation was to become closer still in 1954 with the alliance formed under the treaty establishing the Southeast Asia Treaty Organization. By this treaty Thailand abandoned any pretense of continuing its traditional neutral policy and openly aligned itself with the nations opposed to the Chinese Communists. In return, Thailand expected, despite the highly qualified language of the SEATO agreement, that the United States and Thailand's other SEATO partners would come to its defense against any threatened aggression from the Asian Communist nations. In this expectation the Thai were to be gravely disappointed.

The first major test of what Thailand's SEATO allies would do to assist Thailand's interests came with the Laos dispute and internal fighting in the period from 1959 to 1962. Since Laos became independent in 1954 following the Geneva Conference ending the war between France and its Indo-Chinese colonies, this small, remote, landlocked country, little known in the West except to France, had become a target for Communist infiltration from North Vietnam. Attempts at integrating the indigenous Lao Communist military forces and political leaders into some form of national government had generally foundered on the obstructionist policies of the Pathet Lao (pro-Communist) military group and its political arms. Coups and countercoups accompanied by fighting broke out repeatedly and reached crisis proportions in 1959 and 1960. The country was divided into three major factions: (1) the pro-Communist group supported by North Vietnam and its allies, (2) an anti-Communist group supported by the United States and Thailand, and (3) a neutral group which at one time or another was supported by one or the other of the two larger Lao factions in the disputes.

Laos was not a signatory to the SEATO agreement, but under the agreement's terms the SEATO powers could extend assistance to Laos under certain specified conditions. For Thailand, what happened in Laos was vital to Thailand's position in Asia and to its security. Thai and Lao relationships had been close for centuries. The majority peoples in both countries were ethnically related as were the minority hill tribes in both countries. For long periods of Thai and Lao history the two countries were under the rule or suzerainty of the same Thai princes. Most importantly, however, in the current world situation, Laos provided a buffer, and a narrow buffer at that, between Thailand and Communist China in the north and Communist North Vietnam in the northeast. If Laos were to become Communist, too, the aggressive Asian Communists would be brought to the long Mekong River border between Laos and Thailand and would become a serious menace to Thailand. By the early 1960's the Communists were already using the chaotic situation in Laos to cover their infiltration into North and Northeast Thailand.

Thailand had genuine reason to fear the intentions of the Communist Asian nations. As early as January 1953, the Communist Chinese set up a Thai Autonomous People's Government in southern China. The purpose of this step was to create a group to combat alleged "imperialist" forces in Thailand and to call on all Thai peoples in Thailand, Laos, Burma, and Vietnam to join with those in Yunnan to form a "greater Thai" government under the control of the Communist Chinese. The Communist Chinese by these efforts were trying to do more than had been done by the Chinese emperors. Instead of a nominal suzerainty over the Thai, the current Chinese rulers were trying to extend real control over them. In recent years the Chinese have stepped up their efforts. Late in 1964, Peking announced the formation of a Thai Independence Movement and early in 1965, the formation of a Thailand Patriotic Front. At first cooperating together, these groups are now believed to be merged as the spearhead of Communist efforts to subvert the Thai and to cause internal dissension within Thailand wherever possible.

As the Laos crisis developed in the 1959–62 period a split appeared within the SEATO alliance. On the one side Thailand, with some support from the other Asian nations, urged the United States to give strong support to the anti-Communist faction in Laos. Britain and France, on the other hand, supported by the official representative of the United Nations in Laos, urged the United States to support the neutralist factions. Both sides had their supporters within the military, intelligence, and foreign service communities of the United States government itself. The United States vacillated, and Thailand became disillusioned over what it saw as inaction on the part of its major Western ally on a matter of crucial importance to the security of Thailand. While the debate went on, the anti-Communist forces in Laos were making a poor military showing and were steadily being routed by the Pathet Lao and neutralist forces. The weakness of the anti-Communist forces added strength to those in the West who were arguing against giving all-out support to that faction in Laos.

When the United States did reach a decision, the decision was an unhappy one for the Thai. The United States decided not to use its own military forces in Laos to bolster the anti-Communist forces, but to support the British effort to work out with the Soviet Union (the two were co-chairmen of the 1954 Geneva Conference on Indo-China) an end to the Laos fighting and a new government for the country.

This decision by the United States in 1961 caused Thailand to look anew at its alliances and its membership in SEATO. The Thai had reason to feel that SEATO had failed, in the Thai view, to protect legitimate SEATO interests in Asia, and that this failure was due to strong influence on the United States by European members of SEATO whose interests in Asia had been greatly reduced since the end of World War II. Thailand began to think about forming closer ties to other Asian nations without relying on European states and about getting a bilateral defense commitment from the United States outside the framework of SEATO.

The Thai succeeded in their second goal when Foreign Minister Thanat Khoman and Secretary of State Dean Rusk issued a joint statement on March 6, 1962, which said in part: "The Secretary of State reaffirmed that the United States regards the preservation of the independence and integrity of Thailand as vital to the national interest of the United States and to world peace. He expressed the firm intention of the United States to aid Thailand, its ally and historic friend, in resisting Communist aggression and subversion." After reiterating U.S. intentions to carry out its obligations under the SEATO agreement, the statement continued: "The Secretary of State reaffirmed that this obligation of the United States does not depend upon the prior agreement of all other parties to the treaty [SEATO] since this treaty obligation is individual as well as collective." By this last statement the United States was indicating it could act under the SEATO agreement without waiting for the approval of France, Britain, or any other party to the treaty.

The statement had the effect of easing some Thai fears about the reliability of its principal ally in SEATO. The Thai had historical reasons to be concerned about what support they might get from their Western allies in the face of serious threats. In late 1941, when the Japanese invaded Thailand and coerced it into becoming an ally, the Thai could not get help from France, England, or the United States. Thailand and France, just defeated in Europe, had had a dispute over former Thai territories in Cambodia taken by France early in the century and taken back by the Thai with help from the Japanese in 1940 and 1941. The United States in the Philippines and the British in Malaya, Singapore, and Burma were in deep trouble themselves and could not help the Thai, who were left, therefore, without any possible help from the West, even if the Thai had wanted it, to face the invading Japanese. Many years earlier, in 1893, when France threatened the use of force against Thailand and did use a gunboat and troops, the Thai had turned to the British for assistance only to be advised to proceed cautiously, a caution that led to the surrender of some fringe Thai territories to France and to England, too. With this historical experience and the current disillusionment with SEATO and the United States in Laos, the Thai were to remain understandably wary of the effectiveness in the future of their alliance with the West.

The joint Thanat-Rusk statement was issued at a time when the Communist forces in Laos were renewing their attacks and the anti-Communist forces were again retreating. The United States decided to show its armed might in Southeast Asia without committing its forces to Laos. On May 17, 1962, a force of almost two thousand U.S. Marines landed in Bangkok and was whisked off to Udorn. A U.S. Army group of about a thousand men was near Khorat where it had participated in SEATO exercises in April and had not yet departed. The United States brought in more men until the total of its military forces in Thailand was around ten thousand. In June new agreements were reached in Geneva among the states concerned with Laos to set up a three-pronged coalition government in that strife-torn country. With that new government established in Vientiane, the United States withdrew about half the troops it had brought into Thailand to meet the spring Laos crisis.

By the middle of the 1960's, the United States was devoting most of its efforts in Asia to the Vietnam war, and the Thai were loyal supporters of a strong anti-Communist stand by the United States in Vietnam. When the United States called for military support, the Thai, as they had earlier in the Korean War, sent troops to Vietnam. At first, the Thai contingent was a battalion which was later increased to a division. In 1969, the number of Thai troops in Vietnam was almost twelve thousand.

After the United States began its bombing of North Vietnam in 1965, it requested Thai permission to build air bases in Thailand to make its bombing missions more effective. The Thai granted permission with the understanding that the bases were to continue to remain, at least legally, under Thai control and command, and that the bases were to be used only for the duration of the Vietnam war. The benefits to the United States of these bases only minutes away from the North Vietnamese targets were great enough to justify the heavy United States expenditures in expanding the Thai air bases and building new facilities where needed. Before that time, United States bombers had to fly from bases as far away as Guam and so the number of missions a day was limited. In Thailand the bombers could fly several missions a day and return quickly to their bases.

In the fall of 1969 the United States and Thailand reached an agreement to begin the withdrawal of the first American troops in the immediate future.

12

Phuket

In the spring of 1969, I arrived in Bangkok two days before Songkran, the traditional Thai New Year's festival. The biggest celebration of Songkran each year is held in Chiengmai, to which thousands of people from all over the country go to celebrate the wet and joyous occasion. But to avoid the crushing crowds I had arranged to fly to Phuket at the opposite end of the country for the holiday.

Phuket is a large island in the Andaman Sea off the southwest coast of Thailand's Malay Peninsula area. On early marine maps of the area and in journals of some of the early Western sea captains and explorers of this coast, the island bears the unusual and picturesque name of Junk Ceylon. It is thought that this name came from a mistaken pronunciation and spelling by Westerners of the Malay name for the area which was Ujong (meaning Cape) Salang. Until within the last five years the island could be reached by boat and airplane, but not by road although it is very close to the mainland at its northern end. The Thai government recently built a bridge linking the mainland and the island so that it is possible now to drive all the way there from Bangkok.

I flew to Phuket, and its airport is one of the few I have been in that I find more than routinely interesting. It has only one runway, and when I first visited there eight years earlier that one runway was a stretch of dirt with an unusually steep upgrade for an airport landing strip. When the plane set its wheels down the passengers found themselves climbing a small knoll. At the top of the knoll was the end of the runway and just over the top was the ocean. One had the feeling that if the plane did not stop on its uphill climb, it would plop over the top into the ocean.

Since my first trip there the airport had been much improved with a new terminal building and a newly paved runway. Fortunately for the adven-

236

turous the incline of the runway, a much steeper grade than that found in any airport in the United States, is still there and so is the ocean when you reach the top.

My flight to Phuket was made on Songkran Day, April 13. The beginning of the Thai new year traditionally was set astrologically about the middle of April and in recent years the Thai government has set April 13 as the day of Songkran. Until 1940, April 1 was the official beginning of the Thai year regardless of the date of Songkran. In 1940 the government decreed the year 2483 of the Buddhist Era to be only nine months long running from April 1 through December 31, and the new year B.E. 2484 began on January 1, 1941. By so doing the Buddhist Era years were made to coincide in Thailand with the Western calendar years.

On the eve of Songkran the Thai prepare themselves to begin a fresh new year. Houses are thoroughly cleaned and refuse and garbage is discarded or burned. The wat compounds, too, are cleaned and new sand is spread around. The night before I left for Phuket I visited a small wat near my hotel. In the entrance courtyard I found several men watching some women and children building what looked like sand castles. On closer inspection I saw that what they were building were miniature wat buildings, viharas and chedis, made of fresh sand. This custom of building sand wats as a way of earning some merit by building a symbolic wat by those who cannot afford to build a real wat goes back a great many years. When King Mongkut was making his reforms within Thai Buddhism more than a century ago, he referred to this custom as an innocent one, but one that had no real religious significance and which was in no way sanctioned or called for under the teachings of Buddhism. Since he did not prohibit it, the custom continues today as a pleasant way to decorate the wat though without any real religious meaning.

Near the entrance to the wat compound there were some tables on which had been placed a row of bowls into which the visitor could place a contribution. Each bowl was for a different purpose. A monk who had attended Mahachulalongkorn University and spoke some English came up to talk to me and explained the meaning of the bowls and then conducted me around the wat. Inside the vihara several monks were reading aloud portions from the Buddhist teachings. As usual the services were quite informal with both monks and listeners coming and going. Some listened for a while and others conferred with a senior monk, pointed out to me as the abbot to whom I was later presented, who was seated on a platform in front of the altar. The altar had a main Buddha image about twenty feet high surrounded by about a dozen other Buddhas and several other images of disciples. The Buddhas all faced in the same direction while the disciple images faced the central Buddha as if listening to his words. All of the

Buddha images had new cloth robes around one shoulder. These robes were of a pale saffron color. The robes had been placed on the images to celebrate the beginning of the new year and to gain merit for the donor.

On Songkran itself the Thai begin the day by bringing food to the monks at the wats. Later there are also services and the Buddha images are symbolically bathed by sprinkling with water. Still later, the younger Thai visit their elders, pour scented water over the palms of the old people, and ask for their blessing at the beginning of the new year. Many people will make a special effort to buy captured birds and fish to be released on Songkran as a way of earning special merit.

Up to this point in the celebration the activities are relatively sedate. But then the fun begins. Although probably not a part of the ancient Songkran festivals, many persons over the last few score years have extended the sprinkling of water on the hands of the elders to sprinkling water on other members of the family and on friends and finally on anyone within range. At the same time the amount of water used has increased from sprinkling a few drops, except on the elders, to throwing whole bucketfuls.

The water-throwing custom of Songkran is officially frowned upon in Bangkok because too many foreign visitors were shocked to find themselves doused with water if they wandered outside their hotels on Songkran. Nowadays many residents of Chiengmai who do not want to spend several days getting soaked flee to Bangkok during the festival. The best way to experience the full impact of this holiday is to don one's oldest clothes and get outside Bangkok.

When I arrived in Phuket on Songkran I hired a taxi to drive me around the island to visit some of the island's magnificent beaches and to see its rubber plantations and tin mines. Because of the heat we drove with the car windows down, but with our hands on the window handles ready to roll them up whenever we saw anyone, suspicious or not, standing innocently by the side of the road. For hours we drove past children and adults who showered water on the car with great glee. Usually we managed to get the windows closed, but not always, before the water hit us. One time I did not see a little boy on my side of the road until my driver shouted. I turned to the fully opened window just as the boy, about eight years old, flung a whole pailful of water in. With a perfectly accurate aim the water came through the car window, hit me full in the face, and drenched me from head to lap. I looked back in time to see the little boy jumping with joy and the adults near him doubled up with laughter. I suppose the young man got extra credit for having squarely hit a foreigner. After the first shock I was laughing so hard myself, as well as being envious of the boy's good luck, that I failed to close the window before the next attack and got a second but smaller dousing from the next roadside villain. There is only one real way to participate in Songkran and that is to adopt the Thai philosophy of "mai pen rai," it doesn't matter, and have a good time.

In several villages through which we drove the village population was well organized for its attacks on travelers who ventured within their precincts. About twenty or thirty men would stand across the road forcing all vehicles to a stop. Then women and children came out and poured water on everyone and everything. In a closed car we stayed reasonably dry, but the poor riders on motorcycles, bicycles, and motorscooters, and in small buses without windows soon looked as if they had been swimming fully clothed.

Some victims were well prepared to retaliate. On one motorcycle I saw the driver had replaced his saddlebags with metal five-gallon cans filled with water. With a small dipper he threw back at anyone who threw at him. Two buses I noticed had steel oildrums filled with water strapped to the rear of the bus. Whenever anyone threw at the bus a passenger was ready with a dipper full of water to throw back.

Many older Thai feel this informal water-throwing part of the festival has got out of hand and has little to do with the original purpose of the sprinkling at the festival. Perhaps they are right. But the frenzy of the water throwing does not seem to be abating and no one seems to be seriously disturbed. Indeed, on a hot April day in the middle of Thailand's hottest season, a cool even though unexpected shower can be refreshing.

On my Songkran day ride around Phuket my driver showed me a unique coconut palm tree the likes of which I had never seen before and may never see again. Most persons who have ever seen a coconut palm tree are impressed with the tall graceful trunks bare almost all the way to the top where the coconuts and palm branches are clustered. The unusual tree on Phuket started out from the ground like any other stretching its bare trunk upward in a gentle curve. But about ten feet from the ground the trunk divided, like a giant tuning fork, and from that point upward there were two distinct trees each pushing its fronds and fruit skyward at the top of a separate, fully developed trunk. The local Thai consider this strange tree a lucky one and around its single base trunk were tied many colored ribbons by those who hoped to absorb some of the tree's good luck.

On the road back to Phuket city we saw several womb-shaped concrete tombs built into the hillsides by Chinese families who bury their dead rather than cremate them as is done by Thai Buddhists. The tombs are a visual reminder that Phuket is the home of one of the largest concentrations of Chinese families in Thailand outside the metropolitan Bangkok area. Some of the Chinese businessmen in Phuket are among the richest men in

Thailand. Their fortunes were made mainly in tin mining and to a lesser extent on the rubber plantations and in rubber trading.

Tin is by far the most important mineral found in Thailand and most of it is found in the west coast area of peninsular Thailand although it is profitably mined in other areas of the peninsula and the western border mountains of Northern Thailand as well. Tin mines have been known for centuries in Phuket and references to the tin mines of Junk Ceylon can be found in some of the early journals of Western traders in this area in the seventeenth century. Despite drastic and frequent fluctuations in the world price of tin, the mineral has remained one of the principal exports of Thailand for many decades.

Dotting the entire island of Phuket, looking like narrow, rickety ski slides, are the bamboo frameworks of the sluices used in tin mining. Relying heavily on manpower, these mines were worked by thousands of Chinese laborers imported from China for many, many years. For much of this century, however, the traditional Chinese-operated mines on land have faced growing competition from tin mining in the sea where dredges scoop up tin ore from the sea's bottom. Many of these tin-dredging operations which now account for more of the tin mining than the land mines are owned by foreign, non-Chinese companies. The Australians have been especially prominent leaders in dredge mining. Until very recently within the last decade, Thai exports of tin were in the form of tin ore to smelters in Malaysia, Singapore, and elsewhere. Now the tin can be smelted in Thailand. A company with Thai government support has built an operating smelter on Phuket and most tin sent abroad now is shipped in a refined form.

A second major industry in the South, not only on Phuket, but on the mainland as well, is the production of rubber. There are few large rubber plantations in Thailand, as there are in Malaysia. Most Thai rubber trees are grown on relatively small plots, and unfortunately, Thai rubber in the past at least has not generally been of the best grade. It could not compete well in the world market with the rubber from Malaysia, where the British and later the Malaysian governments made great efforts to raise and preserve the quality of rubber. Recently, Thailand has taken some steps to upgrade the quality of rubber produced in Thailand, but at the very time that Thai raw rubber is improving, the world market for rubber faces increased competition from rubber substitutes.

About a month after Songkran in Phuket I attended another celebration in Bangkok. Like many Thai festivals, this one, called the First Plowing Ceremony, is essentially a Brahmanic ceremony onto which a Buddhist branch has been grafted. The Buddhist portion usually consists of the recitation of an appropriate part of the Buddhist scriptures by a chapter of monks followed by the presentation of gifts to the monks to earn merit.

The First Plowing Ceremony takes place at the beginning of the rainy season usually early in May when the farmers are beginning to prepare their rice fields for planting. The ceremony functions both to call upon the gods and spirits to assist in bringing adequate rains for a good agricultural season and to predict what the season will be like.

In recent years the ceremony, presided over by the king, has taken place on the Phra Mane Ground. In the days preceding the main day a section of ground is prepared for the plowing and pavilions are built for the king and the ceremonial officials and guests. Around the whole area several tent booths are set up in which to demonstrate new agricultural machinery and farming techniques so that the Phra Mane Ground takes on a little of the appearance of a rural fair.

The king, sometime before the ceremonies, appoints a Lord of the Plowing, in the past usually an official of the agricultural ministry, but not necessarily so. An auspicious time for the first plowing is set by the court Brahmin astrologers. In 1969 this time was between 8:32 and 9:02 A.M. on May 9. Shortly before the auspicious time after the guests and officials had assembled, the Lord of the Plowing, dressed in his traditional robes, arrived escorted by four beautiful young women, several court Brahmins in white, and a red-clad guard of honor. The first task of the Lord of the Plowing was to choose one of three folded phanung (the traditional Thai lower garment). Each of the three is a different length. If he chooses the longest, rainfall will be abundant, the shortest means too little rain, and the middle length means average rainfall. The hope is, of course, that he will choose the middle one so that there will be neither too little nor too much rain.

Then the Lord of the Plowing must take hold of a plow pulled by specially trained oxen decked in gorgeous harnesses of red and gold. The four beautiful ladies follow the Lord as he plows three concentric circles. The ladies carry rice in gold and silver baskets. The Lord scatters the rice in the furrows he has plowed while another official scatters holy water prepared by the Brahmins.

When the plowing is completed several vessels are placed before the oxen. Each vessel contains a different product—rice, maize, beans, sesamum, rice liquor, water, and grass. The oxen are expected to choose one and whichever is chosen will be the most plentiful crop. Naturally, most farmers, even if they do not believe in the ceremony, hope that rice and maize, the principal crops, will be chosen.

After the oxen have made their choice the formal ceremony is finished. It is followed by a rush onto the plowed field by the thousands of persons present and each one tries to retrieve some of the blessed grains which have been scattered. They want to mix the blessed grains with their own growing seed. In so doing, their own seed will produce a better and more abundant harvest, so they believe.

Between Songkran and the First Plowing Ceremony is one of the national state holidays. May 5 is Coronation Day celebrating the coronation of King Bhumibol in 1950.

Soon after the First Plowing Ceremony comes what is probably the most important of all Buddhist holidays. By one of those strange coincidences often found in religious histories, according to the Thai the Lord Buddha was born, received Enlightenment at the age of thirty-five, and died at age eighty, all on the same date. This date is called Visakha Puja Day and falls on the full moon day in May. On this date all Buddhists make a special effort to visit the wat to pay special homage to the Buddha and to make merit in many different ways. At night there are usually candlelight or lantern processions around the wat, a colorful and beautiful type of ceremony performed in many Buddhists celebrations.

Buddhist Lent extends from the first day of the waning moon in the eighth lunar month to the full moon day of the eleventh lunar month which means roughly mid-July to mid-October. During this time monks do not travel, but remain in their own monasteries and make special efforts to follow all the rules for monks enunciated by the Buddha. Since this period is often the time during which many young men enter the monastic order, the period is preceded by frequent ordination ceremonies which are celebrated with special festivities by Buddhist households and villages throughout the country.

During Buddhist Lent one national holiday takes place for the Thai. This holiday is the birthday of the Queen on August 12.

At the end of Buddhist Lent comes a month-long period of celebrations which are called *kathin* ceremonies. The monks have been released from the especially strict observation of their rules which they have followed during the Lenten period and they are permitted to travel again around the country. As part of the celebration of the end of Lent extra efforts are made by Thai Buddhists to present new robes to the monks. These ceremonies of the presentation of robes are called kathin ceremonies and may take place at any time in the period from mid-October to mid-November.

Traveling in the countryside of Thailand during this period the visitor will often meet gay, colorful processions headed toward a wat. Often there will be cars and bicycles and samlors decorated with flags and Buddhist banners. Usually a local band will be riding along to enliven the procession with music, and everyone will have a joyful time.

The most famous and most colorful kathin ceremony is the Royal Kathin

Ceremony by Water. It is at this time each year, in a ceremony recently revived, that the long teakwood barges colorfully decorated in gold and with
elaborate carved figureheads are brought out for the trip by the king on the
Chao Phya River. The barges, propelled by sixty or more oarsmen in traditional red costumes, bear the king on a throne and his officials to deliver
robes personally to the monks at the royal wats, such as Wat Arun, on the
river's bank.

Another national state holiday at the end of October pays homage to the
great King Chulalongkorn on the anniversary of his death on October 23.
This day is commemorated with festivities before the equestrian statue of
the king that stands in the wide plaza in front of the National Assembly
building. From early in the morning through much of the first half of the
day units of school children, soldiers, other military services, civil officials,
business organizations, and other groups march to the plaza, kneel before
the king's statue, and present huge wreaths of flowers to pay respect to this
man who ruled Thailand for forty-two years and did so much to make it the
modern nation it has become and to preserve its independence at the time of
European territorial encroachments in the area. By afternoon the statue is
surrounded by hundreds of huge wreaths of flowers, some of which are so
many feet tall that the horse appears to be cantering through a flower-filled
meadow. Once the wreaths are presented the thousands of people wander
around the booths that surround the plaza or else they stroll through the
nearby park and zoo. The whole atmosphere is again one of a fair, and late
at night there are still thousands of people standing to look at the floodlit
statue and its bed of flowers.

In November each year there is my favorite of all Thai holiday festivals—
loy krathong. It is a festival of lights on the water and takes place on the
full moon of the twelfth lunar month which is November, when the rainy
season has come to an end and the rivers and klongs of Thailand are full.
A krathong is a leaf cup and loy means to float, so the loy krathong festival
is one in which tiny boats made of banana or plantain leaves are floated on
the waterways.

The exact meaning and origin of the festival are not known. It may have
some Brahmanic aspects to it connected with worshiping one of the Hindu
gods. Some Thai have suggested it is a way to pay homage to any sacred
footprints of the Buddha which might lie on the beds of rivers and streams.
The most probable meaning, however, is animistic in origin. The festival is
an attempt to give thanks to or to propitiate the spirits of the rivers and
waters.

The krathong may be a simple floating cup of leaves or a large, elaborate,
decorated flower boat. A krathong usually contains a candle, a few incense

sticks, and possibly a small coin or some other gift to the spirits. The last time I was in Bangkok for the loy krathong festival my driver's wife made a krathong for me of green banana leaves and white and pink flowers shaped to look like a large lotus flower. The krathong was about ten inches in diameter and in the center was a large candle. I waited until the night was quite dark and took the krathong to the klong a block or so behind my apartment house. There surrounded by the excited children of the neighborhood I lit the candle and launched the krathong on the klong. For as long as we could see it floating down the canal I stood there quietly with the children hushed and their parents speaking softly in the background. In both directions we could see scattered pinpoints of light floating calmly on the canal until suddenly churned by a speeding water taxi. In its wake the krathong bobbed dangerously and their lights flickered in the spray. But when the waters were smooth again the lights could still be seen riding steadily on the surface glistening in the moonlight.

Later that evening I went to the Phra Mane Ground area to view the krathong, some several feet long, launched on the Chao Phya River and to see other krathong on the klongs near the Grand Palace. People from all over the city came to this area to float hundreds of krathong on these central klongs. The canals were covered with tiny flower boats each with a lighted candle reflected in the water. The odor of sweet burning incense pervaded the air above the klongs. The banks were lined with a large portion of Bangkok's populace—old men with their best white shirts and dark trousers and old women, some with close-cropped hair and wearing the phanung, young couples with their infant children who hugged their krathong closely before standing enchanted by the light of their flower boats floating away— all spellbound by the beauty and, most surprisingly of all, by the quiet of the evening. As long as the floating candles stayed aglow no one seemed to want to go home. For a few minutes the world stood still on a pleasant and peaceful night in Bangkok.

About a month after loy krathong comes another colorful display of lights. That is for the birthday of the present king, on December 5, which is now celebrated world-wide as Thai National Day. For more than two decades after the 1932 revolution, June 24 was observed as Thai National Day, but after the Sarit coup in 1958, National Day was changed to coincide with the king's birthday. Three days of celebrations are highlighted by displays of colored lights put up by merchants and government offices around the capital city. Most spectacular of all is Rajadamnoen Road, where the trees lining the sides are decorated with multicolored lights which make them glow like giant outdoor Christmas trees familiar to Westerners. A few days after the king's birthday is another national holiday on December 10. On that day the Thai observe Constitution Day, celebrating the anniversary of the first permanent constitution on December 10, 1932.

On the full moon day of the third lunar month (February) falls another major Buddhist holy day, Magha Puja, referred to commonly as a kind of Buddhist All Saints' Day. On that date one year during the life of the Buddha on earth a miracle occurred. With no advance planning or invitation 1,250 Buddhist monks coincidentally arrived at a place where the Buddha was staying, and to them he delivered a sermon bringing to them the 227 rules of the monastic order. Like other Buddhist holy days this one is celebrated with special attendance at wat services and with special efforts to perform tasks which will earn merit for the performer.

The holidays and festivals of the year are almost over. April 6 is Chakri Day, honoring the nine kings of the current dynasty whose impressive reigns have brought many changes to Thailand. A week later is Songkran again and another water festival begins a new year.

There are other special occasions which I might just mention. Since changing their calendar year to agree with the West, January 1 is now an official New Year's holiday and is celebrated much as it is in the West. On the first Thursday of each new school year students at all levels of the education system from the elementary schools through the universities pay special homage to their teachers. Throughout most of the year wats all over the country hold fairs which are special occasions to celebrate with fun and amusement for the people of the local and neighboring areas. Some of these fairs are nationally famous, such as the November fair at Wat Saket (the Temple of the Golden Mount) in Bangkok.

The Thai have a word for a quality which they are all seeking to achieve for themselves and looking for in others. That word is *sanuk*. It is both a simple and a complex word in meaning. Simply, it means joy or pleasure; more deeply, it means an all-pervading sense of well-being. Often an event or a person may be judged on the basis of how much it or he contributes to the "sanukness" of participants and friends. Holidays, festivals, and fairs, needless to say, are always sanuk and enjoyed by all.

Across the Malay Peninsula from Phuket is Songkhla at the southern end of a large inland lake which is connected to the Gulf of Thailand by a narrow passage on one side of which is Songkhla City. The area around much of the lake, which is more than fifty miles long, is little known to most visitors or to Thai from Bangkok for that matter. Several years ago I shared a train compartment returning to Bangkok from the South with a police general who told me he had been supervising police efforts to capture pirates who were using the unpopulated and little-known shores of the lake as bases from which they sailed forth into the Gulf to raid small vessels.

Songkhla is one of the major fishing ports to be found along the Gulf coast. Each morning one can watch the small fishing boats chug their way back into the port loaded down with fresh fish for shipping both northward to Bangkok and southward to Penang in Malaysia, which is much closer. A large cold storage warehouse has been built along the Songkhla water-front so that fish can be preserved frozen for a period of time. Dotting the waterfront are small shipyards where the fishing boats can be built and re-paired. Fish is a major item of Thai diet and most farmers catch their own fish to eat with their rice or to make into a fish sauce commonly used in Thai dishes. The rivers and klongs (and during flood the rice fields them-selves) are filled with fish. Still the commercial fisheries are necessary to supply the needs of the cities and to provide some export to neighboring lands.

Several years ago the Thai government began to encourage the develop-ment of Songkhla as a beach resort. The Gulf side of the peninsula on which the city is built has a magnificent long white sandy beach on which a small, completely modern hotel has been built with a small golf course next to it. The city is a little too far distant from Bangkok, however, and few foreigners will travel the five to six hundred miles to get there for a holiday. On my most recent visit there only two rooms in the hotel were occupied by Westerners. The other vacationers were Thai or Malay, but there were not enough of them to fill the hotel.

The people of the most southern provinces of Thailand are ethnically Malay rather than Thai. The Malay language is widely spoken by many per-sons who know no Thai, and the predominant religion is Islam instead of the Theravada Buddhism found in the rest of the country. Although Malay Muslims can be found in many provinces of the country they are most heavily concentrated in the five southernmost provinces of Songkhla, Pattani, Setul, Yala, and Naradhivas. While more than 95 percent of all Thai na-tionals over five years old speak Thai, more than a third of the nationals in these five provinces cannot speak Thai; their only daily language is Malay although they may have learned Arabic in memorizing the *Koran*.

There are variations among and within the five Southern provinces them-selves; they are not homogenous units joined against all outsiders. The provincial capitals often have the largest numbers of non-Malay, non-Muslim people in the persons of Thai government officials and Chinese merchants. Songkhla, which has a major police headquarters and other government offices, has a large number of Thai-speaking people among the Muslims as well as among the Buddhists. Setul, too, although Muslim in religion is

oriented northward rather than southward toward Malaysia due to geographical conditions and has more Thai speakers than Malay speakers. Yet, the
heavily shared Malay language and Islam religion of the five Southern
provinces historically link them together and tend, to some extent, to
separate them from the rest of Thailand. Again, as in the Northeast, in recent years the Thai government has made several efforts, not always with
sensitivity or success, to tie this region more closely to the rest of Thailand.

The entire Southern peninsula area has had a long history distinct from
that of Central or Northern Thailand. Long before the Thai came to
Sukhothai, Ayudhya, and Bangkok there were ancient kingdoms in this
Southern area referred to by ancient Chinese and Arab and Persian writers.
Well known is the Srivijaya kingdom with its central cities believed to
have been in Sumatra and which met the Mons and Khmers at the northern
end of the peninsular area. Even earlier, the exact whereabouts of such
kingdoms as Tambralinga and Langkasuka, mentioned in Chinese chronicles,
are not known yet today. Some researchers believe they may have existed in
present-day Malaysia while others think their locations were in Southern
Thailand.

Both early Chinese and later European traders to this area found thriving
trading ports at Pattani, Songkhla, and Nakornsrithammarat farther north.
All of them served at one time or another (usually under other names) as
the terminals of cross-peninsular trading routes linking the Indian Ocean
and the China Sea and reducing the hazards and amount of time needed by
trips completely around the southern tip of the Malay Peninsula.

When the kings of Ayudhya began to extend their domains southward
they encountered important independent trading states under the rule of
rajas and their queens at Pattani, Songkhla (Singora), and Nakornsrithammarat (Ligor). In time these independent states as well as some still farther
south, which are now an integral part of Malaysia, were incorporated into
the Thai kingdom or made tributary states. Some remained in the status of
tributary states until the beginning of the present century when they were
surrendered to Great Britain.

There is a sign, not often seen, in peninsular Thailand of what is assumed to be a still earlier group of inhabitants. These are the Negrito people
of whom little is known by scholars of either East or West. The number
of Negritos living deep in the mountain forests is probably no more than a
few hundred at most, and they rarely venture into Thai villages or towns.
Called Semang, the Negritos that have been seen are usually compared to
pygmies of Africa. Their dark, short, muscular bodies are topped with heads
covered with a thick woolly hair. They apparently have no settled villages,
but consist of small nomadic groups that depend on hunting and what food
can be gathered in the forests without cultivation. Their principal hunting

weapon is the blowpipe with a poisoned arrow. On their few appearances in Thai villages the purpose is usually to barter forest products for the few items, such as salt, they might want from the villagers.

Scattered groups of Negritos are found in other countries of Southeast Asia, including Malaysia, the Philippines, and Indonesia. The origin of all these groups is a mystery as is their relationship to similar groups in Africa and to each other.

When the Arab and Persian traders came to the Malay Peninsula many centuries ago they brought with them a new religion as a major cultural contribution to the area. They found a local religion, believed to have been animistic, already there. As the Thai farther north imposed Buddhism on a base of animism and achieved a satisfactory mixture so the Malay imposed Islam on an animistic base and created a satisfactory blend. Islam, therefore, in Malaysia is not identical to Islam in North Africa or the Middle East. Many of the old spirit-worshiping practices continue among the Malay peoples, although these practices have been relegated to a position of lesser importance under the dominance of Islam. Yet, spirit doctors may still be summoned to drive out spirits causing illness, but the incantations they use now to exorcize the evil spirits are drawn from the *Koran* rather than from old spirit beliefs.

The religious, ethnic, and to some extent historical differences between the majority Thai Buddhists and the minority Thai-Malay Muslims are the root of the problems in Southern Thailand today. The friend or student of Thailand should make no mistake in underestimating the problems of the minority living in Southern Thailand. Although involving fewer persons in total, the Malay minority may well be a more serious problem to Thailand than that of the ethnic Chinese or the Thai-Lao problem of the Northeast. It is important to remember that while the Communist terrorists operating on both sides of the Thai-Malaysia border have added a dangerous complication to the political scene, the Thai-Malay problem existed long before the Communists were around and is basically separate from the Communist menace. The Communists have latched on to the Thai-Malay problems and are using them for their own ends to the detriment of the Thai and Malay on both sides of the border. But eliminating the Communists from the area will not by itself solve the older problems of the Thai treatment of the Malay minority.

Historically the Malays in Southern Thailand have been oriented toward their fellow Malay-Muslims farther south. Four of the five principal Thai-Malay provinces share a common border with Malaysia; only Pattani does not. At various times in history these provinces were united in independent states ruled by Muslim rajas and these independent states sometimes included districts which are now in Malaysia. During the period of British

rule of the Malay states some of the colonial officials were not averse to let-
ting it be known subtly and openly at times that they thought the Southern
Thai provinces would be better off economically and politically if they were
united with British Malaya. An irredentist movement grew among Malay
on both sides of the border.

Often Thai officials in Bangkok were insensitive to the needs and desires
of their Malay subjects in the South. Officials were sent to the Southern
provinces who did not know the Malay language and customs, and worse,
were completely unfamiliar with Islam, its laws and its meanings for the
everyday life of the Thai Muslims. In other ways the Malay felt they were
discriminated against. At times, the Thai government tried to stop the use
of the Malay language in the schools. Thai laws covering personal and
family relations contrary to the teachings of the *Koran* were sometimes
forcibly imposed on the people without thought. Young men who spoke only
Malay were drafted into the Thai army where only Thai was spoken, which
put the young Malays in an impossible situation. Furthermore, the Thai army
served Thai food based on the diet habits of the majority of the Thai people
and paid no attention to Muslim dietary rules. In many ways, big and
small, the Thai majority frequently antagonized this important minority and
built up a resentment which could be easily utilized by irredentists calling
for reunification with northern Malaysia.

At the end of the 1950's a new factor was introduced into the situation in
the form of the Communists from Malaysia. When the British and later the
independent Malaysians finally managed to suppress the Communist guerilla
movement in Malaysia, a small band of hard-core Communist terrorists
(mainly ethnic Chinese) fled across the border into the jungles of Thailand.
There they have attempted to rebuild their organization and forces so that
they may now number several hundred or more. Although most of the fleeing
Communists, including the leaders, were Malay-Chinese, they have not
hesitated to use the discontent among Southern Thai-Malay to recruit new
members and to gain support for their bands in hiding. The Thai border
patrol police and Malaysian forces have combined efforts at times to root out
the remaining Communist bands with little real success. Often abandoned
camps are found, but much less often are any Communists found. Part of the
Thai effort has had to be diverted to seeking out and trying to destroy a few
indigenous Communist bands farther north in the central Thai part of the
peninsula.

In the last ten years the government of Thailand has taken steps to improve the relations between Bangkok and the Southern provinces. Muslim
leaders from the South have been brought to the capital for training and
indoctrination programs. Efforts have been made to send Malay-speaking
officials to the Southern provinces. The Malay language, under certain con-

ditions, can be used in schools, at least in elementary schools, but all students must also learn Thai. Disputes involving marriage, inheritance, and other family matters, when only Malay are parties to the dispute, can be settled according to Islamic law. The courts generally in the Malay area have a Muslim religious adviser present during the hearings on cases. The adviser is usually of rank equal to the judge and advises the judge on relevant Islamic law applicable in similar cases. A new university is beginning to function in the South with divisions at Songkhla and in other cities. In these ways and many others the Thai government has finally begun to demonstrate its awareness of the problems of the South and its willingness to take some positive steps and make some concessions to bind the Malays of Thailand more closely to the national state and government. Some of the steps have had little success and much, much more needs to be done to win the full support of the Thai-Malay peoples for Thailand, but a beginning has been made.

No visitor to Southern Thailand should miss a trip to Nakornsrithammarat, one of the oldest cities in Thailand. The city, some distance north of Songkhla, is connected to the main Southern railroad line by a short spur line. From the windows of the train one can see evidence of the mixed nature of the population of this city which at one time was a busy cosmopolitan trading port with Chinese, Malay, Arab, Persian, Dutch, Portuguese, French, and British trading vessels coming and going. Along the railroad tracks are Christian and Muslim cemeteries and in the distance are the towering chedis of Wat Mahathad.

Wat Mahathad is one of the largest, oldest, most revered, and most interesting temples in all of Thailand. It dates back hundreds of years and is the home of one of the Buddha images which is claimed to be, in contention with those in Chiengmai's Wat Phra Singh and the National Museum of Bangkok, the original Phra Singh image from Ceylon.

The temple has a large compound at one end of a long main city street. The compound is roughly one city block wide and four or five city blocks long and is carefully sprinkled with sand and shaded by a generous number of trees. More than a score of buildings including residences for the monks are well spaced throughout the compound.

At one end of the compound are the main religious buildings of the wat clustered together and surrounded by a rectangular covered gallery of brick and whitewashed stucco with wooden roof beams a dull red in color. Built up from the floor of the gallery is a platform which is about fifteen inches high and runs the entire length of the four sides of the gallery. On the platform sit more than 170 bigger-than-life-size Buddha images each seated on a lotus flower or naga pedestal. Curiously, the clothes of the images are all painted a dull, fading red which in many spots is peeling to reveal the gray stucco underneath.

The interior area of the wat is a stone garden of chedis ranging in size from a few feet to perhaps thirty feet. Crowded together with the small and large bot and vihara within the rectangular gallery walls there seems hardly enough room to move about. In the center of the area is a giant chedi rising to two hundred feet or more, one of the tallest in Thailand and topped with a gold-covered spire. The steep stairway to the closed entrance of the chedi seems squeezed between a small vihara and the bulk of the chedi's base. The stairway is guarded by seven-headed nagas which form the balustrades and by crocodiles, lions, demons, and humans on horseback, all carved and painted on the sides of the stone stairway. And over the entire complex the standing and seated images of a benign Buddha watch peacefully the Thai who come now to pay their respects as they have come for several centuries.

I have made the trip from Nakornsrithammarat to Bangkok several times by train. On my last journey I was unable to get either first-class accommodations or second-class sleeping accommodations and I traveled by second-class coach for what turned out to be a twenty-two-hour trip. A short train ride connects Nakornsrithammarat with Khao Chum Tong Junction where the spur line meets the main southern line of the railroad. On the way the train made frequent stops for reasons which I could not always discern. A couple of times I saw we had stopped to receive or discharge passengers and one time we had to wait for several buffalo to cross the tracks ahead of us. The engine was a woodburner and with all the windows open in the heat, soot and occasional cinders were continually blowing into the car.

At Khao Chum Tong our second-class coach was to be hooked on to the international express from Penang in Malaysia to Bangkok. The express was late and we had to wait on a siding for about two hours. In the early sunny afternoon of a hot-season day sitting in an old railroad car can become a bit uncomfortable. Most passagers climbed out to find a spot of shade while several, including me, walked into the small junction town's largest coffee shop near the station for some refreshing cold drinks.

Finally, the international express arrived and with considerable jockeying around our car was hooked to it. Express is a misnomer, for the train makes almost every stop and averages only about thirty miles an hour. When we pulled out of Khao Chum Tong we had to climb through a southern mountain ridge and our speed was reduced to around five miles an hour. This "express" also found itself sidetracked from time to time to await the passage of freight trains.

The snail's pace at the beginning of the trip gave me the chance to observe the rugged mountainous countryside through which we traveled. It appeared to have few inhabitants to enjoy what seemed to me from the safe haven of the train to be some of the most beautiful scenery in Thailand, steep hills covered with heavy jungle growth. Only a few villages did we see, and to my surprise we saw houses which seemed to be isolated or in small clusters of two or three in the forest areas rather than in villages. Some of the houses were little more than thatch lean-tos and most were made of thatch and matted palms.

By nightfall our coach had become a temporary community. The car was crowded so that some people sat or stood in the aisles surrounded by a motley collection of baggage piled all over the floor, racks, and seats. Suitcases, boxes, paper bags, bags of woven palm strips, toys, packages, water bottles, food, blankets, and everything else needed on the trip or at the destination were stuffed into some corner or other space in the car. At every station more baggage was loaded usually through the open windows by friends while the passenger boarded at the end of the car and then searched up and down the aisle until he found his baggage.

Young men and boys struggled through the crowds bringing cold soft drinks, beer, and Mekong whisky for those who wanted refreshment. Later, the same boys brought plates of rice and curry for those who wanted to buy a meal. Many of the travelers had brought their own food, however, or waited until we stopped at a station when the train was attacked by an army of women and children selling fruit, rice sweets, barbecued chickens, and cold drinks through the windows all accented by the piercing call of "Olian, Olian, Olian!" Olian is an iced black coffee sold in glasses, paper cups, and plastic bags and drunk with straws. It is a very popular and inexpensive drink and can be found all over Thailand. The plastic bags were an especially practical idea. About the size of refrigerator bags used for storing food in the West, the bags were filled about halfway with ice and the olian was poured over the ice. The tops of the bags were tied together tightly leaving only room for a straw to reach into the bag. The cold mixture of coffee and ice lasted a long time in this form.

Finally the train reached Ban Pong Junction and we entered the Central Plain of Thailand, leaving the southern peninsula behind. At Ban Pong the train turns sharply eastward heading toward Bangkok. Another rail line heads west of the junction toward Kanchanaburi just beyond which it crosses the river Kwai and extends a short distance farther before it comes to an end. This rail line, known by many as "the railway of death" in World War II, was made famous by Pierre Boulle in his novel, *The Bridge Over the River Kwai*. For those who saw the movie, a visit to the actual site may be a little disappointing. Although it is a rugged area, it does not have the dramatic, spectacular ruggedness of the site used in the motion picture which was filmed in another country.

I made my first visit to Kanchanaburi in 1960 to visit the bridge site and the cemetery where lie some seven thousand British, Dutch, and Malay troops who died to build a railroad line to link Thailand and Burma, a line which was never satisfactorily used by the Japanese forces.

Row after row of graves with small bronze plaques identifying those that can be identified fill that well-kept cemetery. On many of the plaques a simple, sentimental, yet deeply moving memorial line from the dead man's family is inscribed. There one can read on these markers such sentiments as: "A vacant chair, an empty place, how we miss his loving face"; "Midst life's changes we never forget. With us always remembered"; "Deep in our hearts his memory is kept"; "At the sinking of the sun and in the morning, we will remember them"; and for a sailor, aged twenty-one, "My darling, so sadly missed by all. Your ever-sorrowing mother."

The Kanchanaburi cemetery is the most vivid and impressive reminder in Thailand of World War II, but the effects on Thailand of the Japanese alliance and subsequent occupation were territorial and economic. The Thai received from the Japanese the four northernmost provinces of Malaya which the Thai had turned over to the British early in the century. The Thai also received from the Japanese armies part of the Shan states in Burma. Earlier, as a result of Japanese arbitration, Thailand had acquired provinces in Cambodia and Laos from the Vichy French government. All of these territories were returned to Britain and France in the postwar peace settlements.

The large numbers of Japanese troops stationed in Thailand during World War II were a heavy drain on the Thai economy. One of the economic measures taken by the Japanese was to reduce the value of the baht until it was at parity with the Japanese yen. The Japanese demanded large loans from the Thai and also paid high prices for what they bought. In time these measures upset the economic stability of the country and inflation quickly took its toll. In the early days of the occupation the Chinese, loyal to China, took what steps they could to disrupt supply shipments to the Japanese and often cheated the Japanese forces in sales to them. In time, the Thai joined in the cheating and corruption. Trickery of the Japanese became widespread and was to leave some bad habits for the postwar generation of Thai people in their relations with their own government.

Under the very noses of the Japanese forces a Thai resistance movement was built. By the end of the war it was estimated that the Thai underground had organized and trained some fifty thousand guerrillas. But they were never called into action. The Japanese were probably aware of these activities, but despite their frustration did nothing to suppress them effectively. The Japanese forces were retreating in Burma and needed an open Thai territory across which they could retreat farther, if need be. They could not afford to fight the Thai at the same time as they were losing in Burma.

In several other countries of Southeast Asia large underground forces had also been built up. In most of them these forces were not immediately disbanded, but frequently became the core of the forces used for the nationalist revolutions against the returning colonialist powers. There, Thailand had a strong advantage. It did not have to worry about a European colonial power coming back into its territory; Thailand could safely disband its guerrilla forces without any nationalist revolutionary aftereffect.

The steady progress of American and allied forces across the Pacific islands and the atomic bombing of Japan resulted in the Japanese surrender. The Japanese troops left Thailand, and within a short time, compared to other areas of Southeast Asia where the Japanese occupation had stimulated nationalist independence movements, Thailand had begun its recovery and resumed its independent station in the community of nations. Today, only scars, such as the cemetery at Kanchanaburi, are there to remind the Thai and others who might visit that off-the-track site of the Japanese occupation a quarter of a century ago.

From Ban Pong Junction our train moved eastward through the bright morning sunlight freshened by a light rain shower. The dry season would soon be over and the rains would begin bringing new life and new green of young rice to the faded, dusty gold of the dry fields of stubble. When we passed through Nakorn Pathom we saw the giant golden chedi rising into the sky. The gold tiles shone with dazzling brightness in the sun.

The train approached Bangkok from the Thonburi side of the river and north of the center of the city. We journeyed through heavy forest growth as if in a dense, lush jungle until we burst onto the bridge crossing the Chao Phya. Then our train turned southward for the last few kilometers, passing railyards, a cement plant, houses, and Chitralada Palace before reaching our destination in the cavernous interior of Hualampong Station.

Epilogue: Fish in the Water, Rice in the Fields

Many of the activities, customs, festivals, and other matters described in this book are changing. Traditional behavior patterns melt before the heat of rapid modernization. Part of the changes in Thailand can be attributed to what may be seen as the natural evolution of any country as its population grows and presses on its natural environment creating new physical, economic, social, and psychological needs and desires. For four centuries Thailand has has had contacts of various sorts with the nations of the Western world and for centuries before that with the Oriental trading nations and ancient empires, some of which have since disappeared. All have left their impact on the Thai people and their country, an impact which has been widened and deepened in the last century and a half and which has contributed significantly to the changes in the country. Added to the impact brought by contacts with other nations are rapid changes in modern science and technology which have had and are having major effects on the development of Thailand, its land, and its people.

Still, no country or society ever changes totally or at once. The Southeast Asia found in the romantic fiction of Joseph Conrad and Somerset Maugham earlier in this century can still be found in many parts of Thailand. The brilliant green rice fields, the slow, lumbering buffalo, the small handsome brown men and beautiful women, the colorful costumes, the sometimes lazy natives interested in producing no more than they need at any particular time, about which these novelists and other writers told, can still be found, although the traveler today may have to search far out of Bangkok and other major Southeast Asian cities to find some of them.

255

Despite these lingering features, which often add much to the feeling of affection one has for the area, there have been many obvious changes in Thailand. Bangkok has grown enormously in population during the 1960's, and with this growth in numbers has come a growth in physical Bangkok. Expanding in all directions over the former rice fields and market gardens, Bangkok has built new roads to link all the sections of the city. Klongs have been filled in to widen older roads. Ten years ago the capital city had a hotel and one apartment building which were ten stories high, the tallest structures except for the graceful chedis which rose above some of the city's wats. Now, new buildings rising up in some cases to heights of twenty or more stories are in all parts of the city, creating monuments to expansion and modernization in this sprawling city surrounded by flat fields as far as the eye can see. Driving through Bangkok one can immediately see the surface impact that Western culture has had on the Thai capital—popular music, American movies, night clubs, new consumer goods of all kinds in countless numbers of new stores and shopping centers, a miniature golf course, a drive-in restaurant, an ice-cube factory.

Beyond the surface glitter of new buildings and gaily lighted colored signs, recent years have also brought deeper, more important, more lasting changes to Thailand. One of the most important changes of the decade in Thailand is the construction of many new all-weather roads linking all major regions of the country together with one another and with the national capital. Much more needs to be done because there are now no more than one or two principal highways in each area. Both main roads and feeder roads must be extended until the whole country has a large unified road network. But much has already been achieved when an automobile or a truck hauling a load of goods can at the beginning of the 1970's cover the distance from Chiengmai to Bangkok or Nongkai to Bangkok in half the time or less than it took in 1960. At the beginning of the last decade there was no through road usable in all weather linking Bangkok and the South, a factor which contributed to the feeling of separation between the Southerners and the Central Thai. Now there is such a road joining these areas and the traveler can make the trip faster by road than by railroad.

Other changes have begun to break down the separation of Bangkok and Central Thailand from the rest of the country. The central government has given increasing emphasis to regional economic development, although many of its efforts are still in initial stages. Encouragement has been given to the diversification of agriculture for the production of new cash crops. While rice has remained number one, far outdistancing any other crop, the 1960's have seen the major increase in production and export of maize and lesser, but significant increases in other products. In upcountry education, too, gains have been made, and of special note is the establishment of higher education institutions in the North, Northeast, and South.

Politically the most important change of the decade is the drafting and announcement of a new permanent constitution which firmly declares Thailand to be a democratic constitutional monarchy. The constitution's provisions are such that leaders dedicated to democracy can create one for their country using its framework. But the constitution has qualifying clauses in many provisions which will permit, if the government is controlled by the wrong hands, the semblance of democracy while perpetuating the military authoritarianism, benevolent though it may appear at times, which has ruled Thailand for most of the last forty years since the revolution of 1932. The final direction of government in Thailand awaits more experience under the new constitution.

For most of the 1960's Thailand has been ruled by an oligarchy of military leaders. They have functioned under an interim constitution which permitted them to restrict many ordinary expressions of a free political society. Political parties, labor unions, mass organizations and assemblies have not been permitted. All of these organizations are expected to function under the new constitution. If they do, undoubtedly one group that will make itself felt will be the young, educated elite both inside and outside of the government. In 1957 the university youth of Thailand, opposing the February rigged election of Marshal Pibun Songgram, helped create the conditions which brought Marshal Sarit to power. Once in control, however, Sarit prohibited mass student organizations and student political activities.

The prohibition of organized opposition by young persons does not mean it did not exist. Private rumblings of discontent were heard frequently among students and many frustrated young government employees, also. Although remaining quiet and disorganized through most of the 1960's, their numbers were increasing. Enrollments in universities were going up and thousands of students were going abroad to study in the United States, the United Kingdom, Australia, and New Zealand. It is difficult to imagine that Thai students spending several years in any of these nations will not be affected by the fundamental beliefs and practices of democracy they witness, and by the basic confrontation, especially in the second half of the 1960's, between the young generation and the established governments.

In the days of King Ramkamheng of Sukhothai, he wrote in his famous inscription on his stone pillar:

During the life of my father I served my father, I served my mother. If I got a piece of game or a piece of fish, I brought it to my father. If I had a fruit that was acid or sweet, delicious and agreeable, I brought it to my father. If I went on a hunt for elephants and got some, I brought them to my father. If I went to attack a village or town and brought back elephants, men, women, silver, gold, I gave them to my father. My father died. There remained my elder brother. I continued to serve my elder brother as I had served my father. My elder brother died, the entire kingdom passed on to me.

While there is no doubt that most young Thai men and women continue to show the same respect toward the elders in their families as did this great king in the thirteenth century, can it be expected that they will show the same respect and patience in the years ahead for an impersonal government of elected men no longer possessing the "fatherly" image previously supporting the absolute monarchy? Can contemporary youth in Thailand be expected to wait its turn, as did King Ramkamheng, or is it going to start making demands for quicker action?

As thousands of Thai students return home from abroad and thousands of others achieve higher levels of education at home, it can be assumed that they will expect their government, functioning under its new constitution, to make the necessary changes in Thai society to make it politically more democratic and free, economically more developed and fulfilling, and socially more modern and open. If the new constitution does not pave the way for desired changes in society, the young may feel it is necessary again to change the constitution or more fundamentally to change the government structure itself.

Some Thai, supported by some Western political leaders and writers, believe that any future change will automatically lead to Communism in Thailand. Under certain conditions there is no doubt that Communism could come to Thailand as it could to any other country in the world. But such need not be the case, and I believe that a study of all relevant factors and signs in Thailand indicates that the direction of change probably will not be toward Communism in the immediate future, unless all attempts to solve Thai problems are blindly frustrated by a stubborn and unyielding and unintelligent governing elite that defines government interests in Thailand narrowly in terms of self-interest of the elite. Any elite surrenders power slowly, but to think of the Thai elite as stubbornly unyielding or unintelligent is to display a lack of knowledge of Thai history and Thai character, for the one political trait most often attributed to the Thai is their flexibility in the face of strong power which can inevitably bring about changes to conform to its will.

In the face of changes in the 1960's and the growing demand for more changes in the years ahead, it should be noted that there are some aspects of Thailand and Thai life that have remained basically unchanged even where some alterations to the surface have appeared. For one thing, Thailand is still an agricultural country with an economy based on a small number of agricultural crops and will probably stay such a country for many years to come. Despite the economic gains that have been made, the country is still underdeveloped. Although few people are starving, many are poor when measured in terms of health, length of life, education, cash income, and other standards besides that of subsistence living.

With more than 90 percent of the Thai population ethnically and racially Thai, speaking the same language or a variation of it, and following the same religious beliefs, Thailand is culturally one of the most homogeneous countries in Asia. There are ethnic minorities in the Chinese, Malay, and hill tribe peoples and to a lesser extent in the Thai-Lao, Cambodian, and Mon peoples, and these ethnic differences should be properly recognized. But these ethnic minorities are nowhere near as numerous or troublesome as one finds between the Malay and Chinese in Malaysia or the Karens, Shans, Chins, Kachins, and Burmans in Burma. Linguistically there are some differences among groups in Thailand, but again the differences are not as pronounced or the numbers so great as one finds in the Philippines, where less than half of the population can speak Tagalog, the national language. In religion there is an important and distinctly different minority of about 4 percent in Thailand who are believers in Islam. This group must be dealt with with greater intelligence than it has in much of Thailand's recent history.

Happily for the visitor to Thailand most personal traits of the Thai which endear them to other people have undergone little or no change over the years. The Thai are still among the most tolerant and independent of peoples. Supported by their principal religion, Buddhism, they still believe that each individual is responsible for his own actions and will be held accountable for them in his next life. Each individual, therefore, makes his own choices in working out his karma, and his responsibility is first of all to himself. Differences, even aberrations not harmful to others, are tolerated as the individual's independent effort to develop his own future life.

The Thai are reluctant to do or say anything that would embarrass others. Lying can be accepted if it helps some person to "save face" or preserves him from unnecessary embarrassment. So as not to embarrass others it is important to keep oneself under internal control, internal discipline. Extremes of thought and behavior should be avoided. Moderation is a positive virtue. Keeping control of one's voice, emotions, behavior is referred to as keeping a "cool heart," and a cool heart in a Thai or a farang is an important asset in the eyes of a Thai.

The recognition that all things change and that few things, thoughts, or actions are of eternal value in themselves, expressed at times in the Thai attitude of "mai pen rai," helps the individual to exercise self-control and to avoid embarrassing others. Finally, the evaluation at one level of everything by the degree to which it is "sanuk," that is, whether or not it contributes to the joyous general sense of well-being for the individual, helps the Thai to shunt aside those activities and persons who might create distressing situations of an unnecessary or ephemeral nature. All of these traits and many others contribute to the approach to life and its problems of these kindly, intelligent, proudly independent, and often frustrating people.

Unchanged, too, during the decade of the 1960's, despite the inroads made against them are the problems the Thai face. None of these problems has been eliminated. Fully realizing the general homogeneity of Thai society, still among Thai problems are the minority groups, small in numbers, but of whom many are more or less disaffected and estranged from the large majority group. The Thai government has begun efforts to promote the integration of the Thai-Malay Muslim of the South, the assimilation of the ubiquitous Chinese, the strengthening of the bonds between the Central Thai and the Thai-Lao, and the recognition that the hill tribes are a significant and integral part of the national community. Much more needs to be done, and it must be done soon and at levels beyond formal government action alone. Ancient behavior patterns and prejudices need changing, for the Thai are learning, as have many other nations, that deeply rooted social divisions are not eliminated by government decisions alone even when those decisions are uniformly and fairly executed.

Thailand continues to face problems of maintaining security for its villages and their people. Part of the security problem is the safeguarding of remote areas against marauding bands of outlaws of one kind or another. In recent months Bangkok newspapers carried stories of buffalo rustling gangs in the Northeast and of extortionist gangs preying on rubber and coconut farmers in the South, including some of the poorest farmers, who must pay for protection against the looting, destructive bandit gangs. If a government is going to hold the allegiance and support of its people, it must first of all protect them from ruthless marauders of all types.

The security problem is complicated in Thailand by the intrusion of Communist activist groups in the North, Northeast, and the South. While no doubt some of the individuals in these groups, which are repeatedly terrorizing remote villages, have been trained locally, others have been trained among the Communists of Laos and North Vietnam. In the South remnants of the old Malay Communist guerrilla bands are still found. While the numbers in all areas are still small, experience in other countries shows that the Communists are adept at using any discontent for their own ends and to build their own strength. The Thai government should recognize this fact and direct its activities not only against Communist insurgents, but against the causes of discontent as well.

The most important factors causing discontent are poverty, corruption, and worn-out traditions. These three are interrelated and solutions to them should be approached simultaneously.

The most often quoted part of King Ramkamheng's inscription almost seven centuries ago is the following:

During the lifetime of King Ramkamheng, Muang Sukhothai was prosperous. In the water there was fish; in the fields there was rice. The lord of the country did not levy taxes on his subjects. . . . Whoever wanted to engage in commerce in elephants could do so; whoever wanted to trade in horses could do so; whoever wanted to engage in commerce in silver, or in gold, could do so.

There is still plenty of fish in the water and rice in the fields, but these are no longer sufficient to meet the rising new demands of the Thai people for better health, better education, more material goods, a more nutritious diet, wider economic opportunities, and better government. Subsistence living is no longer sufficient for a people aware of world developments and taking an increasingly important part in the world. To meet the new needs and demands of the Thai people is a tremendous task for the government and it has far to go. In that sense the Thai people, even though as we have noted several times few are starving, are a poor people, and these unfulfilled demands for higher standards of living need to be satisfied.

One of the signs of poverty is the low salary paid to most government employees who often cannot rely on subsistence farms to provide them with supplementary food and clothing. Working for the government has great prestige, but in times of rising costs prestige is not an adequate substitute for more income. Thailand has several salary categories for civil servants, but more than four out of five are in the lowest category.

Consider the upcountry government employee who earns 1,000 baht a month (approximately U.S. $50) and who has a son he wants to send to college. First, he must get him into a good preparatory school usually in Bangkok. Besides the usual fees traditionally this requires several thousand baht in payment of "tea" money, an unofficial and often disguised illegal payment a school or any other office or individual might demand to get something done that should normally be done as part of the duties of the office or individual. It is a form of bribery. Many Westerners are familiar with the need to pay "tea" money when renting real estate in Bangkok. In order to meet these high demands on his salary, the government official himself may start charging a few extra baht to provide supposedly free government services to the people under his jurisdiction. And so begins another tale of official corruption in a network that extends throughout the entire society. Yet, if salaries of these government officials are raised very much, prices will rise, and a vicious circle begins. In King Ramkamheng's time the lord of the country may not have levied taxes and fees, but the Thai government does now, and the door has been opened to differences in degree of collection and enforcement of other laws dependent often on the amount the citizen can pay on the side to the tax collector or to the law enforcer. This kind of corruption at all levels of government has led to a resigned but cynical and distrustful view by many ordinary Thai citizens of any government official.

King Ramkamheng wrote that anyone who wished to engage in trade in gold or silver or other items could do so. But in the seven hundred years since his reign traditions have grown to restrict that free-trading situation. Today, only Sino-Thai of a particular linguistic group would, in fact, trade in gold or silver. While legally open to all, tradition often dictates who will be employed in certain occupations. To counter these traditional limitations the Thai government has tried by law to restrict some job fields to Thai citizens. Restrictions either by law or tradition can be harmful to an open economy, and while it is comparatively easy to change the law, it is extremely difficult to change traditions of centuries. Yet, these traditions in the economic, social, and political life of Thailand must be altered, if the nation is to solve the problems of poverty and corruption.

For the Thai and for the foreign friends of Thailand nothing I have written here is new. The Thai leaders are fully aware of these problems, and a real sign of hope is the statements these leaders are making and the plans they are announcing for taking steps to solve this full range of problems. The foreigner must understand one fact above all others. While he can suggest, urge, and try to persuade, he cannot dictate to the Thai. For centuries they have acted independently to solve their own problems at their own speed in the light of what they understood their interests to be. There is no reason to believe that they will not continue to do the same, and we should be glad that they will. While changing those worn-out traditions that are hampering the development of their economy and polity, they have no intention, as far as I can see, of changing those traditions which have enabled them to preserve their rich culture and their proud independence. This is as it should be.

Perhaps the most difficult fact about Thailand for any foreigner to accept is the fact that a time will come when he must leave this beautiful country and its delightful people. This description is true despite the foreigner's knowledge of Thailand's problems, the frustrations he often faces, and the doubts he may have that any outsider can ever really know the Thai people, their beliefs, and their feelings. The only consolation the foreigner has is to return again and again, and between visits to hope that the next visit to Thailand will be soon.

FOR FURTHER READING

A vast reservoir of publications about Thailand is available for anyone interested in further reading about that fascinating country and its people. This information is available in Thai and in several Western and Asian languages. For Western materials published before 1960, the reader will find useful a publication in that year of the Central Library of Chulalongkorn University. The publication is entitled, *Bibliography of Material About Thailand in Western Languages*. The list of materials here below is selected to cover a wide range of subjects for the general reader at varying degrees of scholarship and difficulty. In this list are included a few representative articles from recent issues of *The Journal of the Siam Society*, but the reader interested in Thailand will find every issue of the *Journal* filled with interesting articles well worth the reader's time.

Annual Report 1968. Bangkok: Bangkok Bank Ltd., 1969 .

Phya Anuman Rajadhon. *Life and Ritual in Old Siam: Three Studies of Thai Life and Customs*. New Haven: HRAF Press, 1961.

Audric, John. *Siam, Land of Temples*. London: Robert Hale Limited, 1962.

Barnett, David. *The Mask of Siam*. London: Robert Hale Limited, 1959.

Bartlett, Norman. *Land of the Lotus Eaters*. London: Jarrolds, 1959.

Bernatzik, Hugo Adolph and Emmy. *The Spirits of the Yellow Leaves*. London: Robert Hale Limited, 1958.

Blake, W. T. *Thailand Journey*. New York: Taplinger Publishing Co., 1960.

Blanchard, Wendell, et al. *Thailand, Its People, Its Society, Its Culture*. New Haven: HRAF Press, 1958.

Blofeld, John. *People of the Sun, Encounters in Siam*. London: Hutchinson & Co., 1960.

Boulle, Pierre. *The Bridge Over the River Kwai*. New York: Vanguard Press, Inc., 1954. (A novel)

Bowers, Faubion. *Theatre in the East: A Survey of Asian Dance and Drama*. New York: Thomas Nelson & Sons, 1956.

Bowie, Theodore, ed. *The Arts of Thailand*. Bloomington, Ind.: Indiana University, 1960.

Boyd, Dean and Marjorie Martin. *Farang.* New York: Harcourt, Brace & World, 1964. (A novel)

Brandon, James R. *Theatre in Southeast Asia.* Cambridge, Mass.: Harvard University Press, 1967.

Brandt, John H. "The Negrito of Peninsular Thailand," *The Journal of the Siam Society,* Vol. XLIX, Part 2, November 1961, pp. 123–160.

———. "The Southeast Asian Negrito: Further Notes on the Negrito of South Thailand," *The Journal of the Siam Society,* Vol. LIII, Part 1, January 1965, pp. 27–43.

Buchanan, Keith. *The Southeast Asian World: An Introductory Essay.* New York: Taplinger Publishing Company, Inc., 1967.

Busch, Noel F. *Thailand: An Introduction to Modern Siam,* 2nd edition. Princeton, N.J.: D. Van Nostrand Company, Inc., 1964.

Cady, John F. *Thailand, Burma, Laos, & Cambodia.* Englewood Cliffs, N.J.: Prentice-Hall, Inc., 1966.

Caldwell, John C. *Massage Girl and Other Sketches of Thailand.* New York: The John Day Company, 1968.

Chalermnit. *Thai Folk Tales.* Bangkok: Chalermnit Press, 1967.

Ch'en, Kenneth K. S. *Buddhism the Light of Asia.* Woodbury, N.Y.: Barron's Educational Series, Inc., 1968.

Chu, Valentin. *Thailand Today, A Visit to Modern Siam.* New York: Thomas Y. Crowell Company, 1968.

Prince Chula Chakrabongse. *Lords of Life.* New York: Taplinger Publishing Company, Inc., 1960.

Coast, John. *Some Aspects of Siamese Politics.* New York: Institute of Pacific Relations, 1953.

Collis, Maurice. *Siamese White.* London: Faber and Faber Limited, 1936.

———. *Quest for Sita.* New York: The John Day Company, 1947.

Coomaraswamy, Ananda K. and The Sister Nivedita. *Myths of the Hindus and Buddhists.* New York: Dover Publications, Inc., 1967.

Coughlin, Richard J. *Double Identity: The Chinese in Modern Thailand.* Hong Kong: Hong Kong University Press, 1960.

Cripps, Francis. *The Far Province.* London: Hutchinson & Co., Ltd., 1965.

Davies, David M. *The Rice Bowl of Asia.* London: Robert Hale Limited, 1967.

de Young, John E. *Village Life in Modern Thailand.* Berkeley and Los Angeles: University of California Press, 1955.

Prince Dhaninivat, Kromamun Bidyalabh. *A History of Buddhism in Siam.* Bangkok: Reprinted from The Encyclopedia of Buddhism of the Government of Ceylon, 1960.

Ellis, Cynthia. *Mango Summer.* London: Hodder & Stoughton, 1960.

Exell, F. K. *The Land and People of Thailand.* London: Adam & Charles Black, 1960.

———. *Siamese Tapestry.* London: Robert Hale Limited, 1963.

Fraser, Thomas M., Jr. *Fishermen of South Thailand, The Malay Villagers.* New York: Holt, Rinehart and Winston, Inc., 1966.

Griswold, A. B. *King Mongkut of Siam.* New York: The Asia Society, 1961.

Harris, Townsend. *The Complete Journal of Townsend Harris.* Garden City, N.Y.: Doubleday, Doran & Company, Inc. for the Japan Society, N.Y., 1930.

Humphreys, Christmas. *Buddhism,* rev. ed. London: Penguin Books, 1955.

Hunter, Guy. *South-East Asia—Race, Culture, and Nation.* New York: Oxford University Press for the Institute of Race Relations, London, 1966.

Insor, D. *Thailand: A Political, Social, and Economic Analysis.* London: George Allen & Unwin, Ltd., 1963.

Kirkup, James. *Bangkok.* London: Phoenix House, 1968.

Krull, Germaine with Dorothea Melchers. *Tales from Siam.* London: Robert Hale Limited, 1966.

Kunstadter, Peter, ed. *Southeast Asian Tribes, Minorities, and Nations.* Princeton, N.J.: Princeton University Press, 1967. 2 vols.

LeMay, Reginald. *A Concise History of Buddhist Art in Siam.* Rutland, Vt. & Tokyo, Japan: Charles E. Tuttle Company, 2nd. ed., 1963.

Leonowens, Anna. *The English Governess at the Siamese Court.* New York: Roy Publishers, 1954.

Lomax, Louis E. *Thailand: The War That Is, The War That Will Be.* New York: Random House, Inc., 1967.

MacDonald, Malcolm. *Angkor.* London: Jonathan Cape, 1958.

Moerman, Michael. *Agricultural Change and Peasant Choice in a Thai Village.* Berkeley and Los Angeles: University of California Press, 1968.

Moffat, Abbot Low. *Mongkut, the King of Siam.* Ithaca, N.Y.: Cornell University Press, 1961.

Nach, James. *Thailand in Pictures.* New York: Sterling Publishing Co., Inc., 1967.

Nimmanahaeminda, Kraisri and Julian Hartland-Swann. "Expedition to the 'Khon Pa' (or Phi Tong Luang?)," *The Journal of the Siam Society,* Vol. L, Part 2, December 1962, pp. 165–186.

Nuechterlein, Donald E. *Thailand and the Struggle for Southeast Asia.* Ithaca, N.Y.: Cornell University Press, 1965.

Olivier, Tarquin. *Eye of the Day.* New York: William Morrow and Company, 1964.

Pendleton, Robert L., et al. *Thailand, Aspects of Landscape and Life.* New York: Duell, Sloan and Pearce, 1962.

Prabha, C. *Buddhist Holy Days and State Ceremonies of Thailand.* Bangkok: Prae Pittaya Publishing Company, 1964.

The Staff of Pramuan Sarn and Gordon H. Allison. *All About Thailand.* Bangkok: Pramuan Sarn Publishing House, 1967.

H. M. King Rama I. *Ramayana.* Bangkok: Chalermnit Bookshop, 2nd ed., 1967.

Reynolds, Jack. *A Woman of Bangkok.* New York: Ballentine Books, 1956. (A novel)

Riggs, Fred W. *Thailand: The Modernization of a Bureaucratic Polity.* Honolulu: East-West Center Press, 1966.

Seidenfaden, Erik. *The Thai Peoples (Book 1): The Origins and Habitats of the*

Thai Peoples with a Sketch of Their Material and Spiritual Culture. Bangkok: The Siam Society, 1958.

Sewell, W. R. Derrick and Gilbert F. White. "The Lower Mekong, An Experiment in International River Development," *International Conciliation,* No. 558, May 1966.

Silcock, T. H., ed. *Thailand: Social and Economic Studies in Development.* Durham, N.C.: Duke University Press, 1967.

Professor Silpa Bhirasi, et al. *The Origin and Evolution of Thai Murals.* Bangkok: Fine Arts Department, 1959.

Luang Sitsayamkan. *The Greek Favourite of the King of Siam.* Singapore: Donald Moore Press Ltd., 1967.

Siwasariyanon, Witt, ed. *Aspects and Facets of Thailand.* Bangkok: Public Relations Department of Thailand, 4th ed., 1961.

Skinner, G. William. *Chinese Society in Thailand: An Analytical History.* Ithaca, N.Y.: Cornell University Press, 1957.

————. *Leadership and Power in the Chinese Community.* Ithaca, N.Y.: Cornell University Press, 1958.

Smith, Nicol and Blake Clark. *Into Siam, Underground Kingdom.* Indianapolis: The Bobbs-Merrill Company, 1946.

Smith, Ronald Bishop. *Siam or the History of the Thais from Earliest Times to 1569 A.D.* Bethesda, Md.: Published by the author, 1966.

————. *Siam or the History of the Thais from 1569 A.D. to 1824 A.D.* Bethesda, Md.: Published by the author, 1967.

Soonsawad, Thong-in. *Panorama of Thailand.* Bangkok: Panorama of Thailand, 4th rev. ed., 1969.

Stanton, Edwin F. *Brief Authority: Excursions of a Common Man in an Uncommon World.* New York: Harper & Brothers Publishers, 1956.

Tarling, Nicholas. "Harry Parkes' Negotiations in Bangkok in 1856," *The Journal of the Siam Society,* Vol. LIII, Part 2, July 1965, pp. 153–180.

Thai Culture New Series. Bangkok: The Fine Arts Department, 1960 and later years. A series of pamphlets by various authors on several subjects related to Thai culture.

Thai Culture Series. Bangkok: The National Culture Institute, 1956. A series of pamphlets by various authors on several subjects related to Thai culture.

Thailand, A Seminar on Economic Development and Investment Opportunities. Bangkok: Bangkok Bank Ltd., 1968.

Thailand, Facts and Figures, 1966. Bangkok: Department of Technical and Economic Cooperation, Ministry of National Development, 1967.

Thompson, Virginia. *Thailand, The New Siam.* New York: The Macmillan Company, 1941.

Wales, H. G. Quaritch. *Siamese State Ceremonies: Their History and Function.* London: Bernard Quaritch, Ltd., 1931.

Wavell, Stewart. *The Naga King's Daughter.* London: George Allen & Unwin Ltd., 1964.

Wells, Kenneth E. *Thai Buddhism: Its Rites and Activities.* Bangkok: Published by the author, 1960.

Williams, Lea A. *The Future of the Overseas Chinese in Southeast Asia.* New York: McGraw-Hill Book Company for the Council on Foreign Relations, 1966.

Wilson, David A. *Politics in Thailand.* Ithaca, N.Y.: Cornell University Press, 1962.

Wit, Daniel. *Thailand: Another Vietnam?* New York: Charles Scribner's Sons, 1968.

Wood, W. A. R. *A History of Siam from the Earliest Times to the Year A.D. 1781,* with a Supplement Dealing With More Recent Events. Bangkok: Chalermnit Bookstore, 1924.

———. *Consul in Paradise, Sixty-Nine Years in Siam.* London: Souvenir Press, 1965.

Young, Gordon. *The Hill Tribes of Northern Thailand.* Bangkok: The Siam Society, 1962.

Young, Kenneth T. "The Special Role of American Advisers in Thailand 1902–1949," *Asia,* No. 14, Spring 1969, pp. 1–31.

Yupho, Dhanit. *Classical Siamese Theatre.* Bangkok: Hatha Dhip Company, 1952.

———. *Thai Musical Instruments.* Bangkok: 1957.

Index